BEYOND INEQUALITIES

2008

Women
in Southern Africa

Foreword by Magdeline Mathibba-Madibela

SARDC
Southern African Research
and Documentation Centre

WID
Women in
Development
Southern Africa Awareness

SOUTHERN AFRICAN RESEARCH AND DOCUMENTATION CENTRE (SARDC)
Women In Development Southern Africa Awareness (WIDSAA) Programme
P.O. Box 5690, Harare, Zimbabwe
Tel 263-4-791141/3   Fax 263-4-791271
Email widsaa@sardc.net   sardc@sardc.net   sardc@maputo.sardc.net
Website http://www.sardc.net

ISBN 1-77910-032-9

Citation: SARDC WIDSAA, *Beyond Inequalities 2008: Women in Southern Africa*, SARDC,
Harare, 2008.

Accessible in full text at the Virtual Library for Southern Africa on the SARDC website
www.sardc.net   Knowledge for Development

Cover design and Layout   Tonely Ngwenya for SARDC
Origination/Print   DS Print Media, Johannesburg

BEYOND INEQUALITIES

2008

Women
in Southern Africa

A profile on the situation of women in southern Africa
produced by the
Women In Development Southern Africa Awareness (WIDSAA) Programme
of the
Southern African Research and Documentation Centre (SARDC)

Compiled by
Barbara Lopi
Nakatiwa Mulikita
Patience Zirima
Petronella Mugoni

WIDSAA is a southern African partnership initiative with national partners in member countries of the Southern African Development Community (SADC). Production of this profile was funded by the Southern Africa Regional Office of the Humanist Institute for Co-operation with Developing Countries (HIVOS).

BEYOND INEQUALITIES 2008: WOMEN IN SOUTHERN AFRICA
Chapter Writers and Reviewers

Writers

Women, Poverty, and the Economy
Theresa Moyo - Zimbabwe

Women, Agriculture and Food Security
Priscilla Mng'anya - Tanzania

Women, Education, and Technology
Nakatiwa Mulikita - Zambia

Women and Health
Nana Kgosidintsi – South Africa

Women, Governance and Decision-Making
Dr. Fenella Mukangara -Tanzania

Women, Law and Legal Rights
Barbara Lopi - Zambia
Matrine Bbuku Chuulu - Zambia

Women and Gender-Based Violence
Keiso Matashane-Marite - Lesotho

The Girl Child
Naira Khan - Zimbabwe

Women, Gender and Media
Loga Virahswamy - Mauritius

Women and the Environment
Dorothy Mushayavanhu - Zimbabwe

Way Forward and Strategies for the Future
Barbara Lopi

Reviewers
Barbara Lopi
Priscilla Mng'anya
Nakatiwa Mulikita
Patience Zirima
Petronella Mugoni

Research Assistants
Saeanna Chingamuka
Chenai Mufanawejingo

WIDSAA Programme Staff
Barbara Lopi, Head of Programme
Nakatiwa Mulikita, Deputy Head of Programme
Patience Zirima, Researcher Writer
Petronella Mugoni, Researcher Writer
Saeanna Chingamuka, Programme Assistant/Researcher
Chenai Mufanawejingo, Documentalist
Tendai Gandanzara, Project Accountant

Gender Reference Group
Pamela Mhlanga, Former Head of Programme, SARDC WIDSAA
Bookie Kethusegile-Juru, Secretary General, SADC Parliamentary Forum, Namibia
Susan Nkomo, Chief Executive Officer in the Office on the Status of Women, South Africa
Elsie Alexander, Sociology Lecturer, Botswana
Nomboniso Gasa, Researcher/Consultant, South Africa
Thembayena Dhlamini, Consultant/Gender Specialist, Swaziland
Terezinha da Silva, Gender Consultant and Chairperson of Forum Mulher, Mozambique
Professor Ruth Meena, Gender Consultant, Tanzania
Barbara Lopi, WIDSAA Head of Programme
Nakatiwa Mulikita, WIDSAA Deputy Head of Programme

FOREWORD

Southern Africa has made significant progress in achieving gender equality since the Beijing Declaration and Platform for Action (1995) and the SADC Declaration on Gender and Development (1997) were adopted.

In line with these instruments, unprecedented policy frameworks and programme developments on gender in the region have been instituted. These include identification of critical areas of concern; addressing women's empowerment at national and regional levels, and the development of plans of action to address those concerns; formulation of gender/women's policies, as well as establishing institutional mechanisms to drive the implementation of plans and programmes. The institutional mechanisms included the establishment of a Gender Unit at the SADC Secretariat to facilitate and coordinate all gender programmes at the regional level.

Furthermore, the SADC region has recorded milestones in the increase of women in the public sector including the executive, the legislature and the judiciary over the years; for example in political representation, SADC countries had an average of 20 percent women representation in parliaments in 2005, coming second only to the Nordic countries. Some improvements have also been reported in health within SADC Member States, especially in the reduction of maternal mortality rates. In education, it has been noted that some Member States have achieved high retention of girls in schools and have further incorporated gender perspectives in their policies, programmes and curriculum. On gender-based violence, and in particular domestic violence has become a priority area in the legislation policy and programme development of most Member States.

In spite of these positive changes, profound contradictions still remain, with some pervasive problems threatening to reverse the gains that have been made in gender equality and women's empowerment in SADC. The gendered nature and marked increase in HIV and AIDS infections, illness and deaths continue to compromise the lives of women and girls. Policy responses to this pandemic remain limited to cope with magnitude of the problem in a gender sensitive manner. Access to basic socioeconomic rights, in light of the continued HIV and AIDS challenges remain one of the key issues for concerted action for gender equality.

Other major gender challenges for Southern Africa include women's unequal participation in politics and decision-making at all levels; the feminization of poverty; increased cases of gender-based violence; lack of economic empowerment opportunities for women; women's limited access to means of production; gender inequalities in higher and tertiary education for girls and women; constitutional and legal rights that do not adequately protect women; lack of access to information and communication; the negative portrayal of women in the media; and limited support to institutional mechanisms that address gender issues.

An audit on the SADC Declaration commissioned by the SADC Gender Unit an dthe SADC Parliamentary Forum in 2005 noted progress in various areas, but also identified gaps and challenges in achieving gender equality. The Audit further revealed that the implementation of gender commitments is very inconsistent and patchy among SADC Member

SARDC

The Southern African Research and Documentation Centre (SARDC) is an independent regional knowledge resource centre, which seeks to enhance the effectiveness of key development processes in the SADC region through the collection, production and dissemination of information, and enabling the capacity to generate and use information. SARDC has five main areas of focus, which are pursued by specialist departments for environment and water resources, gender, democracy and governance, regional economic development, and human development. SARDC has offices in Harare and Maputo and partners in all SADC member states. Founding Patron was the late *Mwalimu* Julius Nyerere.

WIDSAA

Women In Development Southern Africa Awareness (WIDSAA) is the gender programme of SARDC. The programme was established in 1994 to serve as a catalyst and information service to the SADC region's governments, parliaments, NGOs and agencies, the media and the public in the formulation of policy affecting women.

HIVOS

The Humanist Institute for Co-operation with Developing Countries (HIVOS) is a Dutch non-governmental organisation, which operates on the basis of humanistic values. HIVOS aims to contribute towards a free, just, and sustainable world. The organisation is committed to the poor and marginalised and to organisations with similar interests in countries in the South, including Africa, central Asia and southeast Europe. Sustainable improvement of their situation is the ultimate benchmark for HIVOS work. An important cornerstone is strengthening of the position of women in society.

States, thus creating the need for more robust initiatives to facilitate action.

It is on the above stated challenges Summit 2005 directed the Secretariat to facilitate and coordinate the drafting of the SADC Protocol on Gender and Development. The SADC Protocol on Gender and Develpment is expected to accelerate progress towards gender equality and women's empowerment. The draft Protocol is the climax of all gender equality developments in our region as a protocol is the most legally binding of all SADC legal instruments, and would accelerate the implementation of gender commitments once adopted.

The protocol will also incorporate and bring into one legal instrument all gender commitments from all regional, global and continental instruments to which SADC is party, such as the Beijing Declaration and Platform of Action (1995), the Convention on the Elimination of all forms of Discrimination Against Women (1979), the Millennium Development Goals (2000), the Protocol to the African Union Charter on Human and Peoples Rights on the Rights of Women in Africa. (2003) It is expected to enhance and complement these other instruments by addressing gaps and setting specific, measurable targets where they do not already exist; and to advance gender equality by ensuring accountability at sub-regional level as well as providing a forum for sharing best practices, peer support and review and an effective monitoring and evaluation mechanism.

To enhance a better appreciation of how SADC has progressed so far in terms of gender equality, it is important to gather information on the existing gender gaps and achievements in respect of our critical areas of concern as aregion, and *Beyond Inequalities 2008: Women in Southern Africa* becomes essential in that regard. This publication provides the necessary motivation to Member Statesto accelerate action in implementing the SADC Gender Commitments.

Beyond Inequalities 2008: Women in Southern Africa highlights progress in efforts to improve the status of women as well as challenges, limitations and opportunities for accelerating the pace to achieve gender equality in SADC Member States.

I cannot over-emphasise the importance of relevant and accurate information. It is critical for strategic planning and programming of gender equality activities in our Member States. Therefore, data consolidated in this publication must serve as an important tool in tracking progress, sharing best practices, and monitoring.

I therefore commend the Southern African Research and Documentation Centre (SARDC) and their gender programme Women in Development Southern Africa Awareness (WIDSAA) with all their partners who contributed to the production of this book for their role in the process of advancing the gender agenda in our region.

Magdeline Mathiba-Madibela
Head – SADC Gender Unit
Gaborone, June 2008

ACKNOWLEDGEMENTS

This book is an update of *Beyond Inequalities: Women in Southern Africa* produced in 2000 as part of a series of publications profiling the status of women in southern Africa. SARDC WIDSAA and national partner organisations first published the *Beyond Inequalities* series during the period 1997 - 2000.

Production of this book, *Beyond Inequalities 2008: Women in Southern Africa*, whose conceptualisation and data collection began in 2003, could not have been produced without considerable help and support from a wide variety of people and organisations.

Many people were involved in consultations, drafting, researching, writing, reviewing and rewriting parts of the manuscript. Some of the people involved in the various stages of the process moved on and others joined in and carried the process forward. It has therefore not been easy to allocate precise roles to people as writers and/or reviewers of parts or the whole manuscript. I sincerely regret any omissions or misrepresentations.

I would like to thank all the Gender Reference Group (GRG) members listed elsewhere in this book, for their active participation in a continuing process to provide accessible and current information on gender equality, justice and the challenges and opportunities in realising women's empowerment in southern Africa. The GRG and representatives from national partner organisations gave constructive comments on the outline and thematic issues covered in this book during the 2003 Annual Partners Meeting, held in Maputo, Mozambique, and subsequent meetings.

The Humanist Institute for Co-operation with Developing Countries (HIVOS) is greatly appreciated for its financial support towards the production of this book. Particular recognition goes to Corina Straatsma, the Director of the Southern Africa Regional Office of HIVOS for accepting to fund the proposal to produce seven national gender profiles and this regional one under the *Beyond Inequalities* series.

I am particularly grateful to my predecessors as WIDSAA head of Programme: Bookie Kethusegile-Juru who produced the first edition published in 2000, and Pamela Mhlanga who initiated the process for this one in 2003.

I am also grateful to the SARDC Executive Director, Phyllis Johnson and the Deputy Director, Munetsi Madakufamba, who supported the process throughout and persistently pushed toward deadlines. To colleagues in other SARDC departments, Tafadzwa Ndoro and her team in the Finance Services department, Clever Mafuta, Director of the Environment Resource Centre whose team helped in reviewing the chapter on Women and the Environment. Chipo Muvezwa, Head of the Knowledge Resource Centre whose team supported the processes with relevant reference materials for the researchers and chapter writers; Dambudzo Jambwa, the Head of Facilities Administration whose team provided the conducive working environment, I say thank you all for ensuring that the job undertaken to produce this profile was well done.

Very special thanks are due to those colleagues at SARDC who assist us in presenting and projecting our work. Shiela Chikulo and Tonely Ngwenya of the SARDC publishing unit put their creativity to work on edit and design of this book. Tiwonge Machiwenyika and his team in ICT/Web Development have posted this book in searchable format in the Virtual Library for Southern Africa www.sardc.net Knowledge for Development.

Participants to the SADC Consultative Conference on Gender and Development held in December 2005 in Botswana, and conference convenors, the SADC Gender Unit are acknowledged for their valuable contribution to the process. The SADC Consultative Conference on Gender and Development produced the SADC Gender-Based Regional Integration Plan: Strategic Implementation Framework (SIF) 2006 - 2010, whose contents form part of the Way Forward and Strategies for the Future outlined in this book.

Most of all, recognition goes to my colleagues in the WIDSAA programmes (past and present) whose names are listed in previous pages of this book. Thank you all very much. Always remember that nothing is impossible when we follow our inner guidance.

Barbara Lopi
Head of Programme
SARDC WIDSAA, October 2007

CONTENTS

List of Tables, Figures and Boxes

ACRONYMS

ACHPR	African Commission on Human and People's Rights
ACRWC	African Charter on Rights and Welfare of the Child
AIDS	Acquired Immune Deficiency Syndrome
ALDEP	Arable Lands Development Programme
ANC	African National Congress
ART	Antiretroviral Therapy
ARV	Anti-Retroviral
AU	African Union
BDPFA	Beijing Declaration and Platform for Action
BNCW	Botswana National Council on Women
BPFA	Beijing Platform for Action
CBOs	Community Based Organisations
CEDAW	Convention on the Elimination of All Forms of Discrimination Against Women
CGE	Commission on Gender Equality
COMESA	Common Market for Eastern and Southern Africa
CRC	Convention on the Rights of the Child
CTOPA	Choice On Termination Of Pregnancy Act
DRC	Democratic Republic of Congo
DWA	Department of Women's Affairs
FANR	Food, Agriculture and Natural Resources
FAO	Food and Agriculture Organisation
FAWE	Forum of African Women Educationalists
FemAct	Feminist Activism Coalition
FEMSA	Female Education in Mathematics and Science in Africa
FINCA	Foundation for International Community Assistance
FPTP	First Past The Post
FRELIMO	Mozambique Liberation Front
FWCW	United Nations Fourth World Conference on Women
GBI	Gender Budget Initiative
GBV	Gender Based Violence
GDP	Gross Domestic Product
GEAR	Growth Employment And Redistribution
GETT	Gender and Education Task Team
GFATBM	Global Fund for AIDS, TB and Malaria
GIDD	Gender in Development Division
GNP	Gross National Product
GRB	Gender Responsive Budgeting
HIV	Human Immunodeficiency Virus
ICPD	International Conference on Population and Development
IDD	Iodine Deficiency Disorders
ICT	Information Communication Technologies
IFAD	International Fund for Agricultural Development
IFI	International Financial Institution
ILO	International Labour Organisation
IMERCSA	India Musokotwane Environment Resource Centre for Southern Africa
IMF	International Monetary Fund
IOM	International Organisation for Migration
ITFEMC	Inter-Sectoral Task Force for Educationally Marginalised Children
IUD	Intra- Uterine Devices
MDGs	Millennium Development Goals
MMD	Movement for Multiparty Democracy

MNGP	Malawi National Gender Policy
MONASO	Mozambique Network of AIDS Service Organisations
MPs	Members of Parliament
MRFC	Malawi Rural Finance Company
MTCT	Mother to Child Transmission of HIV
NAC	National Aid Council
NACP	National Aids Control Program
NCDP	National Commission for Development Planning
NCWID	National Commission on Women in Development
NDP	Namibia National Development Plan
NEPAD	New Partnership for Africa's Development
NGOs	Non-Governmental Organisations
NGP	National Gender Policy
OAU	Organisation of African Unity
OSW	Office of the Status of Women (SA)
PEP	Post Exposure Prophylaxis
PER	Public Expenditure Review
PLWHA	People Living With HIV/AIDS
PMTCT	Prevention of Mother to Child Transmission of HIV
PNURC	Urgent National Capacity Strengthening Programme
PNURR	Urgent National Programme for Reconstruction and Rehabilitation
PR	Proportional Representation
PRSP	Poverty Reduction Strategy Paper
RCSA	Regional Centre for Southern Africa's Regional Strategic Plan
RECLISA	Reducing Child Labour in Southern Africa
RHRU	Reproductive Health Research Unit
RISDP	Regional Indicative Strategic Development Plan
SACU	Southern African Customs Union
SADC	Southern African Development Community
SADC GU	Southern African Development Community Gender Unit
SAPs	Structural Adjustment Programmes
SARDC	Southern African Research and Documentation Centre
SEDOM	Small Enterprises Development of Malawi
SIF	Strategic Implementation Framework
SLOCA	Small Livestock Owners Communal Areas
SMME	Small Micro and Medium Enterprises
SPANGP	Strategic Plan of Action for the National Gender Policy
STIs	Sexually Transmitted Infections
SWAPO	South West Africa People's Organisation
TAC	Treatment Action Campaign
TAS	Tanzania Assistance Strategy
TB	Tuberculosis
TGNP	Tanzania Gender Network Programme
TNDP	Transitional National Development Plan
TRIPS	Trade-Related Aspects of Intellectual Property Rights
UDP	United Democratic Party
UIF	Unemployment Insurance Fund
UN	United Nations
UNAIDS	United Nations Programme on HIV/AIDS
UNAM	University of Namibia
UNCDF	United Nations Capital Development Fund
UNCED	United Nations Conference on Environment and Development
UNDESA	United Nations Department of Economic and Social Affairs
UNDP	United Nations Development Programme
UNECA	United Nations Economic Commission for Africa
UNESCO	United Nations Education Scientific and Cultural Organisation
UNICEF	United Nations Children's Fund
UNIFEM	United Nations Development Fund for Women

UPDP	United People's Democratic Party
USAID	United States Agency for International Development
VAT	Value Added Tax
VCT	Voluntary Counselling and Testing (for HIV)
WAD	Women and Development
WHO	World Health Organisation
WID	Women in Development
WIDSAA	Women in Development Southern Africa Awareness
WILDAF	Women in Law and Development in Africa
WLSA	Women and Law in Southern Africa
WTO	World Trade Organisation
YWCA	Young Women's Christian Association
ZARD	Zambia Association for Research and Development
ZDHS	Zambia Demographic and Health Survey
ZWRCN	Zimbabwe Women's Resource Centre and Network

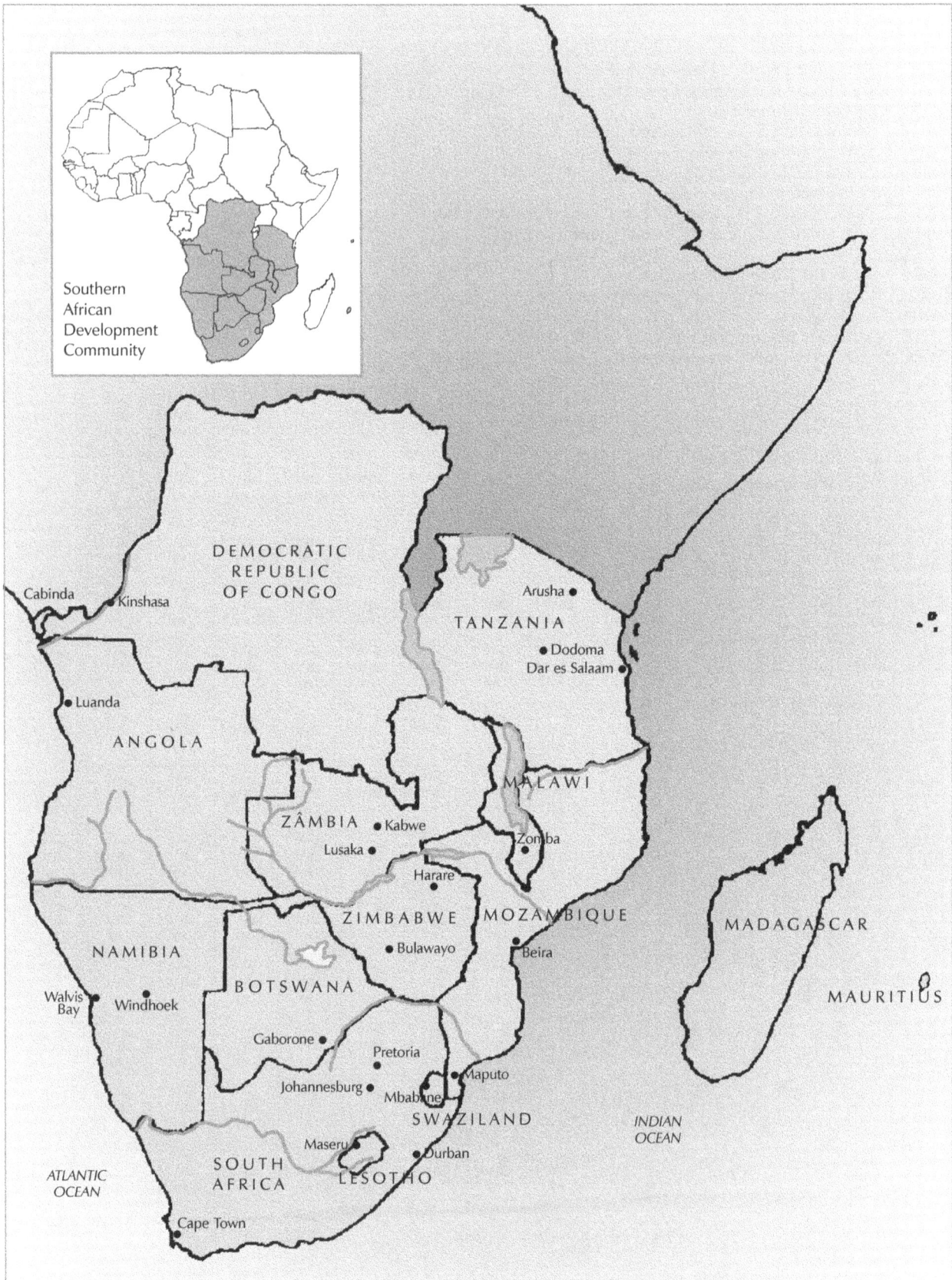

Southern
African
Development
Community

DEMOCRATIC
REPUBLIC
OF CONGO

Cabinda
Kinshasa

Luanda

ANGOLA

Arusha

TANZANIA

Dodoma
Dar es Salaam

MALAWI

ZÁMBIA   Kabwe
Lusaka   Zomba
Harare

ZIMBABWE   MOZAMBIQUE

MADAGASCAR

Bulawayo   Beira

NAMIBIA

MAURITIUS

Walvis
Bay   Windhoek

BOTSWANA

Gaborone
Pretoria
Johannesburg   Maputo
Mbabane
SWAZILAND   INDIAN
OCEAN

Maseru
Durban

ATLANTIC
OCEAN   SOUTH
AFRICA   LESOTHO

Cape Town

INTRODUCTION

*B*eyond Inequalities 2008: Women in Southern Africa is part of a series of publications profiling the status of women in southern Africa. The *Beyond Inequalities* series of books were first published during the period 1997 - 2000 by SARDC WIDSAA and its national partner organisations.

From 2002, SARDC WIDSAA and its partners have been updating the *Beyond Inequalities* books on Botswana, Malawi, Mozambique, Namibia, South Africa, Zambia, Zimbabwe, and southern Africa. The updated *Beyond Inequalities* country profiles provide a gender situational analysis and highlight gender related gaps in the social, economic, political and policy spheres in the various southern African countries.

SARDC WIDSAA believes that knowledge is power, a resource and a strategic tool for socio-economic development. Thus, the *Beyond Inequalities* series aims to provide accessible information to engender development processes in the southern African region. The series has been updated based on the conviction (highlighted in the last series) that information is a strategic resource for socio-economic development. Information can catalyse development, and unless players and stakeholders have access to reliable information on the complexities and nature of gender relations and how they intersect with development, effective responses and the process of positive change will remain slow and ineffective. *Beyond Inequalities 2008: Women in Southern Africa* provides an analysis on the status of women and the various challenges, limitations and opportunities encountered in accelerating the pace to achieve gender equality in SADC, through identifying the roles of men and women and their relationship to economic, political and social resources to achieve the highest level of human development.

The analysis of the status of women in SADC is located within the frameworks of the Beijing Declaration and Platform for Action (BDPFA), resulting from the United Nations Fourth World Conference on Women held in Beijing, China; the 1997 SADC Declaration on Gender and Development, and its 1998 Addendum on the Prevention and Eradication of Violence Against Women and Children; and the Millennium Development Goals (MDGs).

Several developments have taken place in the gender arena in southern Africa since the first *Beyond Inequalities: Women in Southern Africa* book was published in 2000. The development of a Strategic Implementation Framework (SIF) 2006-2010 to serve as a guide for addressing gender issues in southern Africa, and the draft SADC Protocol on Gender and Development are two major landmarks in the process to accelerate implementation of commitments towards gender equality and women's empowerment in the region. A protocol as the most binding of SADC legal instruments would accelerate the implementation of gender commitments.

Drawing from the SADC Declaration on Gender and Development and the SADC Regional Indicative Strategic Development Plan (RISDP), the SIF provides guidelines for stakeholders operating in SADC member states on critical areas needing attention as they plan gender programmes and activities up to 2010.

Most SADC member states now have gender/women's empowerment policies in place. All countries identified critical areas of concern from the BDPFA, and it is significant that a majority identified issues of women's health (later including HIV and AIDS), economic empowerment, and education as key areas for targeted action.

In the political arena, there is a slow but upward trend of women occupying seats of power in SADC, particularly in politics, where representation in the legislatures rose from an average of 17 percent to almost 20 percent in the last six years and continues to rise. Three countries, South Africa, Mozambique and the United Republic of Tanzania had achieved the 30 percent target of women in politics and decision-making positions by 2005.

In southern Africa, the increase of women in decision-making in the ten years since the Beijing conference has been more rapid than anywhere else in the world. As a region, southern Africa is second only to the Scandinavian countries. Despite the many gaps, the political will exists and there is now an unstoppable march towards women's equal participation in decision-making.

There have been advances in legislation, particularly on issues of domestic and sexual violence, with some countries widening the definition of rape to include marital rape, and tightening remedies for survivors of domestic violence to include removal of the abuser from the home. All SADC countries have now ratified the Convention on the Elimination of all forms of Discrimination Against Women (CEDAW), and all have adopted, but few have ratified, the Protocol to the African Charter on Human and Peoples' Rights on the Rights of Women in Africa.

Institutional structures such as gender/women's ministries, departments, units, and gender desks were put in place or their mandates expanded to take on the challenge of implementing the ambitious plans to achieve full equality between men and women, and in particular women's empowerment. The SADC Gender Unit, by virtue of the restructuring exercise of the institution, has also been integrated into the Department of Strategic Planning, Gender, and Policy Harmonisation to ensure that it continues to play a pivotal role in facilitating gender mainstreaming.

Most of these structures, however, are inadequately resourced and skilled, and thus remain relatively weak and unable to implement gender policies and plans adequately, thereby impacting on the effectiveness of post-Beijing plans and initiatives. Gender and/or women's empowerment groups continue to play a role in bridging this implementation divide, and are influential in the policy and programmatic arenas, although they face their own challenges.

Whilst milestones have been achieved, there have been setbacks, and new issues have emerged. Some of the greatest threats to human, and in particular women's development are HIV and AIDS and other communicable diseases such as malaria and tuberculosis. There are an estimated 14 million HIV-infected people in the SADC region, representing approximately 37 percent of the global total; women and girls being the hardest hit as both the infected and affected. The pandemic has placed a heavy toll on women's labour through increased unpaid care work, as well as further compromising their rights by virtue of the imbalance of power intersecting with some cultural beliefs and practices socially, and in intimate relationships. This book seeks to highlight some of these issues, and women's coping mechanisms, as well as government and other stakeholder responses.

Although there is now an acknowledgment that HIV and AIDS is a development challenge, the gender dimension and links to human rights remain a challenge. The SADC Declaration on HIV and AIDS adopted in July 2003 places a premium on increasing access to treatment and awareness and, to some extent, recognises gender as a key variable.

Resource allocation to address the multi-dimensional nature of the pandemic remains weak in most countries and very few countries in SADC are close to reaching the target of universal access to treatment, though some have targeted programmes for pregnant women to prevent parent-to-child transmission.

Poverty remains high, with 40 percent of the population in SADC living in extreme poverty. SADC economies have generally experienced slow growth in recent years, with few exceptions. The average growth rate of 3.23 percent in 2002 falls below half of the seven percent target growth rate set in the MDGs, if poverty and other development indicators are to be effectively addressed in the next few years.

A compromised economic outlook and high poverty hits the most vulnerable hardest, in this case women and children, with a corresponding negative impact on their ability to meet their most basic needs. Poverty remains one of the biggest challenges in the region.

Target

The *Beyond Inequalities* series is targeted to policy makers, researchers, academics, media, co-operating partners, gender focal persons in governments, development agencies, non-governmental organisations, the private sector and other persons interested in gender and development issues.

Format

Beyond Inequalities 2008: Women in Southern Africa is structured in 11 chapters presenting the situation of women under the following headings: Poverty and the Economy, Agriculture and Food Security, Education and Technology, Health, Governance and Decision-Making, Law and Legal Rights, Gender-Based Violence, Children's Rights with emphasis on the Girl-Child, Gender and Media, the Environment and the Way Forward and Strategies For The Future. Each chapter provides a gender situational analysis and highlights gaps in the sector/theme as well as challenges, and progress to address gender inequalities.

Process

The regional Gender Reference Group (GRG) of WIDSAA met in October 2003 at a workshop in Maputo, Mozambique to review the draft outline and identify the issues to be covered. WIDSAA later incorporated issues raised by the GRG members and designed terms of reference for contributors and writers of various chapters. The process was further informed by the SADC Consultative Conference on Gender and Development in Botswana in December 2005, which produced the SADC Gender-based Regional Integration Plan: Strategic Implementation Framework (SIF)2006-2010. See Chapter 11 of this book on the way forward and strategies for the future. During 2003 WIDSAA, through its partner organisations in seven countries, also commissioned an impact analysis on access and utilisation of the first *Beyond inequalities: Women in Botswana, Malawi, Mozambique, Namibia, South Africa, Zambia,* and *Zimbabwe* profiles. The findings of the survey were useful and subsequently incorporated in conceptualising the updated gender profiles.

Impact analysis

In summary, the impact analysis revealed that the *Beyond Inequalities* series:

+ created opportunities for generation of gender analysed data and information sharing on gender and other issues that impact on women in the southern African region;
+ strengthened the capacity to manage, process, and communicate gender information in southern Africa at regional and national levels;.
+ contributed to the monitoring and evaluation of progress on gender and development in the SADC region;
+ has been useful in identifying gender gaps and informing the region on challenges and opportunities regarding women's issues;
+ strengthened the capacity for policy formulation and advocacy towards gender mainstreaming and equality by providing current information on women's situation in the region;
+ greatly enhanced the visibility of the situation of women in southern Africa by providing gendered information on the social, economic, cultural, and political spheres; and
+ enabled WIDSAA and its national partner organisations to establish a knowledge base on the status of women in southern Africa.

The series, including this update, was conceptualised and has been implemented by SARDC WIDSAA, in collaboration with partners at national level. WIDSAA aims to contribute to the improvement of the status of women in the SADC region through awareness-building and collecting, documenting and disseminating relevant, timely, quality, and current information to a range of strategic stakeholders.

The WIDSAA programme believes in the power of information as the mainstay in facilitating the reversal of gendered negative socio-economic, political, and legal trends that continue to grip the region. Gender disaggregated data and gender analysis remains insufficient, yet information access is a key strategic resource for socio-economic development. It is the hope of SARDC and WIDSAA that the information in this book will be widely accessed and shared by all stakeholders in development to facilitate the eradication of gender-based inequalities.

WOMEN, POVERTY AND THE ECONOMY

1

Introduction

The Southern African Development Community (SADC) has identified poverty eradication as the overarching priority and main goal in its 15-year development blueprint.[1] Priority intervention areas to achieve this objective include gender equality, economic liberalisation and development; infrastructure support for regional integration and poverty eradication; trade; sustainable food security; human and social development and combating the HIV and AIDS pandemic.

Gender equality is noted as contributing to economic growth, poverty reduction and overall human development. There are no reliable disaggregated statistics on poverty in the region but it is important to note that women constitute the majority of the poor. This is because there are gendered differences in access to resources, services and opportunities in the economy. Because of the need to reduce pover-

ty, the region has embarked on implementing several reform measures to promote macro-economic stability and high growth, with gender equality as a crosscutting issue in the whole process.

Although most southern African countries have undertaken significant economic reforms, including measures aimed at improving monetary and fiscal policies and management, the economies have failed to achieve sufficiently high and sustainable rates of growth. Unemployment rates and the incidence of poverty remain high, real savings rates are low or negative and few countries are able to attract direct foreign investment. It should be noted however that some of the economic policy reforms undertaken have been responsible for the deepening poverty and worsening conditions for women. This has happened mainly through the removal of subsidies on basic commodities and other price de-control meas-

Selected Basic Indicators for SADC 2004				Table 1.1
	Area Sq Km	Population (million)	Estimated Population growth rate (%)	GDP/annum US$ (billion)	GDP/Capita US$
Angola	1 247 000	15.1		19.1	1 264
Botswana	582 000	1.7	2	8.5	4 959
Democratic Republic of Congo	2 345 095	59.6	3.1	6.6	111
Lesotho	30 355	2.3	2.3	1.4	598
Madagascar	587 000	16.9	2.9	5.8	346
Malawi	118 484	11.9	3.3	1.9	157
Mauritius	2 040	1.2	0.9	6.3	5 099
Mozambique	799 380	19.0	2.4	5.9	313
Namibia	824 116	2.0	2.5	5.5	2 749
South Africa	1 221 000	46.6	0.9	213.1	4 574
Swaziland	17 364	1.1	2.9	1.8	1 629
Tanzania	945 200	35.3	2.9	10.4	294
Zambia	752 612	11.0	2.5	5.4	492
Zimbabwe	390 757	11.9	2.6	3.1	256

http://www.sadc.int/member_states/socio_economic.php and Africa Development Bank Indicators

ures, introduction of user charges on basic social services, such as health and education, and retrenchments in the private and parastatal sectors.[2]

In the face of cuts in social spending (as reflected in some of the fiscal policy strategies of economic reforms), the capacity of those with limited access to resources to cope with the economic hardships is limited. While economic reforms benefit some (especially private capital), unless the government has effective social safety measures in place, these can lead to deepening poverty and the worsening of the situation of women who because of their subordinate status in society, their lack of or limited access to capital, finance and other economic resources become worse-off.

The economies in the region are largely agro-based, with on average, 60 percent of their populations residing in rural areas and deriving a livelihood from subsistence agriculture. A SADC Fact Sheet on HIV and AIDS and the agriculture sector produced in 2004 noted that women account for 70 percent of food production in sub-Saharan Africa and carry out most of the labour intensive farming activities and 60 percent of all those living with HIV and AIDS are women.[3]

Therefore any long-term development plans in the region need to consider the social and economic cost of HIV and AIDS and the vulnerability of women who are affected by the pandemic in terms of HIV infection rates, AIDS-related deaths, and women's roles as care givers in the case of orphan care and other home-based care responsibilities.

Due to HIV and AIDS, the care burden on women is increasingly referred to as the care economy. This "care economy" describes the many tasks carried out mostly by women and girls at home such as cooking, cleaning, fetching water and many other activities associated with caring for the young, sick and elderly in the household.[4] Although the precise size is not known, the value of time, energy and resources required to perform this unpaid work is hardly recognised and accounted for, despite its contribution to the overall economy and society. This care work reduces women's ability to participate in income generation, education and skills building.

A study in the village of Kagabiro in Tanzania, demonstrated that when a household included someone with AIDS, 29 percent of household labour was spent on AIDS-related matters. In two-thirds of the cases women were devoted to nursing duties and on average the total labour lost to households was 43 percent.[5] Much of the care work performed by women and girls remains unpaid and therefore unaccounted for and undervalued in economic terms. A first step towards improving this situation would be to establish women's care burden as an issue. The case must be made that women's care work implies costs to women, households, communities and national economies, and that something can and must be done to reduce women's excessive care burden in the context of HIV and AIDS.

Policy framework

Regional Indicative Strategic Development Plan

SADC's Regional Indicative Strategic Development Plan (RISDP), a 15-year development strategy for the region identifies gender as a crosscutting issue that needs to be addressed in order to eradicate poverty; and improve the quality and standard of living of the majority of citizens in SADC. The plan, though not very explicit, highlights the challenges brought on by gender inequality in regional development making reference to the need to promote women's economic participation, access to, ownership and control over productive resources in the SADC region.

Poverty Reduction Strategies
Economic policies in most of southern Africa since 2000 appear to have been shaped more by the shift towards market reforms.

Since 1999, so-called heavily indebted developing countries have been required by International Financial Institutions (IFIs) to formulate Poverty Reduction Strategy Programmes (PRSPs) in order to qualify to receive concessional lending and debt relief. Several countries in the region such as the Democratic Republic of Congo, Lesotho, Madagascar, Malawi, Mozambique, United Republic of

Gender equality instruments and poverty provisions — Box 1.1

Instrument	Provisions
Convention on the Elimination of all forms of Discrimination Against Women (CEDAW)	Article 11 To promote the right to ◆ Equal remuneration; ◆ Job security, and all benefits and conditions of service. Article 13 On the basis of equality to promote the right to ◆ Family benefits; ◆ Bank loans, mortgages and other forms of financial credit. Article 14 To ensure that ◆ Rural women participate in, and benefit from rural development; ◆ Benefit from social security programmes; ◆ Women have access to agricultural credit and loans, marketing facilities, appropriate technology and equal treatment in land and agrarian reform as well as in land resettlement schemes; and ◆ Women enjoy adequate living conditions.
Beijing Platform for Action	Area of concern A ◆ Analyse from a gender perspective, macro-economic policies and programmes including those on external debt, taxation and employment with respect to their impact on poverty; ◆ Restructure and target the allocation of public expenditure to promote women's economic opportunities to address basic needs of women, particularly those living in poverty; ◆ Create social security systems wherever they do not exist; and ◆ Collect gender and age disaggregated data on poverty and all aspects of economic activities. Area of concern F ◆ Enhance, at the national and local levels, rural women's income-generating potential by facilitating equal access and control over productive resources, credit development programmes and co-operative structures; and ◆ Provide outreach programmes to inform low income and poor women, particularly in rural and remote areas, of opportunities for market and technology access. Area of concern B ◆ Promote education, training and relevant information programmes for rural women through use of affordable technologies; and ◆ Provide non-formal education, especially for rural women.
SADC Declaration on Gender and Development	Section H iii Promote women's full access to, and control over productive resources such as land, livestock, markets, credit, modern technology, formal employment, and a good quality of life in order to reduce the level of poverty among women.
Millennium Development Goal 1	Halve the proportion of people whose income is less than one dollar a day, and Halve the proportion of people who suffer from hunger.
SADC Draft Protocol on Gender and Development	Article 7 ◆ Ensure equal participation of women in economicpolicy formulation and implementation by 2015; ◆ By 2015, adopt policies and enact laws which ensure equal access, benefit and opportunities for women and men in trade and entrepreneurship; and ◆ Review all policies and laws that determine access to, control of, and benefit from productive resources by women.

Tanzania, and Zambia have embarked on Poverty Reduction Strategy Programmes. The PRSPs however, have been criticised for poorly addressing gender concerns. There is also insufficient national data disaggregated by sex. Therefore women's incomes, livelihoods and resource constraints are poorly articulated in PRSPs.

It is important to look at the gendered dimensions of poverty because men and women experience poverty differently and have different capacities to withstand and escape poverty. The challenge for southern Africa is how to embark on economic reforms which lead to economic growth whilst at the same time ensuring that the majority of the region's population, particularly the poor and vulnerable who are mainly women and children, are not left worse off by economic reforms.

Poverty

Poverty can be described as a lack of freedom to meet one's basic needs and those of one's family. Poverty is a violation of the rights and the dignity of human beings.[6] Poverty in SADC manifests itself as deliberate deprivation of access, both to productive assets and to basic social services and facilities such as land, housing and water. Poverty continues to be a serious challenge throughout all of the countries under review. Even in high growth economies such as Botswana, Mozambique, South Africa and the diamond-rich DRC, poverty has been cited by the various countries as a problem. Furthermore, there is overwhelming evidence that the incidence of poverty is higher among women than men and that this is largely due to factors such as:

- lower educational levels among women as compared to men;
- lower skills level and capacity among women as compared to men;
- exclusion from formal labour markets due to discriminatory labour market legislation or in most instances, failure to implement and adhere to new legal provisions which have democratised the workplace and made provisions for equal and fair treatment between women and men;
- the disproportionate burden of care work which is still carried by women alone; and
- dominant attitudes which prevent women from taking up formal paid work even when the labour markets now provide for equal opportunity between women and men.

Access to resources

Women generally lack access to productive resources such as land, technology, credit, education and training, and formal employment thereby resulting in increasing poverty levels amongst women in the region compared to men. As a result, women carry the burden of the reduction of budgetary allocations in the social sectors and unemployment due to social and economic reforms imposed by global macroeconomic policies.

Land

Though many countries in the region have made major strides in addressing the legal barriers to women accessing and owning land, women's rights are still compromised by the existence of customary law operating alongside statutory law, thereby creating mixed tenure systems that often disadvantage women especially in owning land.

In Botswana, a Land Policy Review Committee was set up in 2003 to draft policies on land and a Land Policy Review was ready by the end of that year. However, due to customary practices on inheritance, there are still some practical hurdles for women to access land even though the laws now permit them to do so in their own right. In 1993, chiefs' responsibilities in allocating land were placed with land boards. However, land boards may only allocate land to married women upon receipt of written consent from the husband – a requirement which is not applied to married men. They also require young women to be assisted by their fathers or male guardians if they are to obtain land. Land boards justify their actions by saying that traditionally, a woman did not request property independently from her husband because doing this would be effectively divorcing the couple.[7]

In 2002, Malawi adopted a National Land Policy which called for, among other things, women to have *de-jure* access to and control of land. In practice though, women do not enjoy equal access to land. And although Malawi has a Wills and Inheritance Act, women still face discrimination due to difficulties in the application of the law and the lack of awareness of women in terms of their entitlements under the law.[8]

In Mozambique, issues to do with land are covered in the Land Law of 1997 – *Lei de Terras* (Lei No. 19/97). The law states that men and women shall have equal rights to land. Article 13 also says that individuals can apply for individual titles after division of the respective community areas of land. The law recognises customary rights as long as they do not contradict the Constitution. Women and men's rights to land are also addressed in the new Family Law that was enacted in August 2004. However, for most rural women, land use rights will only be protected if community land registration and customary management practices do not discriminate against women.[9]

Land reform in South Africa has focused mainly on racially skewed land ownership more than gender imbalances. However, the establishment of the Commission on Gender Equality and the Office of the Status of Women in the Presidency and the Land Reform Gender Policy and Implementation Sub-Directorate are important elements of the gender machinery in the country. These have been instrumental in ensuring that gender issues are mainstreamed in all policy and strategic plans of the government. The 2004 Communal Land Rights Act was criticised because it placed too much responsibility for land administration with traditional councils. Since women are already marginalised and discriminated against under customary law, strengthening traditional leaders and customary law risks negative consequences for women especially widows, divorcees and unmarried women. The Act was amended to state that women are entitled to the same land rights and security of tenure as men.[10]

Land legislation enacted in Tanzania in 1999 (the Land Act and the Village Land Act) has provisions that are aimed at strengthening the position of women, while recognising customary law and existing rights. Section 3 (2) in both laws protect the rights of every woman to acquire, hold, use and deal with land to the same extent and subject to the same restrictions as the rights of any man. Since traditional institutions that are given an important role for implementing this legislation are male dominated, the Village Land Act establishes Land Councils, which serve as land manager of the village and the first instance for dispute settlement. The council is required to have at least 3 female members out of the 7 making up the council.[11]

In Zimbabwe's land reform programme women have not benefited as equally as men. There have been allegations that land was allocated based on political party affiliations. Customary law and inherited Roman-Dutch law exist side by side and this causes problems in relation to property. Section 23 of the Constitution gives precedence to customary law if it comes into conflict with gender equality principles in the field of marriage or inheritance. Women may enter contracts to buy land in their own right but when a woman contracts a customary marriage, it is the husband who has legal right to dispose of it on behalf of the family.

Thus, it would appear that on the legal front, most of the region now has legal provisions for equal access to land for all but the challenge lies in implementation and because of entrenched attitudes, it is often difficult for women to have equal access to land.

Employment
Labour markets in the region are still largely the preserve of men although it is acknowledged that access to employment offers opportunities for women to sell their labour resource and earn income to sustain themselves and their families. Most women are employed in the informal sector as they are excluded from formal labour markets by a number of factors cited under the section on poverty above.

Evidence from the different countries in the region shows that whereas labour laws have been introduced or amended to provide for equal and fair treatment in terms of recruitment, remuneration and other conditions of work such as safety, in practice, labour markets are not inclusive in terms of gender. In South Africa, despite the introduction of democratic and egalitarian labour legislation, occupational segregation in terms of gender and race is still an issue. Fifty-eight percent of the labour force is male whilst 42 percent are female.

In Angola, Article 46 of the Constitutional law stipulates that "work is a right and a duty of all citizens and that every worker is entitled to fair remuneration." In practice, most Angolan women are self-employed in informal markets, which have recently been subjected to clampdown by government. Law No. 2/2000 - General Law of Work, which was approved by the National Assembly; guarantees equality between men and women in terms of employment and remuneration.

In the DRC, the dropping in 2003 of marital authorisation prior to taking up employment by married women is seen as a positive and long overdue step in terms of promoting the participation of women in formal employment. The challenge though is to improve educational and skills levels among women to facilitate entry and participation in high paying jobs.

Malawi's constitution provides that every person has the right to "freely engage in economic activity, to work and to pursue a livelihood" anywhere in Malawi. It also guarantees the rights to fair and safe labour practices, to fair wages and equal remuneration for work of equal value without discrimination of any kind, on the basis of gender, disability or race (The Employment Act 2000) but because women are less literate than their male counterparts, they fail to participate equally in the labour market. The UNDP Human Development Report Malawi of 2003 indicates an adult literacy rate of 47.6 percent among women compared to 75 percent among males, this having risen from 30 and 45 percent respectively, in 1995. The formal market therefore still employs more males than females. For example, only 24 percent of women were in formal employment compared to 71 percent males. Unequal pay also seems to be the norm in agriculture where women earn less than their male counterparts.

The United Republic of Tanzania has ratified all the eight

core International Labour Organisation (ILO) conventions, including convention 100 and 101, which are specifically on discrimination against women in employment.

Despite the legislation, employment of women in the region is still largely concentrated in areas considered culturally accepted as women's areas such as nursing, teaching, and administrative positions in the public service whilst males are in senior and middle level management positions in private and public sectors.

The mining industry for example has never been gender-sensitive. Women exist in large-scale mining rarely as workers but as spouses of mine employees. When they are involved, women usually participate as above ground administration staff or nursing staff. There are few opportunities for women in mining communities. Even where women have marketable skills, they sometimes cannot break into the sector because of the isolation of mining sites, lack of credit facilities, and insecure tenure among other problems. More women are involved in small-scale mining and studies in South Africa note that women enter the sector primarily as a means of survival. In South Africa, women in small-scale mining still face problems such as access to finance, access to training and skills development, mine safety and lack of knowledge of environmentally sustainable approaches to mining.[12]

SADC has facilitated the inclusion of women in mining in the region by supporting the formation of the SADC Women in Mining Trust. Among the objectives of the Trust is to help women interested in mining to participate. Having been a highly male-dominated field, women continue to face problems in being actively involved in mining in the region.

SADC women miners seek appropriate technology	Box 1.2

An annual general meeting for a grouping of women miners from the Southern African Development Community (SADC), the SADC Women in Mining Trust, has recommended the need for women small-scale miners to work in cooperatives in order to jointly seek adequate funding from financial institutions to buy advanced mining and processing equipment.

The meeting, which attracted women miners from Malawi, Mozambique, Namibia, South Africa, Swaziland, Tanzania, Zambia and Zimbabwe, came up with the recommendation following complaints from women miners from some countries that lack of appropriate equipment, mining and processing skills are the major stumbling blocks in their quest to produce competitive products for the international market.

"From my experience, we have not been able to sell because at exhibits we display unfinished products while our competitors bring well-cut and polished stones. Our concern is that we do not have proper or appropriate mining equipment to cut the stones in different shapes and polish them," explained Malawi Women in Mining Association president Emma Mphonde at the meeting, which was held in Malawi's lakeshore district of Mangochi.

One of the Malawian women miners, Lydia Chafulumira reported that the Malawian women miners use simple equipment such as hoes, picks and shovels to access the minerals, which is limiting their production.

"We fail to get some precious stones because we cannot dig deep with such simple equipment. We need to be empowered financially so that we can purchase appropriate equipment such as tractors," she said. She also spelt out the need for governments in the region to play a role in providing training to the women miners, especially on value-addition to mineral products, stressing that without such government intervention it would be difficult for the women miners to make headway.

Tanzania Women Mining Association national chairperson Martha Bitwale told the meeting that women miners that still find the going tough in countries such as Malawi should emulate the example of Tanzania, where women miners have worked together not only in buying equipment but also in seeking markets.

She reported that the Tanzanian women miners have established markets for different mineral products with countries like Hong Kong, India and Pakistan.

"Its is my hope that our grouping (the SADC Women in Mining Trust) will come up with deliberate marketing strategies to assist women mining groups from countries like Malawi, where the marketing strategy is poor, and there are no marketing networks," said Bitwala, who is also chairperson of the SADC Women in Mining Trust.

Malawi's Minster of Mines, Natural Resources and Environmental Affairs Davies Katsonage told the women miners at the official opening ceremony for the meeting that his government is ready to assist the women miners in Malawi with skills, equipment and in identifying markets for their products, since the government identified mining as a priority in its economic growth strategy paper.

Marcel Chimwala, Mining Weekly, 15 October 2004 (http://www.miningweekly.co.za/print_version.php?a_id=58038)

Another serious hindrance to women's participation in formal jobs relates to the disproportionately unequal burden of unpaid care work and therefore, any strategies to promote women's participation in paid work should develop strategies to address the issue. Budgetary policies should be introduced so that there are adequate allocations towards social services in particular, those related to home-based care of persons affected with HIV and AIDS, malaria and tuberculosis, care of children orphaned by the pandemic, child care facilities etc. This will release time for women to sell their labour or be engaged in income-earning activities.

Credit

Access to finance is also a critical determinant in improving the social and economic condition of women. Countries in the region have made efforts to improve access to credit for the poor and especially women and other marginalised groups. Despite governments' efforts to link the poor, especially women, to commercial banks and other micro-finance institutions, some financial institutions procedures are still discriminatory as women are considered credit risks, especially due to the nature of their businesses, their capital base and small loans applied for.

The Government of Botswana funds different ministries to support women's economic empowerment. The Financial Assistance Policy (FAP) requires women to provide only 10 percent collateral against the funds they request for projects while men are required to provide 15 percent. Funds available under FAP are now accessible under Small, Medium and Micro-Enterprise programmes (SMME) and a loan programme.

In Malawi, government has put in place an affirmative action strategy to increase women's access to credit through different institutions. Although access to credit increased after 1994, agricultural credit for rural women dwindled because the government stopped provision of credit facilities. Instead, private financial lending institutions such as Malawi Rural Finance Company (MRFC) provided the credit facilities. The government needs to match its commitment with action through mobilising funds.

An impact assessment on financial lending to women has to be conducted to be able to track gains achieved through these programmes. The government's policy aims at strengthening credit mechanisms to enable women's access to credit for both farm and off farm activities. In order to increase credit access to rural women and men, the government through the Ministry of Gender and Community Services established the loan revolving fund in 2001 by entering into an agreement with two commercial banks - Stanbic and Malawi Savings Banks.

Other credit facilities were established through government collaboration with donors such as World Bank, IFAD, USAID, the German Government, UNDP and the European Union (Annual Report on Poverty – 1999). The intention is to facilitate the involvement of 70 percent of poor rural women and 30 percent men to engage in off-farm activities in order to economically empower them and improve their access to food. Some of the micro-finance institutions that have been established with donor funds include: Malawi Rural Finance Company (MRFC), Small Enterprises Development of Malawi (SEDOM) and Pride Malawi with the initial capital from the Government and FINCA, NABW, UNCDF among others.

Available studies have revealed that women's access to credit has improved. The number of micro financing institutions for women increased from three in 1990 to 15 by 2004. The proportion of women borrowers increased by 50 percent in 2004 from 10 percent in 1995; and more than 500,000 women had been trained in business, credit and technology management between 1995 and 2003. As a result, there has been an increase in the number of women engaged in off-farm business activities from 3,000 in 1995 to 95,000 by 2004.

South Africa has made great inroads in making financial resources available to marginalised groups including women. A Financial Sector Charter was introduced in 2002 and financial institutions were asked by the government to improve their allocation of loans and other financial services to the majority of those historically denied and disadvantaged due to apartheid policies. Access to finance is tackled at a very high level as big financial institutions are asked to come together and commit themselves to improving financial support where it is required. This is tied to other benefits such as higher prospects of getting government tenders. It is essentially an incentive-based approach to improving access of marginalised groups to finance. Although no comprehensive study on how successful the programme has been exists to date, this initiative has led to the introduction of products such as the 'Mzansi account' for low-income savers.

Although there is no law that bars women from taking bank loans in their own name, many commercial lending institutions have insisted on a male guarantor, usually a husband in the case of married women, if the woman has insufficient collateral. The requirement for collateral and guarantors is discriminatory against women, as most do not have assets that can be accepted as collateral. Rural households are the most affected by this situation. In order to address this problem, the group acting as guarantor for its members has been used, by 2003 a total of 45,000 groups had been formed.

In countries such as Malawi, the United Republic of Tanzania and Zimbabwe, micro-finance has grown over the last five years and it definitely seems that governments have taken comfort in the growth of the sector - that these institutions would resolve the problem of access to credit by the poor and especially women who dominate the informal sector. Whilst micro finance is a powerful tool to tackle poverty, there needs to be much more concerted and bigger efforts which involve the large banks and financial institutions in the region so that they become innovative enough to develop new products that serve the millions of those who have been marginalised from their multi-billion dollar business in the region. Although micro-finance institutions have mushroomed all over the region, most of them are far from sustainable, being themselves dependent on donor funding. They cannot therefore be relied upon to resolve the big problem of lack of access to finance by millions of women in the region.

Gender-responsive budgeting

Budgets generally appear to be gender-neutral policy instruments as there is no mention of women or men. However, the apparent gender neutrality is more accurately described as "gender blindness" since the national budget generally ignores the different socially determined roles, responsibilities and capabilities of women and men, and usually overlooks the different impacts that budget policies have on women and men. Gender budgeting aims at assisting governments to integrate gender issues into all policies, plans and programmes as well as restructuring and targeting the allocation and collection of public funds to promote gender equality and can thus help alleviate poverty. The process of engendering budgets identifies the implications and impact of the budgets on women and girls as compared to men and boys, and aims to highlight the gap between policy statements and the resources committed to their implementation, including ensuring that public money is spent in more gender equitable ways. Mozambique, Namibia, South Africa, the Republic of Tanzania and Zimbabwe have introduced programmes to engender budgets

National budgets world-wide are often assumed to affect everyone more or less equally, but have been instrumental in perpetrating and reproducing gender biases, yet they also hold the possibility for transforming existing gender inequalities.

In southern Africa, only a few countries, (Mozambique, Namibia, South Africa, the Republic of Tanzania and Zimbabwe) have made notable progress in engendering budgets and budgetary processes. In the rest of the countries in the region much still needs to be done, as their budgetary processes face a number of challenges.

For example, most national budgeting processes do not assess the gender distribution of public spending, revenues, services, outputs and impacts on men and women, and as a result the majority of women and poor people's needs and priorities are inadequately catered for. Ongoing research by the gender programme of the Southern African Research and Documentation Centre (SARDC) reveals that national budgets in most of the countries in the region do not analyse budgetary allocations on who benefits, how spending and revenue is distributed, the implications in the short and long term for the gender distribution of resources including paid and unpaid work, and whether the provisions are adequate for the needs of women and men.

To be able to effectively produce and implement gender-sensitive national budgets, governments need to have statistics disaggregated by sex, and to be sensitive to gender segregation, cultural practices and gender norms.

The lack of gender-disaggregated data and unavailability of trained personnel, including inadequate accountability and transparency by most legislatures in developing and implementing budgets, are among the key challenges that southern African countries face in the quest to realise gender-sensitive budgets.

Government and all stakeholders in budget preparations need to be aware of the scope of gender issues and should be empowered with the skills to be able to search for more hidden aspects of gender inequality. Cooperation across government agencies, civil society groups, non-governmental organisations (NGOs) and across the policy process is also a key component to realising a gender sensitive budget.

In Tanzania, for example, the Tanzania Gender Networking Programme (TGNP), initiated a Gender Budget Initiative (GBI) in mid-1997 in collaboration with the Feminist Activism Coalition (FemAct). Over the past decade, the GBI in Tanzania has transformed planning and budgetary processes to take into account the practical and strategic needs of marginalised communities, particularly women, poor men, and youths.

The coalition and TGNP have gained access into government structures and strategic decision-making bodies and are invited by government and donors to be a part of the Public Expenditure Review (PER) process and the Tanzania Assistance Strategy (TAS) processes.

As a result, two paragraphs on gender were included in the 2000-01 budget, which mandated that all Ministry, Department and Agency (MDA) budget submissions be prepared with a gender focus. A paragraph on gender was also included in the 1999-2000 budget guidelines.

The Ministry of Finance further commissioned TGNP to facilitate a project to mainstream gender in six sectors of the budget namely: Health; Education; Agriculture; Water; Ministry for Community Development, Women Affairs and Children; and Regional Administration and Local Government.

In Zimbabwe, the Zimbabwe Women's Resource Centre and Network (ZWRCN) and Women's Action Group (WAG) with assistance from the United Nations Development Fund for Women (UNIFEM) are spearheading campaigns to ensure that gender concerns are considered in the budgeting processes.

Efforts to engender budgets are also unfolding in Botswana, Malawi, Mauritius, and Zambia, albeit at a very slow pace.

The processes to engender budgets should be initiated in all countries in the region because gender budgeting initiatives can significantly contribute to reshaping policy goals and overall objectives such as equity, equality, efficiency, transparency and good governance.

Barbara Lopi and Priscilla Mng'anya for SARDC, 2004

Women and trade

Economic policies in the region are calling for the promotion of trade both among countries within the region and between the region and the rest of the world. In SADC, there has been a significant increase in trade especially in the textiles, clothing and sugar sectors. It has increased since the SADC Trade Protocol came into effect in 2000. Intra-regional trade was estimated at 25 percent of all international trade and was expected to rise to 35 percent by 2008.[13]

The gender distribution of gains from trade is difficult to quantify due to paucity of gender-disaggregated data on trade flows and distribution of export earnings. However, given the primary nature of exports from the region and the commercial domination of formal trade, benefits largely accrue to private capital, which men control. Although women constitute a significant proportion of the labour force on plantations in agriculture, they are mostly casual labour working on even less than legal minimum wages in that sector and so their net benefits from trade must be much less than the large export companies they work for. This is an area that requires further analysis.

Conclusion

Although there have been improvements in terms of economic growth and other macroeconomic indicators (improved monetary and exchange rate stability) within the region, that growth has not translated into job creation on a scale that could resolve the problems of unemployment and thus poverty in the region. Poverty remains a significant challenge even for those countries which have achieved high rates of GDP growth.

In terms of access to resources, particularly land, there have been significant legislative gains in terms of the introduction of laws which improve the legal position of women in relation to access to land. However, the challenge still remains in terms of implementation and ensuring that women have equal access.

In the area of trade, efforts have been made to improve regional trade and increase the benefits from trade. In terms of participating in trade, women are largely confined to informal cross-border trade and due to trade barriers and restrictions on movement of labour across borders, growth in this sector is limited. Also significant is the fact that women are marginalised from "mainstream trade" where returns are much higher and which is dominated by men by virtue of their larger representation in formal industry.

Women's participation in labour markets is still limited due to the disproportionate burden of unpaid care work, lower literacy levels among women and dominant cultural attitudes where the work place is largely considered a male domain.

At regional level, the policy implications for the above situation are clear. Economic policies should shift from undue focus on economic growth and pay equal attention to redistribution and poverty reduction. Gender mainstreaming also needs to be done in a more holistic and comprehensive manner. Gender machineries and other stakeholders in the different countries need to work hard to ensure implementation of the many new gender-sensitive policies and strategies such as those relating to reforms in land, labour and budgets that are favourable to women.

Whereas small and medium-scale enterprises and micro-finance

A perspective on the SADC Trade Protocol and women's empowerment — Box 1.4

Given that women make up a large percentage of traders at national level and across borders, albeit mostly in the informal sector, the question of how the Trade Protocol will address the existing gender inequalities in access to and control of resources and means of production has arisen.

For women, who account for the majority of small-scale cross-border traders, the Protocol is a welcome move as freedom of movement is likely to increase women's trade and thus enhance their economic empowerment and self-sustenance.

However, as with most regional instruments, agreements and commitment, there is need to ensure that all SADC nationals have access to information on the content of the Protocol. Different strategies can be adopted to enable access to the content of the Protocol, and promote the engendering of trade and investment in the region.

Initiatives such as the Women in Business SADC Network, which has convened Women's Trade Fair and Investment Forums in recent years, and the SADC Women in Mining Trust, aimed at promoting the interests of women in the mining sector in SADC should also serve as platforms for publicising information on regional and continental trade policies.

Whilst there are distinct possibilities for harnessing the potential of the Protocol, there are several concerns as regards its responsiveness to gender concerns. First, there is silence on the gendered impact of trade liberalisation. Free trade demands greater flexibility in shifting of resources from one sector to another and as such there should be a reciprocal movement of individuals. Women cannot therefore take advantage of some opportunities provided by trade liberalisation because of limitations caused by the continued sexual division of labour both within and outside households.

The trade Protocol does not indicate how it will protect people, in particular women, who are likely to be adversely affected by trade liberalization in sectors dominated by women. It is also unclear as to how states and markets in the region can be transformed to strengthen the entitlements of poor women and treat them as individuals in their own right. Women in the region lack access to, and control over productive resources such as credit, markets, modern technology, and formal employment, a fact acknowledged by the SADC Declaration. Furthermore, the Protocol does not recognise that women and men engage in trade and investment processes differently, and this lack of sensitivity therefore limits integration of practical and strategic needs of SADC nationals from a gender point of view.

It remains therefore, that for SADC women to benefit adequately from the Protocol, more work needs to be done to ensure that its implementation conforms with the region's commitments in the SADC Declaration and the regional Platform For Action, in the areas related to the economic empowerment of women and poverty eradication.

Saeanna Chingamuka for SARDC, 2006

are useful strategies to deal with poverty, at a national level more should be done to tackle the root causes of poverty in a more sustainable way. The problem of access to credit for example requires governments and private sector to confront the multibillion-dollar private financial services sector and develop innovative ways in which the private sector would be more responsive to the needs of women for credit and other financial resources.

Endnotes

1   SADC, *Regional Indicative Strategic Development Plan*, SADC, 2003
2   SARDC WIDSAA, *Beyond Inequalities: Women in Southern Africa*, SARDC, Harare, 2000
3   SADC, "Fact Sheet on HIV and AIDS and the Agriculture sector,"
http://sadcpf.org/docs/Agri.pdf
4   UNAIDS, "The Global Coalition on Women and AIDS, Backgrounder- Care, Women and AIDS"
http://data.unaids.org/GCWA/GCWA_BG_Care_en.pdf
5   UNAIDS "The Global Coalition on Women and AIDS"
6   Kjorven O (H.E), Speech at the SADC Consultative Conference, Gaborone, Botswana, 2002
http://www.dep.no/ud/norsk/aktuelt/taler/politisk_ledelse/032171-090083/dok-bn.html
7   6th N-Aerus Conference, 16-17 September 2005, "Promoting social inclusion in urban areas: policies and practices," Housing Development and Management, Lund Institute of Technology, Lund University, Sweden, http://www.naerus.net/sat/workshops/2005/papers/29.doc
8   Kjorven O, Speech at the SADC Consultative Conference
9   "Land Reform Highlights in southern Africa," Independent Land Newsletter June 2004,
www.sarpn.org.za/documents/d0000850/index.php
10   "Land Reform Highlights in southern Africa"
11   "Land Reform Highlights in southern Africa"
12   Ranchod Sarita, "Gender and Mining: Workplace Report,"
http://www.lied.org/mmsd/mmsd_pdfs/165_ranchod.pdf, for the African Institute of Corporate Citizenship, August 2001
13   SARDC REDI, *SADC Today Vol 7 No 4*, October 2004

References

6th N-Aerus Conference, 16-17 September 2005, "Promoting Social Inclusion in Urban Areas: Policies and Practices", *Housing Development and Management*, Lund Institute of Technology, Lund University, Sweden, http://www.naerus.net/sat/workshops/2005/papers/29.doc
African Focus Bulletin, May 14, 2004

Fosu A, "The Global Setting and African Economic Growth," in *Journal of African Economies 10(3) pp 282-310, 2002.*

Kjorven O (H.E), Speech at the SADC Consultative Conference, Gaborone, Botswana, 2002.
http://www.dep.no/ud/norsk/aktuelt/taler/politisk_ledelse/032171-090083/dok-bn.html

Land Reform Highlights in southern Africa", *Independent Land Newsletter June 2004*,
www.sarpn.org.za/documents/d0000850/index.php

Mbaya S, *Land Issues in East and Southern Africa: An Overview. Vol 1: Southern Africa*, Mwengo, 2001

Poverty Reduction Forum, *Zimbabwe Human Development Report (2003)*, Poverty Reduction Forum, Harare, 2003

Ranchod Sarita, "Gender and Mining: Workplace Report",
http://www.lied.org/mmsd/mmsd_pdfs/165_ranchod.pdf, for the African Institute of Corporate Citizenship, August 2001

SADC, "Fact Sheet on HIV and AIDS and the Agriculture Sector," http://sadcpf.org/docs/Agri.pdf

SADC, *Regional Indicative Strategic Development Plan*, SADC, 2003

SADC, SARDC, *SADC Today, Vol. 7 No 4*, SADC, Gabarone SARDC, Harare, 2004

SARDC WIDSAA, *Gender and Development Exchange Issue 39 July-September 2006*, SARDC, Harare, 2006

SARDC WIDSAA, *Beyond Inequalities: Women in Southern Africa*, SARDC, Harare, 2000

SARDC WIDSAA, *Beyond Inequalities, Women in (Angola; Botswana; Lesotho; Malawi; Mozambique; Namibia; South Africa; Swaziland; Tanzania; Zambia; Zimbabwe)*, SARDC, Harare, 2005

UNAIDS, "The Global Coalition on Women and AIDS, Backgrounder- Care, Women and AIDS"
http://data.unaids.org/GCWA/GCWA_BG_Care_en.pdf

UNCTAD, *The Least Developed Countries Report 2002: Escaping the Poverty Trap*, New York and Geneva, UNCTAD, 2003

UNDP, *National Human Development Report*, Maputo 2001

USAID-Regional Centre for Southern Africa, "USAID Regional Strategic Plan 2004-2010", USAID, 2003

2

WOMEN, AGRICULTURE AND FOOD SECURITY

Introduction

Women in SADC play a vital role in ensuring food security and women provide the largest labour contribution in the agricultural sector. On the African continent, about 70 percent of staple foods are produced by women farmers and in SADC, women contribute more than 60 percent to total food production.[1] Analysis of some countries such as Malawi shows that women perform about 70 percent of agricultural work, which includes weeding, harvesting and processing food. Further, women produce 80 percent of all food consumed at household level.

Women peasant farmers in the region engage in a wide range of activities in order to generate and maintain a livelihood. Some of these activities involve exchange processes whereby services are performed or goods produced which may be exchanged for cash or for needed goods and services.[2] In most countries in the region, women rear a range of small livestock such as chickens, ducks and goats while men are responsible for the larger animals.

Women also cultivate small home gardens where they produce supplementary foods such as ground nuts, sweet potatoes and vegetables. Although the motive for carrying out multiple activities revolves around food and cash, food security seems to be of primary concern to many small farmers.[3] For example, a study conducted in 2003 in Murewa, a rural area in Zimbabwe, noted that smallholder farmers grew finger millet for food security purposes. Most farmers interviewed mentioned that they grew finger millet to replenish their stocks, which had been used up during the previous year's drought.[4] According to the study, finger millet is seen as an important food security crop because it can last several years in storage. Despite families benefiting from the production of these supplementary foods, such crops are considered to be "women's crops" and in most cases they are not taken seriously in national agricultural budgets.

Despite the important role that women play in achieving food security in the region, they have limited access to and control over productive resources such as land, livestock, modern technological innovations and information and they lack incentives such as credit and extension services.[5] Women's limited means have generally made them unable to purchase the inputs associated with improved packages of crop production practices, and thus the performance of the agricultural sector and food production in particular has remained poor.[6] Added to this is that in some SADC countries, agricultural development planning, research and extension services appear to have overlooked the importance of improving small-scale production, especially food related production because of the mistaken belief that this sector is incapable of making any major contribution to national development.[7]

Given the vital role women play in agriculture, one of the necessary conditions to achieving sustainable agricultural development and improving food security in the region is the provision of sufficient attention and support to women farmers, who form a majority of the farming population, both as

workers and food producers. This chapter thus discusses different aspects within the context of agriculture and food security with emphasis on women peasant farmers in the SADC region. The pertinent issues discussed include the current food security situation, women's access to agricultural inputs, the impact of HIV and AIDS on food security and various measures taken to ensure food security in the SADC region.

Policy Framework

Regional Indicative Strategic Development Plan

The Regional Indicative Strategic Development Plan (RISDP) is among the policy frameworks within SADC that seek to promote agriculture and food security and eradicate or minimise poverty among its people. The RISDP has identified agriculture and sustainable food security as an important sector, which can speed up economic development in the region. Improving food availability, nutrition and access to food through rural non-farm income generation, strengthening disaster preparedness and enhancing the institutional framework are some of the key issues addressed by the RISDP. In line with its objectives, the RISDP urges governments to adopt policies/measures, which will generate maximum employment and improve income stability and equity. The development of safety nets such as food/cash for work and distribution of agricultural inputs or food for vulnerable groups are also expected to contribute immensely to improving access to food.

The RISDP however, does not detail specific gender-sensitive indicators for monitoring progress across the key areas identified. Lack of such indicators presents an important challenge as it becomes difficult to ensure that women farmers' concerns are systematical-

ly mainstreamed within the proposed mechanisms. Assuming that gender will be taken into account without identifying specific indicators ignores the role, contribution, and gender related problems faced by women farmers in the agricultural sector.

The proposed interventions in RISDP must be based on a gender perspective to be effective. An effective gender mainstreaming approach that would make every effort to understand the complex set of socially determined roles among women and men and which focuses on equity, and gender differences rather than just equal treatment would be required.[8] Unfortunately, experience has shown that despite the existence of good policies and strategies, interpretation of development strategies through common social conventions often lead to difficulties and compromised understandings of the contents.

Dar es Salaam Declaration

The adoption of the Dar es Salaam Declaration is a milestone towards addressing food insecurity in the region. SADC held an Extraordinary Summit in May 2004, dedicated to finding solutions towards sustainable food security. At this important summit, Heads of State and Government adopted and signed the Dar es Salaam Declaration on Agriculture and Food Security in the SADC Region.

Like the RISDP, the Declaration prioritises a number of areas for SADC to focus on as medium to long-term activities. Importantly, the declaration calls on each country in the region to increase investments and budgetary allocations for agriculture to at least 10 percent of the national budgets as recommended in the African Union's Declaration on Agriculture and Food Security which was made in Maputo, Mozambique in 2003.[9]

The Declaration outlines provisions for the development of gender-sensitive agricultural policies. It seeks to promote agriculture through the provision of key inputs and among these to "promote labour-saving and gender-sensitive technologies and improve infrastructure in the rural areas" and "accelerate land policy reform initiatives, share experiences of best practices and ensure women's equitable access to land."

Food security situation in SADC

The 1996 Rome Declaration on World Food Security defines food security as "food that is available at all times, to which all persons have means of access, that is nutritionally adequate in terms of quantity, quality and variety, and is acceptable within the given culture."[10] Food security is thus not just a matter of availability, but also includes a wide range of factors. For instance, while South Africa has been reported to be a food surplus nation, this has not necessarily translated into household food security. The Human Science Research Council in 2004 noted that approximately 14 million people were vulnerable to food insecurity and 43 percent of households suffered from food poverty in South Africa.

A trend analysis of the food security situation in the SADC region shows that, in 2001 about 15 million people experienced acute food shortage. In 2003, the region continued experiencing food insecurity and approximately 76 million people still lived in extreme poverty.[11] Although in 2005 the proportion of the population facing food shortage had been reduced, the food security situation in many parts of the region has not yet improved or stabilised due to adverse weather conditions.

The table shows cereal production trends from 1990 to 2003 produced by the Food, Agriculture and Natural Resources (FANR)

Directorate of SADC. It reveals that production has remained relatively constant from 1990 to 2003. In the same period however, the region's population increased by almost 40 percent from 152 million to 212 million.

The food security conditions in the region remain mixed, according to the Famine Early Warning Systems Network (FEWSNET), reflecting the mixed production

Cereal Production by Crop					Table 2.1
Year	Maize	Wheat	Rice	Sorghum/Millet	Total
1990	17348	2516	603	1595	22062
1991	15474	2154	491	1642	19761
1992	6783	2365	311	1247	10707
1993	17137	1778	523	2079	21517
1994	20074	2231	562	1838	24705
1995	11097	2490	603	2049	16239
1996	20345	3170	529	2776	26820
1997	17054	2763	533	2032	22382
1998	15835	2201	922	1905	20863
1999	17052	2032	633	1586	21303
2000	20501	2729	730	2124	26084
2001	15880	3053	745	1909	21587
2002	16323	2629	595	1999	21546
2003	18418	1888	767	1680	22753

FANR Directorate 2004

pattern of the 2006/2007 season. Crop production in Tanzania, Zambia, northern Mozambique and parts of Angola are said to be high. However, other countries such as Zimbabwe, southern Mozambique, Lesotho and Swaziland that were affected by drought have seen a decrease in crop production and increased food insecurity. Serious floods occurring in Mozambique, Zambia and Zimbabwe in 2007/2008 have raised concerns that cereal production in these countries may be affected by water logging and leaching conditions that will reduce crop production.

SADC has noted that priority intervention areas in food security should take gender into consideration. This is because women constitute the majority of farmers and consumers in the region but lack control over agricultural output, have limited access to and control of land, markets and technology and extension and information services

Major factors contributing to food insecurity

SADC has identified factors that contribute to food insecurity in the region such as:

- susceptibility to droughts, floods and other natural disasters
- inadequate access by farmers to key agricultural inputs and markets
- vulnerability of the farming community to HIV and AIDS
- lack of advanced farming techniques and equipment
- lack of resources such as credit
- a poor transport network, and
- insufficient natural disaster management.[12]

As with any other developmental issue, these factors have different impacts on the different social groups and on women and men. For instance, due to the gen-der-specific division of labour in agriculture and a strong male bias in the control and allocation of resources including the main capital assets such as tangible property and agricultural equipment which cannot easily be converted into cash and are usually held for a long period, women and men are differently affected by food insecurity. Critics from civil society and women's organisations have cautioned that continuing women's limited access to these important assets is a threat to food security, which can lead to serious consequences, not only for women themselves but also for their families and societies.

Addressing food insecurity in the region

Commendable efforts towards reversing the current food situation are evident. SADC has in place a food policy that guides the regional food and agricultural planning process and setting of priorities in achieving food security. The overall objective of the SADC Food Security Policy is to "ensure that people have access to an adequate diet, to lead an active and normal life." In keeping with its objectives, SADC has been identifying, adopting and implementing various measures that seek to accelerate agricultural productivity in order to guarantee food security and reduce poverty at household, national and regional levels.

Regionally, a number of projects aimed at fostering food security have been implemented. These include the Regional Early Warning System and the Famine Early Warning System Network (FEWSNET). These projects aim at strengthening the ability of SADC countries to monitor food security through the provision of timely early warning and other essential food security information, mainly on availability, accessibility and vulnerability. In addition, national

---

Recommendations to address gender disparities and achieve food security in SADC   Box 2.1

1 Policy, planning and research
- Agricultural research must be directed at food crops for which women are responsible and technologies to improve women's productivity.
- Gender disaggregated agricultural statistical data should be collected to aid policy, planning and research to create gender-relevant programmes.
- Social and economic gender awareness and sensitisation training for planners, policy-makers and researchers in agricultural and environmental issues to be undertaken.

2 Institutional strengthening
- Agricultural extension programmes need to reorient services to support women farmers as well as men.
- Retraining of extension workers to strengthen their skills in working with women farmers should be conducted.
- National credit and financial policies including relaxing the requirements for collateral and co-signing by a woman's husband for a loan should be changed and women allowed to provide alternative forms of collateral.
- Encouraging marketing of surplus food by women, including improved access to marketing groups, small-scale traders' cooperatives and expanded availability of appropriate storage in local and regional markets.

2 Direct assistance to rural women
- Women's human resources development should be improved and strengthened, and women themselves and their families should be supported. Training programmes should adapt to women's needs and take into account the time constraints women face as a result of their triple responsibilities for agricultural production, family and community responsibilities.

Adapted from Templeman D.E., *Rural women and food security: current situation and perspectives*, FAO, Rome, 1998

action plans and programmes on food security are in place in all SADC countries but these have varying degrees of success in implementation.

However, a critical factor in achieving food security in the region is addressing the roles, responsibilities and needs of women farmers.

Nutritional status

Statistics on malnutrition in the region remain alarming. Available information from across the region indicates that protein and energy malnutrition, iron deficiency, anaemia, goitre and other iodine deficiency disorders and vitamin deficiency have remained serious health problems. For instance, according to the Ministry of Gender and Community Service in Malawi, 49 percent of children below five years were stunted and 50 percent were severely stunted, 25 percent of the children were under weight in 2004.[13] The report adds that there has not been any improvement on nutritional status since the adoption of the Beijing Declaration and Platform for Action (BDPFA) in 1995. In Mozambique, the government report on MDGs in 2002 noted that more than 62 percent of the urban population and 71 percent of the rural population live in absolute poverty and suffer food shortage for most of the year.[14] Estimates show that in South Africa, despite the major food surplus, about 1.5 million children were experiencing malnutrition.[15]

According to information collected by SARDC WIDSAA, 10 percent of pregnant women in Namibia suffer from anaemia, primarily due to poor nutrition and illness and 12 percent of all newborn babies have low birth weight.[16] Recurrent droughts, occasional floods and the HIV and AIDS pandemic are severe impediments to improved nutritional sta-

tus. The current plan is to come up with emergency programmes on food security and nutrition to prevent deterioration in the health and nutrition status of the most vulnerable in the population. It is important to stress that in a drought prone region such as southern Africa, the building of dams to store water for irrigation and adoption of simple and advanced technology such as drip irrigation are important projects towards improving food security, be they small scale or large scale. High malnutrition levels indicate acute food shortages not just at the national but in particular at household level therefore increasing the vulnerability of women and children to experience food insecurity. There is need therefore for immediate action to develop programmes that are geared towards improving the quality of women's lives and their families.

Impact of HIV and AIDS on food security

HIV and AIDS pose a serious threat to food security in the region. SADC estimates that women are responsible for 70 percent of food production and carry out most of the labour intensive farming, yet approximately 60 percent of all those living with HIV and AIDS in southern Africa are women.[17]

The increasing number of AIDS-related illnesses in many countries in the region has resulted in reduction in productivity, increasing poverty, rising infant mortality and child mortality as well as the growing number of orphans in the region. The rising incidence of illnesses and home-based care, mostly undertaken by women, is therefore drastically affecting food production and food security, because women's labour is further split between looking after the sick, and working in the fields, in addition to the "traditional" daily household chores.

Food security presupposes access by everybody and at all times to sufficient food for an active and healthy life. It is thus a basic condition for the human organism to create conditions to defend itself from possible infirmities. The lack of resources to produce or acquire food leads to food insecurity. While those infected by HIV need special attention in food and nutritional terms, pregnant women who are infected need to ensure an optimal nutritional status in order to reduce the likelihood of transmitting the virus to their babies, and so that they can have a safer birth. HIV-positive children have social nutritional needs so as to avoid retarding their normal development and help them survive.

HIV and AIDS increase vulnerability to food insecurity. In turn, food insecurity contributes to susceptibility to HIV infection and its progression to AIDS. Food security is part of a concentric chain of the provision of interlinked services, which includes the production, availability and access to food, as well as standards of food consumption.

Bearing in mind that AIDS affects, to a large extent, those of productive age, the death of a household member weakens the household's productive capacity, by reducing the work force needed to cultivate the fields. The subsequent reduction in the area under cultivation will in practice be expressed in a decline in income.

With the sickness or death of the main household providers of resources, a chain of complications arises in managing the life of the surviving members, namely the crisis in family agricultural work, management skills, changes in cultivation systems, an increase in the number of orphans, medical costs, diversion of labour in order to look after the sick, loss of productive income, and reduced ability to buy agricultural inputs (seeds, fertilizer, etc). These aggregate factors often end up generating situations of chronic food insecurity.

Adapted from Mozambique National Human Development Report 2007

The HIV and AIDS pandemic poses significant challenges, not only to individual households but also to the extended chain of individuals, and institutions engaged in agricultural development: governments, farmers, extension workers, ministries of agriculture and finance among others. The HIV pandemic may negatively impact on regional development efforts by undermining the ability of the agricultural sector to produce food owing to high levels of HIV and AIDS related morbidity and mortality, further resulting in AIDS related famine and starvation. This situation has been made more severe by the impact of prolonged drought in some areas of the SADC region, most notably in Lesotho, Swaziland, Mozambique and Zimbabwe.

The ultimate challenge for the region is to improve the well-being of people whose principal occupation and way of life is based on agriculture. A major challenge is to overcome the entrenched gender inequalities in agriculture and the food production sector, including obstacles that prevent women from participating in food production.

To sustain food security, mechanisms will need to be found for mainstreaming gender in planning for agricultural development and ensuring that due attention is paid to gender issues, the impact of HIV and AIDS and orphaned children on rural infrastructure as a whole.

Access to and control of means of production

Women in SADC have limited access to and use of production inputs and support services in agriculture such as land, technology, credit and transportation as compared to men and this has the consequence of limiting their production and agricultural outputs.

Land

Despite the social and economic role of land, and also a noticeable improvement in gender awareness in the region, women's access to and control over land has remained a big challenge. Since colonialism, women's rights to land have been undermined because of lingering colonial policies that introduced the private ownership of land, new legal systems and undermined women's traditional land rights.

In line with the 1995 BDPFA recommendations and the 1997 SADC Declaration on Gender and Development, which call for governments to ensure that women have access to economic structures and control over resources, mechanisms to manage land rights are being developed throughout the region.

While some countries have taken measures to enact new land laws, others are reviewing the existing laws with the view to guaranteeing equality between women and men on the right to access and control land. In South Africa, the government has been planning and implementing several land reform policies which seek to enable individual or group land rights to be

---

What can be done to improve food security in the region?　　　　　　　Box 2.3

- Provide vulnerable farmers with key inputs such as improved seed varieties, fertilisers, agrochemicals, tillage services and farm implements;
- Provide food assistance to all persons in need as a preventative measure. Relieve children and the elderly of their responsibilities as care-givers and breadwinners, and take measures to improve the quality of life of people living with AIDS;
- Expand and integrate HIV and AIDS prevention within school feeding programmes;
- Review legislation relating to access to finance, credit, property and inheritance rights, and ensure that the rights of women and children are protected;
- Integrate HIV prevention and management into the work of agricultural extension workers including making available information and educational materials, condom distribution and information on healthy living;
- Develop nutritional policies and protocols to inform the implementation of nutrition programmes for the general population, including people living with HIV and AIDS, and integrate these within national health systems;
- Establish regional centres of excellence to study crops that can withstand poor weather and water shortages and encourage their use in agricultural production; and
- Integrate information on healthy and balanced nutrition within counselling, care and treatment programmes and routinely monitor the nutritional problems and concerns of people living with HIV and AIDS.

Extract from SADC, *Fact Sheet: HIV and AIDS and the Agricultural Sector*, SADC HIV and AIDS Unit, 2004

registered and protected.[18] The Communal Land Rights Act (2005) for example, recognises women's rights to land. Further, the government, through the Department of Land Affairs has put in place a gender policy which seeks to ensure that gender equality is addressed within all three aspects of land reform. However, the 2004 SADC report on the implementation of the BDPFA noted that some policies, especially, the "Restitution of Land Rights Act of 1994 may disadvantage women as the Act aims to restore land to those who had rights before, most of whom are men."[19]

In Botswana, the government has amended land laws, but women do not as yet enjoy equal access to business lease plots and commercial/industrial licenses. Until recently, only 35.6 percent of commercial and industrial plot holders were females, as compared to 60.5 percent males.[20]

Similarly, the Tanzanian government has amended its Land Act (1999) and the Village Act (1999). The Land Law was "revised in 2004 to create value for land, allow mortgage of land with the consent of spouses and establish land tribunals whose composition must include not less than 43 percent of women." In Mozambique, the most fertile land continues to be controlled mainly by men, with women only having access to it through marriage.[21]

Although there has been an attempt to review and remove gender discrimination in land rights, land rights policies and laws have been implemented with varying levels of success but often, the majority of women still do not have control over land. Women are often denied some of their rights, particularly where customary laws or tenure systems run contrary to statutory laws.

Unlike other SADC countries such as Botswana, Mozambique and Tanzania, which have tried to review or reform their constitutions so as to provide for women's right to own and access land, other countries, such as Zimbabwe provide no guarantee for women to own communal land. Although in 1998, the government adopted equity as a key principle in its land reform agenda, women have not been guaranteed access to land rights in their own right and in proportion to their numbers. Although females heading households can access land and be given permits in resettlement areas, married women still have to access land through their husbands and have no security of tenure should their husbands die. In the absence of such constitutional provisions, women's claims to resources are made even more difficult.[22]

Since land is one asset that is bound to overcome the basic needs of the poor majority, its distribution is of vital concern to every citizen as it affects basic human rights, especially access to food. To this end, it is clear that sustainable food security in the SADC region will depend on how efficiently the land is used, its accessibility to all and how is it fully utilised or under utilised. Land is the heart of sustainable food security and all SADC people, men and women, need to own or lease land as a means of earning a living.

The views expressed in the box above, provide evidence that problems associated with land issues are multifaceted, and one institution cannot provide all the solutions. There is need for a holistic approach, to focus on legal frameworks and ensure that societies' attitudes change. One necessary condition is to ensure that society's attitude towards women's status is changed. Unless women who produce most of the food consumed in the region have access to key productive resources such as land, achieving gender justice, lifting women out of a spiral of increasing

Reasons for holding land	Box 2.4

In a market economy, land has many values other than its value for agriculture. For example, it often:
- Has value as collateral; holding it may benefit non-agricultural enterprises owned by the same person or organisation;
- Contributes to social prestige or political power;
- Has value as a speculative asset, particularly in peri-urban areas, where future use for property development raises its value well above the value derived from its agricultural usage;
- Provides a better hedge against inflation than financial assets;
- Is bound up with identity, membership of a particular community and ancestral and/or spiritual roots; and
- Fulfils a security, welfare or insurance role, for example where other livelihood options are foreclosed.

Adapted from Turner, Stephen and Adams, Martin, "A note on food security and land tenure security in Lesotho," 5 December 2004

Voices on land rights   Box 2.5

In addressing the challenge of access to, and control over land, women throughout the region have been working tirelessly to ensure that their rights are restored and voices are heard. As such a diversity of approaches to management of land rights at all levels has been recommended. These include:

- Redressing gender imbalances and changing the attitudes of policy makers, civil society groupings and communities in relation to women's access to secure land rights;
- Increasing women's participation in decision-making processes that relate to land. This includes having a balanced gender representation in all structures involved in land administration;
- Increasing women's access to critical information on the procedures and policies that are restricting women's greater access to land resources;
- Improving women's access to markets. If they lack this access they continue to grow traditional crops such as maize whilst their capacity to engage in export activities is greatly constrained;
- Improving skills training and provision of technical assistance to women;
- Enacting or amending laws as these have a key role to play in improving women's rights in land and property, and setting standards for good practices;
- Securing ownership or co-ownership of land by women as well as ensuring women's access to land;
- Ensuring women's representation in the policy process, as well as land boards and other local bodies; and
- Removing contradictions that may exist between new gender-equitable land laws and religious and customary laws.

Extracts from various publications on land issues in Africa and SADC[xxiii]

Enabling women's access to agricultural credit   Box 2.6

Women have generally been disadvantaged in most material respects with societal values depicting them as being of secondary importance. When it comes to participating in the formal monetary economy and access to institutionalised credit, the sentimental relegation becomes even worse. However despite these views, experience has shown that women are better credit recipients and tend to perform better in terms of loan repayment.

Women play a major role in the rural community, bearing a large burden of the work within the household unit, from the time-consuming tasks of collecting firewood and water and child bearing, to most of the physical labour activities associated with crop and livestock production. Despite the fact that these women invest more time and labour in farming activities than men do, they continue to have limited access to credit and other inputs primarily due to traditional and cultural patterns, as well as gender-insensitive attitudes on the part of the financial sector.

Where women have gained access to credit institutions, it is important to assess the degree to which the women actually control the usage of the loans and this partly depends on the societal values and norms of a particular community. Research on this issue has found that a significant proportion of women's loans are directly invested by their male relatives, while the women themselves bear the liability of repayment.

Ideal control by women over the productive process would include what activity to invest in, where to source the inputs and productive assets, who would procure them and at what cost, how they would be put to use, where the outputs would be marketed, by whom and at what price, who would provide labour, and the issue of controlling accounts and general management.

The implications of these findings are that it cannot simply be assumed that individual control over a loan is equivalent to empowerment, nor does the phenomenon of transferring it signal a loss of power for women. Conventional banking assumptions about individual loan use and responsibility may be misplaced in the context of gender division of labour within some rural communities. In most of these, the household is a joint venture and most functions are complimentary. On the whole, it is important that the person bearing the liability of repayment be the one to have control over loan use and the productive process.

In the Zimbabwean scenario, more and more women are getting access to credit as individuals and in groups and having control in a number of cases, over the entire productive process as a result of a deliberate affirmative action policy as well as positive attitudinal changes on the part of men induced by education, training and empowerment programmes.

Extract from Chikwera N, "Agribank in Zimbabwe,"
http://www.zoic.co.zw/Documents/05%20Chakwera%20EMERGING%20RURAL%20FINANCE%20MODELS.pdf

poverty and realising the Millennium Development Goals will remain the main challenge in the 21st century.

Agricultural credit

Access to agricultural credit is often much easier for men than for women in the region. As a greater percent of women in SADC countries continue to live in absolute poverty, SADC member states have realised that providing agricultural credit to food producers and especially to women is a necessary condition for attaining sustainable agricultural development and food security. Progress reports on the implementation of the BDPFA 2004 highlight a number of structures and mechanisms in place that facilitate women's access to credit for both small ad medium scale enterprises. Currently, throughout the region there are different structures that facilitate access to cash and agricultural credit including government, NGO programmes and private companies. In all countries women are being encouraged to form groups and set up savings and credit societies so that they can access credit and loans for their enterprises.

In Botswana, the government has set up programmes to facilitate access to cash and credit, including the Financial Assistance Policy (FAP) and Small Micro and Medium Enterprises (SMME), which facilitate cash and credit facilities to small enterprises.[24] In Tanzania, apart from having a Women's Development Fund and credit for women in rural enterprises, the government is facilitating the formation of a women's bank where women will have easy access to credit.[25]

Whilst there are many credit schemes run by community-based organisations and local and international NGOs throughout the region, women have not yet been able to take full advantage of these opportunities. The low educational level of women in agri-business has continued to hinder their development and advancement. It is difficult for women with limited education or training to access information which may be beneficial to them.

There have been efforts to address the problem by SADC governments. A meeting of Ministers of food, agriculture and natural resources, held in Dar es Salaam in the United Republic of Tanzania in 2004, acknowledged the role of women peasant farmers in agriculture and food security, and agreed to support the empowerment of women, to promote equal access for men and women as well as child-headed households to land, credit, and other key agricultural inputs. Providing credit to women farmers will enable them to access more advanced agricultural implements such as tractors and inputs such as fertilizers, seeds and subsequently to improve production and food security at the household, national and regional levels.

Appropriate technology and irrigation

Women's lack of access to improved agricultural technology is another problem affecting agriculture and food production in the region. In most parts of the region, women smallholders use mainly traditional methods such as hand hoes to plough the land. Some of the reasons for women's lack of access to improved agricultural technology include a lack of financial assistance in acquiring inputs such as fertilizers and certified seeds and also, the focus on agricultural technology in Africa is on commercial crops which are traditionally grown by men, rather than food crops which are primarily the concern of women farmers.

In many cases, men usually claim ownership or co-ownership

of water rights and so women are particularly at risk since they cannot retain any rights as female heads of households if they become divorced or widowed. In view of this situation, the World Water Forum emphasises that women must be given equal rights and obtain better access to decision-making roles in governance and general administration of water resources, at both local and basin level, as well as to jobs in operational systems management.[26]

Although irrigation is not a universal panacea to food security problems, if managed properly, can be a lever for reducing poverty and boosting the economy. It is therefore important that agricultural experts and extension officers start prioritising food crops; food security cannot be achieved unless women as food producers have greater access to the technologies of modern agriculture.

Rural transportation

Transport and, most importantly, rural transport is a crucial factor in the development of agriculture and of the economy as a whole. Since the signing of the SADC Protocol on Transport, Communication and Metrology in 1996, which came into effect in 1998, there has been significant progress in ensuring that transport systems are integrated at the regional level.[27] However, the rural population is still disadvantaged, as poor infrastructure and an unreliable transport system in rural areas affects timely delivery of agricultural inputs as well as the distribution and marketing of agricultural products.

This situation is a major constraint to peasant farmers' production levels as it raises transport costs and discourages market production, resulting in farmers incurring losses on agricultural produce. In SADC, as in other parts of

25

Africa, people use bicycles or carry loads on their heads and shoulders to transport goods. A study of the management and financial framework for rural transport infrastructure in sub-Saharan Africa, argues, "Transport is characterised by female portage" and that women transport an "equivalent of 20 kilograms over 10 kilometres everyday of the year."[28] As a result, time which could be used in other productive work is spent transporting goods, significantly increasing women's workload and negatively affecting their health. SADC faces a challenge to ensure the development of a more comprehensive rural transport system, which responds more effectively to the needs of the rural population as well as minimising the transport burden of women and the rural population as a whole.

Visibility of women in agricultural development

At any planning level, gender-disaggregated data plays a critical role in determining how much/what resources individuals and communities need for their social, political and economical well-being. Despite this, several studies on the status of women in the region, implemented by SARDC WIDSAA and its national partner organisations in SADC countries reveal that there is still inadequate gender-disaggregated information in national statistics.[29] These findings point to the fact that most of the existing systems of collecting agricultural statistics in the region ignore a large part of the work done by women.[30]

This has been a contributing factor to the invisible role of women in agricultural development. Subsequently, women's challenges and experiences in agricultural production are not adequately considered in agricultural planning and implementation of programmes. Involving women as full partners and agents of development in main-

stream agriculture will not be possible unless there is gender-disaggregated data which demonstrates the role and contribution of women in agricultural production.

In order to target projects on women, it is necessary to make the role of women in agriculture visible through ensuring availability of adequate gender-disaggregated data on agricultural activities that encompass data on intra-household dynamics and data concerning access to resources. While such data is important for agricultural planning and programmes, there is also a need to have policy-makers who are able to demonstrate the usefulness of such information by formulating programmes which take into consideration issues impacting on women.

Way forward

A broad overview of the policy trends in agriculture in SADC reveals that the region as a whole has been making efforts towards improving food security and nutrition, but in most cases such efforts have not benefited the food production sector, more specifically women across the region.

Factors such as unreliable market information, inadequate infrastructure and lack of women's access to productive services in rural areas and the additional burden placed on women in caring for the sick continue to pose several obstacles. The following recommendations can be helpful for future policy:

- the establishment of policies that will enable sustained improvement of peasant agriculture in terms of incentives and resources. In designing such policies, explicit attention needs to be paid to create opportunities for the participation of women peasant farmers. Such policies must be a means to achieving equity, redistribution and growth.

This means that there is need for governments to undertake gender-mainstreaming to strengthen agriculture and food security.

* measures need to be put in place to assist women peasant farmers with financial resources. Agricultural food policies need to promote the development of financial rural markets. This assistance can be in the form of micro banks, credit unions and credit groups. SADC governments should remember that the private sector is profit-oriented therefore they would not necessarily give priority to poor people's immediate needs.
* implement measures to enhance and facilitate women's access to means of production such as land, agricultural inputs and equipment.
* encourage local processing of agricultural produce through on-farm micro enterprises.
* water and childcare facilities must be given priority.
* there should be a more holistic understanding of the socio-cultural context of women's lives. New and innovative strategies which work towards gender equality and improve women's income without affecting their health, family health, nutrition and welfare are important.
* policies for sustainable agriculture that respond to locally identified needs which harness indigenous knowledge and practices and which involve local participation and organisation need to be given priority on the agenda for development.

SADC governments can meet the ambitious Millennium Development Goals (MDGs) of eradicating extreme poverty and hunger if emphasis is placed on irrigation, rural transport, research, adequate communication technology and financial credit. Redressing the deteriorated physical and social infrastructure and improving institutional performance and education of women are absolutely critical if SADC's agricultural development objectives are to be achieved.

Endnotes

1   SARDC WIDSAA, *Beyond Inequalities: Women in Southern Africa*, SARDC WIDSAA, 2000.

2   Vijhuizen Carin, "Women farmers make the markets Gender, value and performance of a smallholder irrigation scheme"

3   Mitumba J. "Towards an understanding of technology needs of smallholder farmers" University of Zimbabwe Publications, Harare, Zimbabwe, 2003.

4   Ibid

5   Mng'anya, P. "SADC urged to improve the plight of women peasant farmers" The Gad Exchange: A *Gender and Development Newsletter*, SARDC-WIDSAA, 2004.

6   Ngware S., 1996, 'The Agrarian Question in Tanzania: Historical Legacies and Contemporary Challenges', in Suleiman Ngware et al (eds.) *Gender and Agrarian Change in Tanzania with a Kenya Case Study*, Dar es Salaam, University Press.

7   Mbilinyi M., Big slavery: Agribusiness and Crisis in Women's Employment in Tanzania; Dar es Salaam University Press, 1991.

8   Gender mainstreaming as used here implies a deliberate process of transforming systems and agricultural institutions to ensure that gender concerns and needs, implications and experiences of men and women are integrated in all planned actions, including agricultural policies and programmes, from the beginning to the end of the plan/programme.

9   See appendix, medium to long term (2004-2010) (6)

10 http://www.fao.org/documents/show_cdr.asp

11 UNECA, Southern Africa Development Bulletin, issue, No.13, December, UNECA, 2003.

12 SADC, Food Security Situation for 2003/2004 Marketing Season, SADC Secretariat paper presented at Summit, Dar es Salaam, August 2003 and SADC, Dar es Salaam Declaration on Agriculture and Food Security in the SADC Region, Gaborone 2004

13 Ministry of Gender and Community Services (Malawi), Progress on the Beijing +10 Report (Unpublished), Lilongwe, 2004.

14 Forum Mulher and SARDC WIDSAA, Beyond Inequalities 2005: Women in Mozambique, Forum Mulher/SARDC, Maputo and Harare, 2006

15 Human Science research Council 2004 cited in AIDC.

16 UNAM and SARDC WIDSAA, Beyond Inequalities 2005: Women in Namibia, UNAM/SARDC, Windhoek and Harare, 2005.

17 SADC, Fact Sheet: HIV and AIDS and the Agricultural Sector, SADC HIV and AIDS Unit, 2004

18 Kotch and De Beer, 1999.

19 Ministry of Gender and Community Services (Malawi), Progress on the Beijing +10 Report (Unpublished), Lilongwe, 2004.

20 Women's NGO Coalition and SARDC WIDSAA, Beyond Inequalities 2005: Women in Botswana, WNGOC/ SARDC, Gaborone and Harare, 2005.

21 Centre for African Studies, University of Eduardo Mondlane University, Forum Mulher and SARDC-WIDSAA, Beyond Inequalities: Women in Mozambique, CEA/ FM/ SARDC, Maputo and Harare, 2005 (Draft).

22 Zimbabwe Women's Resource Centre and Network, and SARDC-WIDSAA, Beyond Inequalities 2005: Women in Zimbabwe, ZWRCN/SARDC, Harare, 2005.

23 ZERO, Setting the foundations for building capacities, networking and research on land reforms in Southern Africa, ZERO, Harare, Zimbabwe, 1998.

24 Women's NGO Coalition and SARDC WIDSAA, Beyond Inequalities 2005: Women in Botswana, WNGOC/ SARDC, Gaborone and Harare, 2005.

25 Tanzania country report on the progress on the implementation of BPFA, 2004

26 World Water Forum, A vision of water for Food and Rural Development, World Water Forum, France, 2000.

27 SADC RISDP, SADC, Gaborone, Botswana, 2004. p 30-31

28 Banjo G, Management and Financial Framework for Rural Transport Infrastructure: A tool for Poverty Reduction. The food Chain in Sub-Saharan Africa, CASIN/SAA/Global, 2000.

29 See for example SARDC WIDSAA, Beyond Inequalities: Women in Southern Africa, SARDC WIDSAA, 2000 and also Centre for African Studies, University of Eduardo Mondlane, Forum Mulher and SARDC-WIDSAA, Beyond Inequalities: Women in Mozambique, CEA/ FM/ SARDC, Maputo and Harare, 2005 (Draft).

30 SARDC WIDSAA, Beyond Inequalities: Women in Southern Africa, SARDC WIDSAA, 2000.

References

Ashby, J. "Poverty and Gender: A Proposal for Action Research, a paper prepared for the CGIAR Conference on poverty", Costa Rica, September 1999. Cited in *ILRI's Research Strategy to 2010*

Banjo, G. "Management and Financial Framework for Rural Transport Infrastructure: A Tool for Poverty Reduction. *The food Chain in Sub-Saharan Africa*, CASIN/SAA/Global, 2000

Banjo, A. G. "Management and Financial Framework for Rural Transport Infrastructure: A Tool for Poverty Reduction" in *The Food Chain in Sub-Saharan Africa Proceedings of The Workshop Held in Bamako, Mali, October 15-19 1999*. CASIN/SAA/Global, 2000.

Bulletin of the drylands: People, Policies, Programmes, No. 34, International Institute for Environment and Development, London, 1999

Human Science Research Council 2004 cited in AIDC.

International Livestock Research Institute. www.ilri.org

Mbilinyi, M. *Big slavery: Agribusiness and Crisis in Women's Employment in Tanzania*, Dar es Salaam, 1991

Ministry of Agriculture and Food Security, *Agricultural Sector Development Strategy, Dar es Salaam*, 2001

Ministry of Gender and Community Services, *Progress on the Beijing +10 Report* (Unpublished), Lilongwe, 2004

Mitumba, J. "Towards An Understanding of Technology Needs of Smallholder Farmers" in Bolding, A, Mitumba J, Zaag, P. (Eds), *Interventions in smallholder Agriculture Implications for Extension in Zimbabwe*, Harare, Zimbabwe, 2003

Mutepfa, F, Dengu, E, and Chenje, M (Eds.), *Enhancing Land Reforms in Southern Africa. Case Studies on Land Reform Strategies and community based natural resource management*, ZERO-Environment Organisation, 1998

Ngware, S. "The Agrarian Question in Tanzania: Historical Legacies and Contemporary Challenges." In Suleiman Ngware et al (Eds.) *Gender and Agrarian Change in Tanzania with a Kenya Case Study*, Dar es Salaam, 1996

Rome Declaration on World Food Security, November 1996

SADC, "Food Security Situation for 2003/2004 Marketing Season," SADC Secretariat paper presented at Summit, Dar es Salaam, August 2003

SADC, Dar *es Salaam Declaration on Agriculture and Food Security in the SADC Region*, Gaborone 2004

SADC FANR, "Special Agromet update on drought, March 2005," SADC FANR, Gaborone, 2005

SADC, *Regional Indicative Strategic Development Plan*, SADC, Gaborone, Botswana, 2004

SADC Secretariat, SADC Guidelines on GMOs, Biotechnology and Biosafety, SADC Secretariat, Gaborone, 2003

SADC, SARDC , *SADC Today Vol. 7 No.2, June 2004*, SADC, Gabarone and SARDC Harare, 2004

SADC, SARDC REDI, "AU to Create Agriculture Fund" in *SADC Today Vol.7 No.1, April 2004*, SADC, Gabarone and SARDC Harare, 2004

SADC, SARDC, "SADC unveils historic blueprint to fight poverty" in *SADC Today, Vol.7 No.1 April 2004*, Harare, 2004

SARDC WIDSAA, *Beyond Inequalities: Women in Southern Africa*, SARDC, Harare, 2000

SARDC WIDSAA, "SADC urged to improve the plight of women peasant farmers" in*The GAD Exchange*: A *Gender and Development Newsletter*, SARDC, Harare, 2004

SARDC WIDSAA, Centre for African Studies, University of Eduardo Mondlane and Forum Mulhr, *Beyond Inequalities: Women in Mozambique*, CEA/ FM/ SARDC, Maputo and Harare, 2005

SARDC WIDSAA and Tanzania Gender Networking Programme, *Beyond Inequalities: Women in Tanzania*, TGNP/SARDC, Dar es Salaam and Harare, 1997

SARDC WIDSAA and Women's NGO Coalition, *Beyond Inequalities 2005: Women in Botswana,* WNGOC/ SARDC, Gaborone and Harare, 2005

SARDC WIDSAA and Zimbabwe Women's Resource Centre and Network, *Beyond Inequalities 2005: Women in Zimbabwe,* ZWRCN/SARDC, Harare, 2005.

SARDC, INE, ISRE,, Mozambique National Human Development Report 2007: "Challenges and Opportunities: The Response to HIV and AIDS," UNDP, Maputo, 2007

Schreiner, B., van Koppen, B, "From bucket to basin: Poverty, gender, and integrated water management in South Africa." In Abernethy, C. L. (Ed.), *Intersectoral Management of River Basins: Proceedings of an International Workshop on "Integrated Water Management in Water-Stressed River Basins in Developing Countries: Strategies for Poverty Alleviation and Agricultural Growth,"* Loskop Dam, South Africa, 2001

Schuh, G. "Globalisation, Institutional Change, and Food Security." In Breth G (Ed), *Food Security in a Changing Africa,* CASIN/SAA/Global 2000, 2002
The Guardian (Tanzania), Monday, August 25, 2005, SADC Supplement.

Thomson, A, J. *Genes for Africa Genetically Modified Crops in the Developing World,* UCT Press, Lansdowne, 2002

UNECA, *National country reports on the progress on the Beijing +10 presented to the Sub-regional Intergovernmental Meeting of Experts for the Decade Review of the Beijing Platform for Action in Southern Africa. Lusaka, Zambia, 26 – 28 April 2004*

UNECA, *Southern Africa Development Bulletin, issue, No.13, December,* UNECA, 2003

United Nations Secretary General's Task Force on Women, Girls and HIV and AIDS in Southern Africa, Botswana Abridged Version, prepared by Lucy Dixon-Clarke, United Nations in Botswana, June, 2004

Vijhuizen, C. "Women Farmers Make the Markets Gender, Value and Performance of a Smallholder Irrigation Scheme" in Bolding, A, Mutimba J, Zaag, P. (Eds), *Interventions in smallholder Agriculture Implications for Extension in Zimbabwe,* University of Zimbabwe Publications, Harare, Zimbabwe, 2003

WIPSU, "Women and Political Participation in Zimbabwe" 2004, www.wipsu.org.zw (19 May 2006)

World Water Forum, *A vision of water for Food and Rural Development,* France, 2000.

www.fao.org (19 May 2006)

ZERO, *Setting the foundations for building capacities, networking and research on land reforms in Southern Africa,* Harare, 1998

Women, Education and Technology

3

Introduction

Education is a major factor in enhancing a country's social and economic development and helps determine a person's ability to access knowledge, jobs and to effectively make decisions and life choices. Most SADC governments have invested in education programmes, expanded education infrastructure and embarked on literacy programmes for a cross section of citizens.

However, due to various reasons, education is not always accessible to women in southern Africa. When resources are scarce, families have to make decisions as to which child/children to send to school. The norm is for the family to decide on boys going to or attending school. In addition to this, for girls, "domestic responsibilities, sexual harassment, abuse and pregnancies are among other factors hindering females in the region from acquiring an education."[1]

Significant progress in girls' education is critical to meeting the Millennium Development Goals (MDGs) because education creates choices and opportunities for people and reduces the twin burdens of poverty and disease. Education is a way of making sure that girls and boys have an equal start in life and the chance to grow and develop according to their potential which would not be the case where girls cannot go to school for whatever reasons.

Generally, educated mothers are more likely to send their girls to school, to look after the health of their family better, to have smaller families, and educated women are less exposed to exploitation and risks such as HIV and AIDS.

Education has been identified as key to women's participation in national and regional development and as crucial in enhancing women's life opportunities. The 2004 UNICEF State of the World's Children Report maintains, "Girls' education is an ideal investment. It adds value to other social development sectors, eases the strain in the heath-care system, reduces poverty and strengthens national economies."[2] Education for women and girls is critically important, not only for harnessing different nations' human resources for development, but also for raising self-esteem and confidence, and widening women's life choices and their access to information and knowledge.

Obstacles to education may prevent women from exercising their human rights, for example in:
- political participation and voting - Illiterate women may be unable to understand the processes and/or what the political parties stand for. Illiterate women are far less likely to be candidates for office or to be active in political parties, especially at high levels.
- health care - Illiterate women may be less able to access information on where to access health care.
- employment - Illiterate women may be unable to apply for skilled jobs as they cannot read information about potential positions or fill out a job application.
- legal capacity, property ownership and right to contract - Illiterate women cannot read contracts or the papers needed to buy or sell property or to manage a business.

31

- non-discrimination and equality - In many societies, disabled, migrant, racial and ethnic minorities are disproportionately represented among the poor, unemployed and illiterate, and thus a lack of educational opportunities for women and girls perpetuates inequalities and discrimination in these groups.

Education also has a positive impact in the fight against HIV and AIDS. Available data on the link between education level and HIV and AIDS underscore what people know intuitively, that education is one of the best defences against HIV infection. To change the course of the pandemic, good quality basic education and skills-based HIV and AIDS prevention education must be extended to girls and boys equally. Education presents the best opportunity not only for delivering crucial information on HIV and AIDS, but also for chipping away at the ignorance and fear, the attitudes and practices that perpetuate infection, stigma and discrimination.[3]

Data from the Zambia Demographic Health Survey (ZDHS) 2001 shows that education plays a major role in promoting less risky sexual behaviour. According to the ZDHS, women and men with more education are more likely to have sex with one partner, use a condom, had no sex in the last 12 months, and abstained or never had sex (less risky behaviour). This is in comparison with women and men with no education or just primary level education, who are more likely to engage in risky sexual behaviour by having sex with multiple partners without using a condom.[4]

Policy framework

The right to education is recognised in many national, regional and international laws. These include the Convention on the Elimination of All Forms of Discrimination Against Women (CEDAW), the Beijing Declaration and Platform for Action (BDPFA), the SADC Declaration on Gender and Development, the MDGs and the Dakar Framework for Action.[5]

Goals two and three of the MDGs call for universal primary education and gender equality in education respectively, while CEDAW and the BDFPA place education within the human rights discourse.

The SADC Declaration on Gender and Development notes that disparities between women and men still exist in education. This understanding underpins commitments by SADC member states to "enhance access to quality education by women and men, and remove gender stereotyping in the curriculum, career choices and professions" (Section H: v). Countries in the region have worked towards implementing prescriptions contained in this instrument. Progress is recognised in some countries, which have increased literacy levels; primary, secondary and tertiary education enrolments; education of orphans and non-formal adult education.

Article 10 of CEDAW prohibits discrimination in education. The article states that parties shall take all appropriate measures to eliminate discrimination against women in order to ensure equal rights in education. [6]

The Beijing Platform for Action recognises education as a basic human right and an essential tool for achieving equal relations between women and men. It recommends investing in formal and non-formal education and training for girls and women as one of the best means of achieving economic growth and development. The Platform for Action proposes the following strategic objectives:

- ensuring equal access to education;

- ensuring the completion of primary education by at least 80 percent of children, with special emphasis on girls, by the year 2000;
- closing the gender gap in primary and secondary education by the year 2005 and achieving universal primary education in all countries before the year 2015;
- reducing the female illiteracy rate, especially among rural, migrant refugee, internally displaced and disabled women to at least half the 1990 level;
- eradicating illiteracy among women worldwide;
- improving women's access to vocational training, science and technology and continuing education;
- developing non-discriminatory education and training by developing and using curriculum, textbooks and teaching aids free of sex-stereotyping for all levels of education;
- allocating sufficient resources for and monitoring the implementation of educational reforms;
- maintaining or increasing funding levels for education in structural adjustment and economic recovery programmes; and
- promoting lifelong education and training for girls and women, and creating flexible educational programmes to meet their needs.

Levels of literacy

Although literacy levels[7] for women and men have improved significantly over the last decade, there still exist wide gaps between female and male literacy rates in the region. As outlined in Table 3.1, Angola, the Democratic Republic of the Congo and Malawi have the widest gaps between female and male literacy rates.

Primary school enrolments

Millennium Development Goals two and three call for universal or free primary education for all, and promotion of gender equality respectively. There have been varied levels of success in achieving these goals across the region. While Swaziland and South Africa recorded 50/50 enrolment ratios of girls and boys in 2001, in South Africa, racial disparities in access to formal education still exist. Whereas less than one percent of white women and men do not have formal schooling, 21 percent of black women and 13 percent of black men do not have formal schooling.[8]

In Angola, women have lagged behind in attaining formal education. Female literacy stands at 29 percent whereas for males it is 56 percent. Further, only 34 percent of females reach the fifth grade.[9] In Zambia, gains in education made shortly after independence have been eroded due to various reasons including poverty which limits access to education. In the country, primary school enrolment levels have been on the decline, despite the policy on free primary education. *Beyond Inequalities 2005: Women in Zambia* reveals that the primary school net enrolment ratio which had stood at about 80 percent since 1997 dropped to 66.5 percent in 2000, before slightly rising again to 67.9 percent in 2002.

Table 3.2 presents data for 2000-2004 male and female gross primary school enrolments in selected southern African countries.

Botswana, Malawi, Mauritius, Namibia, the United Republic of Tanzania and Zimbabwe are listed in a UNESCO report from 2003/2004, using national data obtained in 2000, as countries that had achieved the enrolment of an equal number of boys and girls in primary education and had thus achieved gender parity in primary education in 2000.

Literacy Levels for Women in Selected Countries in SADC 2004 — Table 3.1		
Country	F (%)	M (%)
Angola	54	83
Botswana	82	80
Congo, DRC	54	81
Lesotho	90	74
Malawi	54	75
Mozambique	34	66
Namibia	83	87
Swaziland	78	81
South Africa	81	84
Tanzania	62	78
Zambia	60	76
Zimbabwe	92	86

Compiled from UNICEF, *The State of the World's Children 2007, Women and Children: The Double Dividend of Gender Equality*, 2006;
INE, *Anuario Estatisco*, 2004, Maputo, Mozambique, 2004 and
ZWRCN, "Gender Budgets Watch – Education," on www.kubatana.net, Harare, 2004

Gross Primary School Enrolment Ratio by Sex — Table 3.2		
Country	Gross Primary school enrolment ratio 2000-2004	
	M	F
Angola	80	69
Botswana	103	103
Congo DRC	52	47
Lesotho	123	125
Madagascar	106	102
Malawi	149	143
Mauritius	106	106
Mozambique	110	87
Namibia	106	106
Swaziland	103	98
South Africa	107	103
Tanzania	70	69
Zambia	81	76
Zimbabwe	100	98

UNICEF, *Childhood under threat: State of the Worlds Children*, UNICEF, 2006

Gender Parity Ratio in Secondary Education				Table 3.3
Countries	Total	Girls	Boys	Gender Parity Index
Angola	75.9	71.6	80.3	0.89
DRC	64.3	56.6	72.0	0.79
Lesotho	73.0	77.6	68.6	1.13
Madagascar	48.9	47.4	50.3	0.94
Malawi	73.4	77.0	62.6	0.90
Mozambique	43.1	31.7	54.0	0.59
Namibia	84.0	86.3	81.5	1.06
South Africa	91.2	91.1	91.2	1.00
Swaziland	70.9	69.4	72.1	0.96
Tanzania	40.1	38.2	42.4	0.90
Zambia	58.6	49.6	67.3	0.74
Zimbabwe	70.7	66.3	74.7	0.89

UNICEF, Progress for Children: A Report Card on Gender Parity and Primary Education, Number 2, April 2005.

Access to secondary school education

In most countries in the region, there are fewer females than males enrolled in secondary and tertiary educational institutions, as more emphasis is placed on ensuring that females access and complete primary education. The same factors hindering girls' prospects for completing basic school further hamper their chances of enrolling in secondary school. Rural areas are the worst affected by this state of affairs as secondary schools are almost non-existent and attendance requires the movement, along long distances, to the next biggest settlement, something that many families cannot afford.

Figures for gender parity in secondary school enrolments indicate that more males are likely to be enrolled in secondary school as compared to females. As indicated in Table 3.3, South Africa and Swaziland are the only two SADC countries that are on course to meet the MDG goal of achieving gender parity in secondary education (GP from 0.96-1.04)."[13]

Access to tertiary and university education

Tertiary level enrolments, including those at university level, follow a similar pattern as that of second-

Access to Tertiary Education by Sex (ratios) (2000)			Table 3.4
Countries	Males	Females	Gender Parity Index
Angola	0.8	0.5	0.63
Botswana	4.9	4.4	0.89
Lesotho	1.9	3.3	1.76
Madagascar	2.3	2.0	0.84
Mauritius	9.7	13.1	1.36
Mozambique	0.6	0.5	0.79
Namibia	5.3	6.6	1.24
South Africa	13.7	16.8	1.23
Swaziland	5.5	4.8	0.87
Zambia	3.4	1.6	0.47
Zimbabwe	4.9	3.0	0.60

UNICEF, Gender and Education for All-The Leap to Equality: 2003-4

ary school enrolments where there are more men than women enrolled. In Zambia, a decrease in government support for students to study at university is making it difficult for many school leavers to get education at this level. Table 3.4 presents data on selected countries in the region showing very low levels of female enrolment in tertiary institutions. The three countries closest to achieving gender parity in tertiary education are Botswana, Madagascar and Swaziland with scores that are close to the 0.96-1.04 gender parity index, a score that indicates progress in enrolments.

In general, more women take up subjects in the social science or non-technical fields while fewer female scholars are to be found enrolled in the natural or pure sciences. In South Africa, a Gender Equality Task Team report noted that women who attend university are more likely to be enrolled in education (65 percent), humanities (59 percent) applied humanities (62 percent) and social sciences (56 percent).[14] Fewer women are enrolled in science and technology (39 percent), business and commerce (32 percent) and law (36 percent).[15] A similar pattern exists in Zambia, where females account for only 14 percent of students enrolled in the school of agriculture and only five percent of all scholars in the faculty of engineering. As indicated in Table 3.3, the only area in which females outnumber males is in the school of education; here female enrolment is at 68 percent.[16]

The Minister of Education in South Africa Naledi Pandor sums up the regional situation adequately when she states; "Although overall gender equality has been achieved in higher education, women remain underrepresented in a number of crucial study areas such as science, technology and post-graduate studies. A further concern is that women are under-represented in the senior echelons of academic institutions."[17] These trends indicate that the Beijing Platform for Action's calls on governments to improve women's access to vocational training, science and technology, and continuing education still remains a major challenge.

Non-formal adult education

Non-formal education provides an opportunity for women who may have missed out on formal education to improve their life chances and social status. Most courses on offer are aimed at helping women and men improve their economic prospects whilst improving their literacy skills. Namibia has a notably high enrolment of women in literacy programmes in the northern part of the country (Katima, Mulilo and Rundu) were enrolment of women is as high as 79 percent.[18] In other parts of the country the figures stand between 44 and 53 per cent. Similarly, a study initiated in Malawi by the National Economic Council (NEC) in 2003 indicates that more women than men benefit from adult literacy classes.[19]

Several non-formal programmes in skills training for adults exist across the region to try and improve the economic opportunities of citizens who have not benefited from formal education. In Namibia, there are courses run by community centres offering a variety of courses to men and women. However, these courses tend to direct women to activities centred around traditional female roles such as sewing, knitting and cookery and males to the more technical areas of woodwork and mechanics. In one course in Namibia, 142 women enrolled in needlework and dressmaking compared to two men and out of a class of 35 taking motor mechanics only one scholar was a woman.[20] A similar pattern is evident in Zambia, where wide gender gaps also exist

Tertiary Education Field of Study and Percent Female Share in Selected Countries 2000			Table 3.5
Country	Education	Science	Engineering/ Manufacturing/ Construction
Angola	37.3	37.6	20.5
Botswana	57.7	26.4	22.2
Lesotho	72.0	35.2	-
Madagascar	42.5	32.5	21.6
Mauritius	49.8	48.6	18.4
Swaziland	51.2	40.4	5.8

UNICEF, Gender and Education for All-The Leap to Equality: 2003-4

between females and males in technical and vocational training institutes. The only institute where females outnumber males is in secretarial training institutions where no men are enrolled.

Non-formal educational institutions are generally under-funded, understaffed and poorly resourced, making learning a challenge. In addition, many are not able to assist graduates with financial and other resources to set up on their own after they finish their courses, leaving many to fend for themselves. Due to these challenges, life changes for the better for only a few of those participating in these programmes, the benefits accrued are even less for women who acquire mainly traditional female skills that are less economically rewarding and not as competitive on the economic market.

Education and disability

Students requiring special education such as the physically, mentally and visually challenged have their education provided for mainly in special schools. The physically impaired though, depending on their physical condition, are also likely to be absorbed in the normal formal schooling system. Even here, gender disparities exist in access to education with disabled male children having better opportunities to access education than

Radios teach Zambian children under trees   Box 3.1

The children have trekked through mud and overgrown grass to sit under a guava tree and be taught via radio. A cool breeze lifts their spirits as a brilliant blue, solar-powered radio perched on a tree branch crackles with basic lessons in arithmetic or biology, tutoring Zambia's future doctors, accountants, lawyers or business leaders.

Thousands of children who cannot afford to attend public or private schools have turned to informal classes, where the radio is the main learning tool available. Volunteers equipped with Freeplay Lifeline radios - bright, robust sets powered by wind-up energy or the sun - and makeshift blackboards hold classes just about anywhere, including under trees.

The scheme to provide radios for use in these informal classes was launched five years ago by the UK charity Freeplay Foundation, the state Zambia Educational Broadcasting Service and other local and international partners.

"I would like to become a medical doctor once I have completed my education," said 17-year-old Isaac Mwale, a model radio-school student who recently passed national examinations.

More than 4,000 Freeplay radios are used to broadcast primary school subjects in around 850 community schools, and demand is growing as the informal classes attract children who might otherwise end up on the streets. Freeplay Foundation executive director Kristine Pearson says at least 100,000 Zambian children have benefited so far, easing pressure on schools where the teacher to pupil ratio is one to 60, and also catering for some of Zambia's poorest children.

Many families simply cannot afford the average $157 needed each term to send a child to school in a country where around 65 percent of 10 million people live on less than $1 a day.

The programmes the children listen to are called "Learning at *Taonga* Market", or "Thank You" Market. And Mwale, who dropped out of school because his father could not afford to pay, is one of the grateful ones.

Usually 17-year-olds in Zambia are preparing to go to university or other third-level institutions, but although Mwale is only getting ready to go to high school now, he is not fazed.

"*Taonga* has brought hope to many of us and I want to use it as a springboard to achieve greater heights in life," he said, adding he could compete with children taught in regular schools.

Freeplay says nearly a third of *Taonga* pupils are orphans and almost 50 percent are girls. Most have missed years of schooling after dropping out or may never have taken classes before, because of poverty or isolation.

"The (*Taonga*) programme has proved to be popular. The children appreciate the lessons and so do their parents," said Mwenya Mvula, a volunteer teacher since 2001. Of the first batch of pupils to sit primary school leavers' examinations under the *Taonga* system, five out of seven passed and qualified for high school, further boosting the credibility of the informal system. "*Taonga* has proved so successful that some centres also offer adult groups the opportunity to use the Freeplay Lifeline radios after school hours for community health projects" Pearson said.

Lusaka's government-run Ngwelele School said the performance of students tutored by Taonga was impressive. "The children we have integrated into our system have performed very well, in most instances better than those we started with because they are mature," Givers Nyoni, deputy head teacher at Ngwelele, told Reuters.

www.alertnet.org

females. *Beyond Inequalities 2005: Women in Malawi* reveals that integration into ordinary schools for persons with disabilities and special schools to cater for specific disabilities is limited in Malawi.

It is also important to acknowledge the heterogeneity of disabled girls. Their access to education is affected not only by their gender and disability but also their type of disability, the socio-economic status of their family, their race/ ethnicity, whether they live in an urban or rural area, and a host of other factors. The educational needs of women and girls with disabilities have gone largely unnoticed by those committed to promoting gender equity.

In addition, HIV and AIDS messages are usually packaged in print and electronic formats. Visually and hearing impaired girls therefore face challenges in accessing this information and may not be able to adequately protect themselves against sexually transmitted infections and HIV. Although many countries in the region have HIV and AIDS policies in place, most of them do not adequately deal with provision of information to people living with disabilities.

Community radios for education

Community radio is one of the vehicles for empowering citizens to participate in education (especially in rural areas). Community radio stations operate on a small level, mostly broadcasting with relatively little power. Many community radios work with the concept "by the community and for the community." Community radios have been an alternative source of providing education to disadvantaged children in the region. One advantage is that community radio is affordable, most stations are supported through donor funds.

Information Communication Technologies for development

Inadequate participation and access of women to Information Communication Technologies (ICT) is placed by the United Nations as the third most important issue affecting women globally, after poverty and violence against women. SADC recognises the importance of ICT and states that, "this paradigm shift from the industrial to the digital economy is the very foundation of the new economy." In order to derive benefits from the new economy it is imperative for the SADC region to review and refocus development strategies and approaches by aggressively using ICT as a catalyst for socio-economic development and prosperity."[22] At policy level, in 2001, SADC published policy guidelines in making ICT a priority in SADC and this was followed by an ICT Declaration in 2001. The declaration is a commitment by member states to embark on in-depth reforms to take maximum advantage of the new technologies.

ICT is described as a forceful tool to improve governance and strengthen democracy. ICTs are particularly powerful for giving a voice to women who so frequently have been isolated, invisible and without a voice. ICT has been identified as important in enhancing education and providing an effective means of reaching large numbers of people. Further, early experience suggests that they can widen access, improve quality of education and help introduce new ideas into the curriculum."[23] ICTs can also help women make incredible progress, obtaining better economic and bargaining power both at home and in the market. Having access to the internet permits women from developing regions, who commonly work in areas linked closely to global markets, to have more control over their products than they would when forced to use a middle person.

In the SADC region, access to and use of ICTs is still de-linked from social and economic development, with more men than women accessing and using the technologies. For the few women accessing and using ICTs, their contact is

mainly in end user, lower skilled ICT jobs related to word processing or data entry.

The term 'digital divide' has become synonymous with the wide variations in access to ICTs, not only in the North-South or urban-rural context, but also in the case of men and women. The gender divide adversely affects women, who make up the majority of the rural poor in developing countries. Issues of time, language and literacy limit their ability to use modern ICTs. Biased cultural views also prevent them from visiting public access points that are frequented mostly by men.

Botswana, Lesotho, Malawi, Mozambique, Tanzania, Zambia and Zimbabwe have developed ICT policies in recent years. Unfortunately, where policies have been developed, the gender dimensions of ICT use are not clearly articulated. Zambia's ICT policy, adopted in 2003, identifies mainstreaming youth and gender issues but gender concerns and issues do not feature in any of the policy goals. Gender is listed as a priority and the policy notes that a threat to using ICTs is women's low interest in science and technology courses. The policy thus ignores the historical and structural inequalities between women and men in accessing education. The non-articulation of these inequalities makes it difficult to put in place strategies to address the issues. The policy is thus not likely to benefit women in accessing ICTs.

ICTs have also been seen as an alternative to mainstream media, which does not adequately cover women's issues. The increasing use of internet communication technology as well as women centred websites are assisting women in Botswana to network and air their views. However, gender aspects of the medium have not been thoroughly investigated and women's access and use could still be limited.[24]

Increasing women's access to ICT remains a huge task for most countries in southern Africa as it involves increasing availability of communication in areas where a majority of women live - the rural areas. Leaders attending the 2001 SADC summit in Malawi pledged to improve delivery of ICTs as a catalyst for improved living standards for its entire people. The reality reveals that much needs to be done for that pledge to be realised, especially for women in the region.

Extensions of infrastructure, particularly wireless and satellite communications, to rural areas and peri-urban areas remain crucial to increasing women's access. While ICT can offer significant opportunities for the majority of women and girls, including poor women living in rural areas, regrettably, the ability of southern African women to take advantage of the opportunities that ICT can offer is inhibited by policies, and limited enabling environments in their countries to extend communication infrastructure to rural areas.

Other factors constraining women's access to ICT include literacy and education, language, time, cost, geographical location of facilities, social and cultural norms, and women's lack of computer and information search and dissemination skills.

To ensure women's ability to effectively take advantage of opportunities presented by information technologies, gender and development policy makers need to be sensitised on ICT issues. ICT and gender policy makers need to enter into dialogue so that ICT programmes meet the needs of women and so that women-targeted programmes contain ICT training and awareness.

Further education at all levels, from literacy through scientific and technological education needs to be improved. Such improvement requires interventions at all levels of education. Information technologies could be integrated into literacy programs in order to expose girls and women to new technologies at the early stages, and allow for much-needed integration of these two programmes.

Beyond access to basic education, girls and women must be equipped with skills to prepare them for a range of roles in information technology as users, creators, designers, and managers. Therefore, efforts should focus on increasing the number of girls and women studying ICT- related subjects in formal schooling and seeking ICT training outside of school, as well as related areas to help them fully utilise information technology skills.

Washington Midzi for SARDC, 2003

Challenges to education provision for women and girls

The challenges hampering the promotion of education for women and girls in southern Africa include poverty, violence, civil war and discriminatory regimes. South Africa has had to address the imbalances in education brought about by many years of the apartheid system. The apartheid system resulted in an education system that was racialised and gendered with major differences existing between rural and urban areas.

In countries such as Angola, the Democratic Republic of Congo (DRC) and Mozambique there have been serious political, economic and social crises brought about by protracted civil war and social unrest, resulting in destruction of social infrastructure including education infrastructure. In the Democratic Republic of Congo, the situation is further compounded by intermittent civil unrest in neighbouring Rwanda and Burundi. In the DRC, children's rights to education have been seriously violated because a lot of children and minors were conscripted as child soldiers and sex slaves during the civil war. The girl child's prospects for education have also been affected by this social upheaval in that many have become mothers before their time through rape and abduction by the military. Available figures indicate that illiteracy rates for females in DRC stand at 44.1 percent and that of males at 18.1 percent, 35.7 percent for girls and 21.7 percent for boys.[25]

Angola, which went through a long protracted national war, also faces challenges in providing education for its citizens. During the many years of civil war that ended and left the country's education system in shambles, an estimated one million children were deprived of educational opportunities. To redress this situation, in February 2003, the Angolan government launched the "Back to School" campaign. The project aims to introduce 250,000 children to formal education in Bie and Malanje, two provinces that particularly suffered during the war.

In an effort to correct past imbalances, post apartheid South Africa provides for compulsory education for all children and disallows discrimination on the basis of sex in access to education. According to the South African Census 2001 figures, women over the age of 20 constitute 60 percent of those without schooling.

In the other southern African countries where war and racial discrimination have not been a major factor, disparities amongst females and males arise more from higher dropout rates for females due to pregnancy and early marriage and discriminatory social practices.

Practices that discriminate against girls include certain types of socialisation practices such as initiation ceremonies and early marriages that continue to negatively impact on girl's education. Socialisation practices that orient females to traditional female roles tend to lead to early pregnancies and at times girls are then taken out of school for marriage. In the United Republic of Tanzania, young girls dropping out of school to be married to older men is not uncommon. For example, research from Koshika Women's Group has shown that in 1994 about 15 girls below 16 were forced out of school for early marriage. The same happened in Tandale Ward, where 18 girls were already married before their 15th birthday.[26] In many instances, circumstances such as this are behind the high school dropout rates amongst girls across the region.

Other factors impacting on access to education are poverty at the household level, brought on in the main by structural adjustment programmes, high national debts, and the HIV and AIDS pandemic which has meant the loss of breadwinners and the availability of fewer resources at household level. The pandemic has also impacted on the quality of education as some qualified teaching staff are infected or affected by HIV.

Poverty is a major barrier to females attaining education. When resources are scarce, girls are the first to be taken out of school, often because they are considered to have the option to get married and their education is therefore a waste of resources. Poverty across the region has taken a toll on the quality of education, generally impacting negatively on education infrastructure and on teaching resources. In addition despite "free education policies" in most countries, hidden costs exist in the form of school uniforms, books, writing materials and transport, resulting

in some families being unable to keep children in school. Instead of sending them to school, affected families are likely to keep children at home to assist in raising household incomes. Girls in particular will be kept back to take care of household chores and look after younger siblings. As noted in the 2000 SIDA Regional Report on primary school dropouts in Mozambique, "The single most important factor that contributed to bad school achievement was work for the family survival."

In the last 10 to 15 years, the impact of HIV and AIDS and its connection to increasing poverty in the family caused by the death of a breadwinner has also determined how much education the girl child can get. In countries hard–hit by HIV and AIDS, school availability has fallen precipitously. Substantial numbers of teachers are ill, dying or caring for family members. In Malawi for example, the pupil teacher ratio in some schools swelled to 96:1. As a result of AIDS related illnesses, quality has been a casualty of overcrowded classes, limited resources, and untrained teachers and administrators. Loss of parents to AIDS is also detrimental to a child's education. Recent data from sub-Saharan Africa found that children aged between 10 and 14 who had lost both of their parents are less likely to be in school than their peers who were living with at least one parent. Studies in Kenya, Tanzania and Zambia found that even when orphans attended school, they were less likely than non-orphans to be at the correct grade level for their age group. The irony is that orphans are frequently deprived of quality education, which is the very thing they need to help protect themselves from HIV.[27]

Cases of violence in schools are also an issue affecting female enrolments in schools. Concerning violence in schools, a UNICEF report notes that some schools fail to provide the necessary protection for children to flourish and, in fact may expose young people, especially girls to violence. School cultures contribute to gender violence in schools. Often, gender stereotypes and inequities abound in the classroom, where different behaviours and roles are expected from girls and boys. Gender-based school violence takes many forms, of which the most explicit are sexual harassment, aggressive or unsolicited sexual advances, touching, groping, intimidation, verbal abuse or sexual assaults. Perpetrators of gender-based school violence are generally older male classmates, but teachers are also offenders.[28]

Of all countries in the region, South Africa identifies school violence as a major concern. Violence in schools remains a problem although the constitution enshrines the fundamental human rights principle of bodily and psychological integrity. Violence in schools is a direct violation of this basic human right. When the Human Rights Watch released their research report, "Scared at school: sexual violence against girls in South African schools," the problem of harassment, other forms of gender–based violence, sexually transmitted infections and the increase of HIV and AIDS amongst young girls were highlighted as major problems.[29]

Policies and programmes on women and girls' education

In recognition of the various factors impacting negatively on women and girls' education, countries across the region have implemented various policies and programmes. Many policies have taken cognisance of international and regional instruments, which emphasise the importance of education for girls and women. As indicated, school enrolments, espe-cially girls' education is under threat. The Mozambique Strategic Plan for Education outlines three main areas of focus:

- expansion of access and equity
- improvement of quality of education
- institutional capacity building

Under expansion of access and equity, the Mozambican government is looking for ways and means to stimulate access and success in training and education. Some of the initiatives towards this end are "The Sara Implementation Initiative" which is aimed at raising community awareness on the importance of girls' education, including gender issues and upgrading teachers' skills. The government is also working towards setting annual targets for enrolments of girls in all districts where there are gender disparities and the establishment of counselling offices to prevent girls from dropping out of schools. Under non-formal and vocational training, the government runs literacy education for pregnant teenagers, single mothers and adult women.[30]

In response to decreasing school enrolments, the Zambian government has introduced free basic education (grade one to seven) and embarked on programmes to expand basic school infrastructure.[31] The government has also introduced special bursary schemes for girls at primary and secondary school levels; lower pass mark for girls to compensate for gender imbalances and 25 percent bursaries allocated to female students at university.

Zimbabwe has put in place a universal primary education policy and the Basic Education Assistance Module (BEAM) to help children from disadvantaged communities. The programme targets children facing economic difficulties and orphans and stipulates that 50 percent of all beneficiaries attending secondary school must be female.

Various education reforms have also been implemented touching on the curriculum, where gender stereotyping is being removed from all textbooks and gender mainstreamed. For example, the social sciences curriculum has been reviewed to include children's rights and human rights in general and has been made more gender responsive.

In order to tackle dropout rates due to school pregnancy, many countries in the region have embarked on programmes to allow girls to re-enter the school system after they have delivered. Malawi has a policy of girls re-entering the formal school system after pregnancy, after one academic year. Re-admittance however is dependent upon assurance of safe custody of the child. However, some parents fear that their daughters will fall pregnant again and stop them from going back to school.[32]Further, the policy is characterised by lack of detailed implementation guidelines, lack of publicity, opposition to timing of re-admission as well as negative attitudes towards mothers. Other challenges have to do with girls not being able to get back to school because they have no one to care for their babies.

Botswana, South Africa, Zambia and Zimbabwe have also implemented re-entry policies. Botswana supplements their programmes with the Young Women's Christian Association Teen Mothers and *Diphalana* Projects (UNICEF), initiated to enrol young mothers who had to leave school due to pregnancy. The re-admission policy however faces many implementation challenges. *Beyond Inequalities: Women in Southern Africa* (2000) report noted that girls who fell pregnant in Namibia were expelled from school. However, *Beyond Inequalities 2005: Women in Namibia* report notes a shift in policy. A new government policy on pregnancy among learners in school was developed to allow girls to return to school after their babies are a year old. In practice though, most school girls who fall pregnant are expelled from school for a period of two years and thereafter might be allowed to resume studies in a different school.[33] South Africa goes a step further by allowing girls to continue schooling even while they are pregnant and to readmit them after they deliver.

School based violence is a major factor hindering education of girls in South Africa. In different provinces, the Department of Education has made concerted efforts to address the increasing violence in schools. The Western Cape Education Department drafted a procedure to deal with complaints of sexual harassment and child abuse by students, educators and school employees. The Western Cape has started the flagship programme, called the "Safer School Project" and learners can phone in and report any kind of harassment in secondary schools.[34] Through the Nelson Mandela Children's Fund, a manual has been developed to "assist educators in handling situations where they either suspect that a student has been sexually abused or when the student discloses abuse." [35]

The government of Swaziland is ensuring gender sensitivity in the curriculum and the elimination of gender stereotypes. There are also programmes to encourage and empower girls to enrol for science and technical subjects. Partners in this programme are the Forum for African Women Educationalists (FAWE) Swaziland chapter and Female Education in Mathematics and Science in Africa (FEMSA). Through partnerships such as this, programmes involving career guidance, counselling, health education, HIV and AIDS education, and sensitisation sessions on gender violence, rights and life skills can be successfully implemented and maintained. UNICEF also supports education programmes that incorporate a gender perspective, with special emphasis on the girl child under the African Girl Education Initiative Project. In order to support orphaned children and in line with Millennium Development Goal targets, the Swaziland government has mobilised funds to ensure orphans have access to education.[36]

Way forward

Based on the above overview, the following are suggested as the way forward:

◆ countries in the region need to capitalise on initiatives to ensure girls are retained in the school system. This could be done through special bursaries, lower pass marks and encouraging all-girls schools where females reportedly do better than in mixed schools.

◆ national education plans should work towards scraping school fees and other hidden costs through well planned education reform strategies. Towards this end, governments may need to support poor and vulnerable children. In addition, governments need to support school food and nutrition programmes as these among other things help alleviate short-term hunger and provide required nutrients. In poor families, even when education is free, it is not uncommon for children to be taken out of school to work to supplement family incomes or to search for food.

◆ programmes directed at teenage mothers should be well supported so as to help girls get back into schools.

◆ there needs to be more committed, effective and concerted efforts in ending war and conflict in the region as it sets back achievements gained not only in education but hinders development as a whole. In times of war and conflict, education of children is disrupted and whole generations miss out on education thereby raising illiteracy levels. In situations such as these, women and girls invariably come out worse off.

◆ in light of the HIV and AIDS pandemic, life skills based education needs to be increased. Life skills education improves critical thinking, problem solving, self-management and improves interpersonal skills that allow young people to acquire knowledge and attitudes that support the adoption of healthy behaviours. The importance of these skills to women and girls cannot be overemphasised.

◆ education for HIV and AIDS orphans and other vulnerable children needs to be made a priority and adequate resources allocated for this effort. A generation of uneducated girls and boys is a sure way of producing another generation of uneducated young people.

◆ girls need to be protected from gender-based violence. The home and school environments need to be safe and healthy. Schools that offer a secure environment that encourages children to attend and reassures parents that their daughters and sons are safe should be established.

◆ the poor quality of education in rural areas hinders school attendance and discourages parents. Many rural pupils who fail to get places in secondary school invariably slip back into illiteracy. Efforts should be made to improve provision of education in rural areas.

◆ the girl child with disabilities must be afforded an equal opportunity to get an education and opportunities for further training.

the potential for ICTs to enhance education must be developed, especially for the benefit of rural areas where education is of poorer quality.

Conclusion

Issues such as gender equity in education, career counselling, girls' and women's access to higher education, education of girls with disabilities and access to ICTs remain a challenge to the provision of education for all. Of particular emphasis in this report is the fact that on the whole, the quality of education is going down across the region and that where 50/50 ratios between girls and boys have been reached; there still exist high dropout rates for females. By about grade five, a number of girls will have dropped out of the school system compared to the numbers that will have been there in grade one. This has resulted in the gains in enrolments being lost along the way. The implication of this is that fewer girls move on to secondary school and even fewer enrol in tertiary institutions and university. When females make it to tertiary institutions and university they are marginalised in the less technical subjects, a factor that limits women's access to ICTs.

The disabled girl child faces major challenges in accessing education as she is discriminated against because of her sex and disability thus disabled girls must have opportunities to access education and complete it availed to them. The chapter has also highlighted the importance of ICTs in education and development, noting that this is an area that is yet to be fully utilised but has great potential for contributing to education.

More needs to be done to mainstream issues of gender, HIV and AIDS, human rights and education on sexuality for awareness raising and empowerment of girls, challenging gender stereotypes and discarding negative practices. Access and use of ICTs for education also need to be enhanced and gender mainstreamed in ICT policies. Another major area of concern is that of school based violence, which in countries like South Africa is a major issue impacting on girls' and women's education. The region also has to grapple with war and conflict and its devastating impact on education provision.

Endnotes

2 UNICEF, *The State of the World's Children 2004 – Girls, Education and Development*, UNICEF, New York, 2004

3 UNICEF, Girls HIV and AIDS and Education

4 Zambia Demographic and Health Survey Data 2001. Cited in Girls, HIV/AIDS and Education UNICEF

5 The CRC is the most widely accepted human rights treaty. It reaffirms the right of every child without discrimination of any kind to free and compulsory primary schooling, and states that the higher levels shall be accessible to all. The CRC contains a strong emphasis on measures to promote free primary education and financial support, human rights, education, sex education and reproductive health information, educational counselling, and a gender aware curriculum. The MDGs Goal number 2 is specific on prescriptions on education: Ensure that by 2015, children everywhere, boys and girls alike, will be able to complete a full course of primary education. The Beijing Platform for Action recommends among other things providing equal access to education by year 2015 and eradicating illiteracy among women at least to half its 1990 levels. The Dakar Platform for Action on Education (2000) re-affirms the Jomteim (Thailand 1990) World Conference on Education for All prescribes that governments commit themselves to achieving quality basic education for all by 2015 or earlier with particular emphasis on girls' education.

6 UNESCO, *EFA Global Monitoring Report 2005, Education For All, The Quality Imperative,* UNESCO, Paris, 2005, p130

7 For about a third of the developing countries, there are no observed data on literacy more than 1985. Literacy Assessment and Monitoring Programme: Background and Approaches , UNESCO Institute For Statistics (Internet Source)

8 UWC Gender Equity Unit and SARDC-WID-SAA, *Beyond Inequalities: Women in South Africa*(draft), UWC/ SARDC, Bellville and Harare, 2004, p40

9 UNDP-Angola, *UNDP Country Cooperative Assessment*, UNDP, Luanda, 2002
Angola HDR/UNDP 1988 - 1999, cited in UNDP/Country Cooperative Assessment: 2002).Angola data is estimate for 1998

10 INDICATOR: (Gross Primary school enrolment ratio-The number of children enrolled in a primary or secondary level regardless of the age, divided by the population of the age group that officially corresponds to the same level)

11 UNICEF, *Progress for Children: A Report card on Gender Parity and Primary, Education,* UNICEF, New York, 2005

12 United Republic of Tanzania Millennium Development Goal Report,2005

13 UNICEF, *Progress for Children: A Report Card on Gender Parity and Primary Education*

14 Secondary net attendance rates based on household surveys of demography and health surveys and Multiple Cluster Surveys 1999- 2003.

Cited in UNICEF, *Progress for Children: A Report Card on Gender Parity and Primary Education,* Number 2, April 2005

15 UWC Gender Equity Unit and SARDC- WID-SAA, *Beyond Inequalities: Women in South Africa* (draft), UWC/SARDC, Bellville and Harare, 2004

16 ZARD and SARDC-WIDSAA, *Beyond Inequalities 2005: Women in Zambia,* ZARD/SARDC, Lusaka and Harare, 2005

17 UWC Gender Equity Unit and SARDC, *Beyond Inequalities: Women in South Africa* (draft)

18 UNAM and SARDC WIDSAA, *Beyond Inequalities 2005: Women in Namibia,* UNAM/SARDC, Windhoek and Harare, 2005

19 WLSA Malawi and SARDC WIDSAA, *Beyond Inequalities 2005: Women in Malawi,* WLSA/SARDC, Limbe and Harare, 2005

20 UNAM and SARDC WIDSAA, *Beyond Inequalities 2005: Women in Namibia*

21 WLSA Malawi and SARDC WIDSAA, *Beyond Inequalities 2005: Women in Malawi*

22 SADC, *Southern African Development Community Regional Indicative Strategic Development Plan,* SADC, Gaborone, 2004

23 Impact, Isis WICCE, an Annual Publication Isis-WICCE, Uganda, Vol. No 5

24 Women's NGO Coalition and SARDC WID-SAA, *Beyond Inequalities 2005: Women in Botswana,* WNGOC/SARDC, Gaborone and Harare, 2005

25 Ministry of the Condition of Women and the Family, *National Report of the Democratic Republic of Congo on the Review and Evaluation of the Beijing +10 Plan of Action,* Ministry of the Condition of Women and the Family, Kinshasa, 2004

26 SARDC WIDSAA, *Beyond Inequalities, Women in Southern Africa,*

27 Demographic Health Surveys 1997-2001 cited in UNICEF Girls HIV/AIDS and Education Internet Source).

28 UNICEF, Demographic Health Surveys.

29 Human Rights Watch, *Scared at school: Sexual Violence against Girls in South African Schools,* Human Rights Watch, South Africa, 2001.

30 Ministry of Women and Social Welfare Coordination, Mozambique Review of Beijing + 10 Report, Ministry of Women and Social Welfare Coordination, Maputo, 2004

31 ZARD and SARDC WIDSAA, *Beyond Inequalities 2005: Women in Zambia,* ZARD/SARDC, Lusaka and Harare, 2005

32 WLSA Malawi and SARDC WIDSAA, *Beyond Inequalities 2005: Women in Malawi*

33 UNAM and SARDC WIDSAA, *Beyond Inequalities 2005: Women in Namibia*

34 UWC Gender Equity Unit and SARDC WID-SAA, *Beyond Inequalities 2005: Women in South Africa*

35 UWC GEU and SARDC WIDSAA, Beyond Inequalities 2005: Women in South Africa

36 Ministry of Home Affairs: Gender Coordination Unit, *Report for Swaziland on the Review of Beijing +10,* Ministry of Home Affairs: Gender Coordination Unit, Mbabane, 2004

References

Gender in Development Division: Cabinet Office, *Progress on the Implementation of the Beijing Platform for Action*, Gender In Development Division: Cabinet Office, Lusaka, 2004

Human Rights Watch, *Scared At School: Sexual Violence Against Girls in South African Schools*, Human Rights Watch, South Africa, 2001

INE, *Anuario Estatisco*, 2004, Maputo, Mozambique, 2004

Ministry of Community Development, Gender and Children, *Review and Appraisal of the Progress in the Implementation of the Beijing Platform for Action*, Ministry of Community Development, Gender and Children, Dodoma, 2004

Ministry of Home Affairs: Gender Coordination Unit, *Report For Swaziland On The Review Of Beijing +10*, Ministry of Home Affairs: Gender Coordination Unit, Mbabane, 2004

Ministry of Labour and Home Affairs: Women's Affairs Department, *Botswana's Response To The Questionnaire to Governments On Implementation Of The Beijing Platform for Action*, Women's Affairs Department, Gaborone, 2004

Ministry of Public Service, Labour and Social Welfare and UNDP, *Zimbabwe Millennium Development Goals: 2004 Progress Report*, Ministry of Public Service, Labour and Social Welfare and UNDP, Harare, 2005

Ministry of the Condition of Women and the Family, *National Report of the Democratic Republic of Congo On The Review and Evaluation of the Beijing +10 Plan of Action*, Ministry of the Condition of Women and the Family, Kinshasa, 2004

Ministry of Women Affairs and Child Welfare, *Namibia National Progress Report On The Implementation Of The Beijing Platform for Action*, Ministry of Women Affairs and Child Welfare, Windhoek, 2004

Ministry of Youth Development, Gender and Employment Creation, *Report on the Implementation Of The African and Beijing Platforms For Action*, Ministry of Youth Development, Gender and Employment Creation, Harare, 2004

SARDC WIDSAA, *Beyond Inequalities: Women in Southern Africa*, SARDC, Harare, 2000

SARDC WIDSAA and the University of Namibia, *Beyond Inequalities 2005: Women in Namibia*, UNAM/SARDC, Windhoek and Harare, 2005

SARDC WIDSSA and the University of the Western Cape Gender Equity Unit, *Beyond Inequalities Women in South Africa*, UWC/ SARDC, Bellville and Harare, 1997

SARDC WIDSSA and the University of the Western Cape Gender Equity Unit, *Beyond Inequalities 2005: Women in South Africa*, UWC/ SARDC, Bellville and Harare, 2005

SARDC WIDSAA and Women and Law in Southern Africa Malawi, *Beyond Inequalities 2005: Women in Malawi*, WLSA/ SARDC, Limbe and Harare, 2005

SARDC WIDSAA and Women's NGO Coalition, *Beyond Inequalities 2005: Women in Botswana*, WNGOC/SARDC, Gaborone and Harare, 2005

SARDC WIDSAA and ZARD and, *Beyond Inequalities 2005: Women in Zambia*, ZARD / SARDC, Lusaka and Harare, 2005

UNDP/GRZ, *Zambia Human Development Report*, UNDP/GRZ, Lusaka, 2003

UNDP-Angola, *UNDP Country Cooperative Assessment*, UNDP, Luanda, 2002

UNESCO, *EFA Global Monitoring Report 2005, Education For All, The Quality Imperative*, UNESCO, Paris, 2005

UNICEF, *The State of the World's Children – Childhood Under Threat*, UNICEF, New York, 2005

UNICEF, *The State of the World's Children 2004 – Girls, Education and Development*, UNICEF, New York, 2004

UNICEF, *UNICEF Progress for Children: A Report Card On Gender Parity and Primary, Education*, UNICEF, New York, 2005

ZWRCN, "Gender Budgets Watch – Education," on *www.kubatana.net*, Harare, 2004
1 SARDC WIDSAA, *Beyond Inequalities: Women in Southern Africa*, SARDC, Harare, 2000, p239

WOMEN AND HEALTH

4

Introduction

Impressive gains in child health and access to primary health care realised in most SADC countries up to the end of the 20th century have largely been reversed due to various challenges, the greatest of which is the increasing maternal mortality rates in most of the 14 countries of the region. In general, the first five years of the 21st century have been characterised by under-investment in the health sector, resulting in deteriorating health infrastructure, skilled human resource crises as a result of migration of highly trained health workers to western nations, increasing burden of morbidity and mortality as a result of HIV and AIDS, and impoverished communities unable to cope with the costs and burden of caring for the ill and dying.

In addition to this, the last two decades have seen a resurgence and spread of "old" communicable diseases once thought to be well controlled, for example cholera, tuberculosis (TB), malaria and yellow fever, while "new" epidemics, notably HIV and AIDS, threaten last century's health gains. The world's three worst communicable diseases in terms of morbidity and mortality are AIDS, TB and malaria. HIV and AIDS, TB and malaria are now recognised as playing a significant role in slowing and even reversing hard-won economic growth and development gains in countries in the region.

Communicable diseases tend to affect mostly poor and malnourished communities and these diseases often exacerbate malnutrition due to their effect on food intake and also because nutritional deficiencies occur during the course of these illnesses. They also affect women disproportionately. In the countries of southern Africa for example, at least two thirds of young people (15-25) with HIV are women. In addition to the biological and physiological factors that increase the susceptibility of women to HIV, gender inequality and sexual violence also contribute to the disparity in infection rates. In SADC countries, TB is a leading cause of death among women of reproductive age. Furthermore, TB and HIV co-infection is reported to

---

Status and impact of tuberculosis, HIV and AIDS and malaria | Box 4.1

- Each episode of malaria may cost up to three percent of a household's annual income and a household may experience many episodes per year; the average annual loss of income in the poorest households in Malawi is 20 percent.
- The long and expensive treatment for TB can cost from five to 21 percent of annual household income.
- Terminal AIDS cases cost from eight to 100 percent of household income.
- In Swaziland, the average hospital stay is six days long, but in 80 percent of cases this increases to 30 days for TB patients with HIV.[2]
- In some countries, health workers are at greater risk of contracting HIV simply due to inadequate provision of basic medical supplies such as latex gloves.
- In Botswana, up to one third of health workers are HIV positive and the figure was expected to rise to 40 percent by 2005.
- In Lusaka, Zambia, it is estimated that 39 percent of midwives and 44 percent of nurses are living with HIV.
- Further, all three diseases impose burdens on already weak health systems, especially on staffing, drug supplies, laboratory services and infrastructure.

The Global Fund to Fight AIDS, "The Status and Impact of the three diseases, Tuberculosis, HIV and AIDS and Malaria," 2005

be high in the region and estimated to be 66.4 percent in South Africa. A recent report on mortality and causes of death in South Africa confirmed that TB was the leading cause of death for both men and women aged 15-49.[1]

The last decade of the 20th century was characterised by the adoption of a number of global and regional commitments and targets for the improvement of the health of people in developing countries. Key among these were the SADC Health Protocol (1999), the International Conference on Population and Development (ICPD) Program of Action adopted in 1994, the 12 Global Critical Areas of Concern emanating from the Beijing World Conference on Women in 1995, the SADC Declaration on Gender and Development (1997), and the Maseru Declaration on HIV and AIDS (2003). In keeping with these goals, SADC countries identified the improvement of health services and provision of adequate health infrastructure for the overall improvement of the health of the population among areas needing attention in order to improve the situation of women.

It is increasingly evident that while some of the regions of the world are on track to meet most of the goals, many countries in sub-Saharan Africa will not meet the targets for advancing development and reducing poverty by 2015. Even more troubling is the evidence that an increasing number of countries in sub-Saharan Africa, including SADC countries, have experienced a drop in the human development index between 1990 and 2002.[3]

While much of this decline is attributed to HIV and AIDS, the conflicts of the last two decades in Angola and the Democratic Republic of the Congo (DRC) have had a devastating impact on the health status of their populations and hampered progress in making health facilities accessible. In addition, post-conflict countries, notably Mozambique, have faced the challenge of incurring massive debt in order to improve health infrastructure among other national priorities.

The threat of epidemics continues in many countries of the region, incidents include cholera outbreaks in different countries in the region. In addition to disease outbreaks, some countries in the region have been hard hit by drought and floods increasing food insecurity, particularly among vulnerable households dependent on subsistence agriculture.

The food insecurity which escalated into a humanitarian crisis affecting countries of the region from 2002 has also highlighted the persistent nutritional problems among people in the region, particularly women and children. The food crisis has also refocused attention on the insidious and previously ignored problem of micronutrient deficiencies most evident in children and women. Nutritional insecurity is also reported to be on the increase in most of the countries of the region, despite successful reductions in child malnutrition in a number of countries in the early 1990s.

With the exception of Botswana and South Africa, which had 50.04 percent and 50.4 percent respectively of people living in urban areas in 2000[4], the majority of people in southern Africa still live in rural areas. Improving access to basic services and economic opportunities, especially to the rural majority, still remains a challenge for most of the countries were infrastructure has always been underdeveloped. While some countries have increased their health expenditure in line with the pledge made in Abuja in April 2001 to allocate at least 15 percent of government budgets to the improvement of the health sector, some are clearly lagging behind.

A review conducted by the Human Science Research Council of South Africa on government expenditure of six countries in the region during 2001 and 2002 found that only South Africa and Zimbabwe fulfilled their commitment to allocate 15 percent of government expenditure to health. Lesotho, Mozambique and Swaziland had spent about half of the 15 percent target, while Botswana spent 10.4 percent.[5] The review questioned whether the 15 percent target is adequate to meet the challenges posed by the HIV and AIDS epidemic to the health sector.

Provision of health services and infrastructure has also declined in countries that implemented Structural Adjustment Programmes (SAPs) in line with International Monetary Fund (IMF) and World Bank reforms. A recent review of available studies on structural adjustment and health for a World Health Organisation (WHO) commission states, "The majority of studies in Africa, whether theoretical or empirical, are negative towards structural adjustment and its effects on health outcomes."[6]

Policy framework

A number of regional and global commitments and targets for the improvement of women's health are in place. These include:

SADC Health Protocol

Among its objectives, the Health Protocol seeks to offer cost effective and quality integrated health care services through regional co-operation. Some of its priorities are targeted at combating malaria, tuberculosis and HIV and AIDS. The protocol recognises that regional co-operation and integration are essential for effective control of communicable and non-communicable diseases. Under the section on reproductive health, the protocol calls on Member States to formulate policies, strategies, programmes and procedures in:

- developing a surveillance system for monitoring maternal mortality;
- reduction of maternal mortality;
- reduction of the incidence of birth defects; and
- empowerment of women and men to have access to safe, effective, affordable and acceptable methods for regulation of fertility.

International Conference on Population and Development

The conference broadened the narrow definition of family planning to one that focuses on reproductive rights as basic human rights. It noted the need for men and women to be informed about and have access to family planning services and health care services. The conference made commitments to make reproductive health care accessible to all individuals through the primary health care system no later than 2015.

Services provided are to include family planning counselling, information, education, communication and services; education and services for pre-natal care; safe delivery and post-natal care, especially breast-feeding and infant and women's health care; prevention and appropriate treatment of infertility; abortion including prevention of abortion, management of consequences of abortion, treatment of reproductive health infections, STDs and other reproductive health conditions; and information, education and counselling as appropriate, on human sexuality, reproductive health and responsible parenting. The role that women play as primary custodians of family health was recognised and high priority was placed on programmes that reduce HIV infection, giving priority to information, education and communication campaigns.

Beijing Declaration and Platform for Action (BDPFA)

One of the 12 critical areas of concern in the BDPFA is women's health. The declaration recognises and re-affirms the right of all women to control all aspects of their health, in particular their own fertility, and that this is basic to women's empowerment. It notes the decrease in public health spending and how Structural Adjustment Programmes (SAPs) have led to the deterioration of health services in countries of the South. The BDPFA urges governments to address health challenges that include unequal access to and use of basic health resources, including primary health services for the prevention and treatment of childhood diseases, malnutrition, anaemia, diarrhoeal diseases, communicable diseases, malaria and TB.

Millennium Development Goals

Goal number 5 of the MDGs calls for improved maternal health and sets a target for countries to reduce maternal mortality rates by three-quarters between 1990 and 2015. Goal 6 calls for a reduction in HIV and AIDS, malaria and other diseases by 2015.

SADC Declaration on Gender and Development

In the SADC Declaration on Gender and Development, member states committed themselves to protect and promote the reproductive and sexual rights of women and girls. Violence against women has also been recognised the world over as a major health issue. The addendum on the Prevention and Eradication of Violence Against Women and Children commits member states to, among other measures, enact laws such as sexual offences and domestic violence legislation that criminalise all forms of violence against women and take appropriate measures to impose penalties for the prevention and eradication of violence against women.

Maseru Declaration (2003-2007) on HIV and AIDS

In recognition of the devastating impact of HIV and AIDS, SADC Heads of State and Government in 2003 signed the Maseru Declaration (2003-2007) on HIV and AIDS. To facilitate operationalisation of this declaration and to fast track the implementation of the SADC HIV and AIDS Strategic Framework and Programme of Action (2003-2007), an HIV and AIDS Unit was established at the SADC Secretariat in the Department of Strategic Planning, Gender and Development and Policy Harmonisation. The Maseru Declaration has also fuelled governments in the region to intensify resource mobilisation by calling on governments to allocate at least 15 percent of annual state budgets to improving the health sector.

SADC has also revised and strengthened its multi-sectoral HIV and AIDS Strategic Framework and Programme of Action, to ensure a multi-sectoral, participatory approach that aims to strengthen partnerships with civil society organisations, faith-based organisations, business, labour and international cooperating partners. SADC identifies five priority areas/goals in the AIDS Strategic Framework and Programme of Action. These are:
- prevention and social mobilisation;
- improving care and access to testing and counselling services, treatment and support;
- accelerating development of programmes for the mitigation of the impact of HIV and AIDS;
- intensifying regional and country resource mobilisation programmes; and
- strengthening institutional monitoring and evaluation mechanisms.

The timelines for achieving these goals are:
- mainstream HIV and AIDS in all programmes of the various SADC directorates by 2006;

- establish a regional prevalence database by 2005;
- develop and harmonise regional programmes for the prevention, treatment and care of people living with HIV and AIDS by 2005;
- develop a regional policy and guidelines for the mitigation of the social impacts of HIV and AIDS by 2006;
- develop a regional policy on the incorporation of HIV and AIDS into all levels of curriculum by 2006; and
- develop a regional framework for facilitating the implementation of international declarations and targets by 2007.

Access to health care services

In southern Africa, there have generally been mixed results in the provision of health care services to citizens. In Botswana, the primary health care approach to the provision of health care facilities has improved access to health services by the majority of people, especially as health services have been brought closer to the people. Evidence shows that nearly all urban residents and over 80 percent of rural residents are within 15 km of a primary health care facility.[7] The country is however still faced with health problems that can be linked to issues related to inadequate food, low levels of education, lack of access to clean water and long distances to health centres in some rural areas.

Namibia has increased its area of health care coverage and now 80 percent of the population lives within a 10 km radius of a healthcare facility and 20 percent of mostly remote rural dwellers live further than 10 km from a health care facility.[8] In some countries however, the budget allocated for primary health care is inadequate. In Malawi for instance, eighteen percent of the health budget is spent on primary health services and the majority of the budget goes to tertiary services.

This is worrying as the majority of poor women normally go to a primary health care facility.

Zimbabwe's public health sector has been in decline since 2000. *Beyond Inequalities: Women in Zimbabwe 2005* reveals that the public health sector has been unable to meet the demands of a growing impoverished population whose only hope of accessible and affordable health care is from the State. Although the health budget has been increased, in real terms, it has decreased due to rising inflation.

In South Africa, the government has made efforts to make primary health care services available to the majority of the people. Although there has been improved access, there remains a lot of work that needs to be done. In studies carried out in three districts in the Limpopo area, women complained that clinics are located far from residential areas and many women lack financial resources to get to the local clinic. Sometimes the state of the roads is poor, hindering public transport services. Community members then have to walk long distances to major roads so as to access transport in order to reach health facilities. This is especially true in rural areas were women also complained of a shortage of drugs in rural health centres.

Inadequate financing, weak management systems, lack of accountability, skills shortages and the devastating reduction in health care facilities plague the public health sector. In Malawi for example, even though health care in government-funded hospitals is free, health care is inadequate and does not meet the needs of the people, drugs are scarce and there is rampant corruption, meaning that only those with money can access drugs and medical facilities. The private health sector operates largely in urban areas and people in rural areas who are the majority of the population have limited

51

Government hospitals in Zimbabwe have been granted permission to commercialise some of their operations after tight budgets saw them fail to provide essential services to patients.

This comes after government hospital administrators around the country had indicated during a meeting held in Bulawayo a few weeks ago that they had scaled down operations due to lack of funding.

Failure to purchase key hospital equipment has become a nationwide problem with hospitals now having to compromise their operations. Most hospital administrators yesterday attributed the challenges being faced by public health institutions to lack of business focus by the ministry of Health and Child Welfare. Hospitals are still charging a consultation fee of between Z$250 and $300.

"The charges are not commensurate with the hyper-inflationary environment the country is currently experiencing."

In an interview, Health and Child Welfare Deputy Minister Dr Edwin Muguti yesterday said his ministry was aware of the challenges facing the health sector.

"After assessing the situation, we gave them the permission to raise the extra money through the commercialisation of some of their services to be able to maintain expected standards," Dr Muguti said.

He said all hospital managers were expected to be innovative by, among other measures, finding ways of recovering money owed to them by many patients and medical aid societies.

"The new concept will see some hospitals, such as Harare and Chitungwiza central hospitals providing private care wards that are not very expensive but have a certain class of people that can afford such services and help boost the hospitals' finances."

Dr Muguti said the ministry acknowledged that consultation fees being charged by all Government hospitals were "ridiculous."

"We are aware that what is being charged is too little and we will soon announce an upward review of fees. There are channels and procedures to be followed when reviewing medical fees and so far we have done everything. We will also need to protect and find ways to help the poor who will still require our services but would not be able to pay the new fees."

Harare Central Hospital, which is now being run by a new executive officer, Mr Jealous Batsirai Nderere, a pharmacist, is the hardest hit due to the non-availability of essential drugs, food and laboratory equipment. The hospital is also facing problems with obsolete lifts and unreliable laundry machines.

"Harare Central Hospital is challenging. I am aware that no one is actually coping in the health sector, but all stakeholders have to work together and find ways to do with the little resources that we have," Mr Nderere said.

The Herald, 20 March 2006, Zimbabwe, 2006

access.[9] This lack of access leads to high death rates from preventable and treatable infectious diseases. Studies also show that with the introduction of health user fees in many countries in the region in a bid to improve health delivery, there has been reduced utilisation of these services by the poor, the majority of whom are women.[10]

Access to medicines

Access to medicines is one of the major challenges facing the health sector in southern Africa. Medicines are unaffordable to many people, supplies are unreliable and the quality of medicines that are available is poor. There is also a need for new medicines.[11]

In some parts of southern Africa, the first source of medicines is the informal drug seller. Though these sources are easily accessible, customers often receive inappropriate and poor quality medicines. In the United Republic of Tanzania, the informal drug seller reaches over 60 percent of the population. In a bid to improve services in these shops, staff is now being trained in dispensing medicines and in business skills. The shops are also regularly inspected and stock a reliable supply of medicines. Policies are needed to improve access to medicines, for example there is a need to reduce taxes and tariffs on essential medicines and increase investment in the health sector.[12]

At the global level, challenges in accessing drugs exist through unequal trade relations between the North and the South. Drug patents imposed by international pharmaceutical companies have maintained the high cost of drugs for African countries. Under World Trade Organisation (WTO) Trade-Related Aspects of Intellectual Property Rights (TRIPS) Agreements, member states are allowed to produce drugs without the consent of the patent owner as long as these drugs are for the domestic market. Pharmaceutical companies do not favour this position. For example, in 2001, 40 pharmaceutical companies took the South African government to court over the Medicines Amendment Act of 1997, which permits the importation of cheap generic anti-AIDS drugs into South Africa. Among other benefits, the Act effectively reduces the cost of anti-AIDS drugs to pregnant women. The Act also calls for the creation of a committee to monitor drug prices and compels pharmaceutical companies to justify their prices and allow for the prescription of cheaper generic drugs.

SADC has come up with a four-year Draft Business Plan for

the SADC Pharmaceutical Programme (2006-2010). The Programme is expected to improve availability of safe, quality and affordable essential medicines, including traditional medicines, and their rational use.

Improving access to reproductive health services

The SADC Gender Unit together with the Social Human Development and Special Programmes Unit of SADC has come up with guidelines on sexual and reproductive health with the following targets:

- provision of free health care for poor and vulnerable sections of society;
- provision of education on emergency contraception including dissemination of information in local languages to communities by 2008;
- development of guidelines for a minimum package on sexual and reproductive health in the region by 2008; and
- reduction of maternal mortality rate by three-quarters between 2006 and 2015.

Family planning

There has been a general increase in awareness about family planning methods in the various countries of the region since 2000. In Lesotho, access to family planning methods is hampered by the lack of an explicit family planning policy. For example, for surgical contraceptive methods, some providers require the consent of partners.

In Malawi, available statistics show that women know at least one method of family planning, 39 percent of women and 56 percent of men have ever used a modern method and only 26 percent of married women are currently using modern contraceptive methods. Increasingly, women are choosing to use injectables, which are the predominant method, fol-

South African women protest medicine court case — Box 4.3

The African National Congress Women's League has called upon all women of South Africa to come out in support of the South African Department of Health as it came under legal attack from 41 multinational drug manufacturing companies in the Pretoria High Court. If the companies were to win the case, this would jeopardise government programmes that aid pregnant HIV-infected women.

The drug companies, most of whom are local subsidiaries of foreign multi-billion dollar corporations, are taking the South African government to court, contesting sections of the country's Medicines and Related Substances Control Amendment Act. These sections of the Act are aimed at making drugs affordable and thus accessible. They also call for the import of so-called generic medicines rather than name-brand drugs. Indian companies offer generic AIDS medicines at one tenth of the price, but multinationals argue that importing those would violate the intellectual property rights of the drug companies.

Women are more exposed to HIV and AIDS in South Africa and also more dependent on cheap, government provided medicines. South Africa, facing a veritable AIDS disaster, has limited resources to medicate its estimated 10 million HIV positive people. The government, however, has launched programmes to provide free anti-retroviral drugs to pregnant women and mothers. The government program is to distribute generic Nevirapine, which is known to significantly decrease the chances of babies becoming HIV infected during birth.

These programs are in danger if the drug companies win the Pretoria lawsuit, as the costs of anti-retroviral drugs would become unsustainable. The ANC Women's League has come out strongly against the lawsuit and is calling "for affordable health care." The Pretoria lawsuit has significance far beyond the borders of South Africa, as it might provide a legal framework for other poor nations to import cheap, generic drugs under emergency situations like the AIDS epidemic.

The South African government is also gaining international support for its fight to get sustainable prices so that it can be able to provide drugs through the public health system. Also, humanitarian organisations came out in support of the South African government. In a joint statement, international aid agencies Oxfam and Médecins Sans Frontières (MSF) said, "many lives could be saved if people had access to affordable medicines, which the South African Medicines and Related Substances Control Amendment Act 1997 would permit."

http://www.afrol.com/News2001/sa010_women_aidsdrugs.htm

lowed by female sterilisation and the pill. There was also a small rise in the use of condoms. Access to these methods is however affected by beliefs that contraceptives are bad for women's health and that they cause cancer.[13] In Namibia, knowledge of the male condom increased from 71 percent in 1992 to 92 percent in 2000. Knowledge of IUDs increased from 41 to 56 percent and injectables from 85 to 96 percent. The Demographic Health Survey revealed that 67 percent of all women interviewed had heard about the female condom. However, accessibility and affordability of the female condom compared to the male condom remains a challenge. The highest rate of female condom use was shown to be amongst women aged 20-24 years old.[14]

Cheaper female condoms will increase accessibility Box 4.4

Women in sub-Saharan Africa will soon benefit from a cheaper version of the female condom, enabling them to negotiate safer sex with their male partners. The prohibitive cost of the female condom has prevented many women in developing countries from accessing the prevention device, but a new second-generation female condom made of synthetic latex could change this. Female Health Company (FHC), announced in October 2005 that the second generation female condom (FC2) would be made available to developing countries, and that smaller, and poorer nations would be able to purchase the product by forming a coalition.

"If countries in the region came together as a collective and place a large order (with FHC) this will allow the smallest country to get the best possible price," said Ann Leeper, president of the US-based FHC.

Depending on the volume of condoms purchased, the FC2 could be sold for as little as US$0.22 per unit. The existing female condom, made from the more expensive polyurethane, sells at US$0.72 per unit. Researchers at the Reproductive Health Research Unit (RHRU) in Durban, South Africa, conducted studies to assess the performance and acceptability of the new female condom and found that there was no difference in performance. "About a third of women who used both condoms said they were the same," Mags Beksinska, RHRU deputy executive director commented. Last year between six and nine billion male condoms were distributed globally, but only 12 million female condoms were made available during the same period. Women in urban areas have more education and thus are more likely to be aware of and use modern contraception.

The Daily Mirror, South Africa, 18 October 2005.

Maternal Mortality

Maternal mortality rates for countries in the region remain high, with UNICEF estimates showing that a woman in sub-Saharan Africa has a one in 16 chance of dying in pregnancy or childbirth, compared to a one in 4,000 risk in a developing country – the largest difference between poor and rich countries of any health indicator.[xv] Because of such disparities, world leaders resolved to improve maternal health as part of the Millennium Development Goals. The target is to reduce the maternal mortality ratio between 1990 and 2015 by three-quarters. Most deaths related to childbirth are preventable as they are due mostly to the lack of sufficient care during pregnancy and delivery. Some pregnancies need emergency obstetric care, which is lacking, particularly in rural health centres.

The current state of maternal morbidity and mortality in southern Africa is an indicator of lack of access to reproductive health services for women and poor quality of care. Such care would ensure that young women have access to information and services to prevent unwanted pregnancies as well as closely spaced births. Furthermore, such services would ensure that pregnant women have access to quality care during pregnancy, labour and after childbirth, as well as access to emergency obstetric services for complicated pregnancies.

The lack of emergency obstetric care is in turn exacerbated by acute skill shortages as a result of the exodus of health workers from the countries of the South, including the SADC region, to the countries of the North. Studies in Zambia show that the proportion of women who deliver with the assistance of a skilled professional has declined from 48 percent in 1996, to 43 percent in 2001/2002. It has also been suggested that distance to health facilities and the high cost of care are contributing factors.[16] Most of the other countries of the region also have very low proportions of births attended by skilled professionals. While countries are focusing efforts in training and improving infrastructure, retaining skilled health workers at current remuneration levels in many of the countries of the region is a challenge.

While the causes of maternal deaths have not changed, there is general agreement that HIV and AIDS has contributed to the increasing mortality as well as low availability of emergency obstetric care. Furthermore, resources going into AIDS care may have detracted from other areas of care including maternal health.

According to the ICPD Program of Action, countries with the highest levels of maternal mortality should aim to achieve by 2005, a maternal mortality rate below 125 per 100,000 live births and by 2015 a maternal mortality rate below 75 per 100,000 live births. However, all countries should "reduce maternal morbidity and mortality to levels where they are no longer considered to constitute a public health problem." [17]

Termination of pregnancy services
The Mozambique national gender profile, *Beyond Inequalities 2005: Women in Mozambique* reveals that Africa has the highest abortion-related mortality ratio in the world. It is estimated that over five million women in Africa undergo unsafe abortions and that a significant proportion of them die from abortion-related causes. The different countries of SADC have different laws concerning abortion. In Zambia for example, the 1972 Termination of Pregnancy Act allows access to safe abortion on medical or social grounds. Despite this law, complications from unsafe abortions are reported to account for a high number of maternal deaths.

The South African legal and service provision context are somewhat different. On the 22nd of November 1996, the South African Parliament passed the Choice on Termination of Pregnancy Act (CTOPA) No 92. The CTOPA gives women of any age or marital status access to abortion services upon request during the first 12 weeks of pregnancy, and under certain conditions, extends access to the first 20 weeks of pregnancy. This Act recognises women's rights to make the full range of reproductive choices including termination of pregnancy. Pro-life groups who continue to campaign against abortions and sometimes target health providers have challenged the Act twice in the constitutional courts.

The CTOPA was implemented from February 1 1997 at designated health facilities. The number of designated public health facilities that may provide TOP services has been increasing yearly, although designation does not necessarily mean that the facility actually provides the service. Due to limited access in rural areas, women may miss the 12-week cut-off that allows a termination to be provided at a community health centre or district hospital. In rural areas the nearest facility where a second trimester abortion may be performed may not be accessible due to distance and cost considerations for poor women.

One of the main causes of unsafe abortions is the high incidence of unwanted adolescent pregnancies. Traditional society and its values are increasingly undermined; especially in urban areas were adolescents are involved in freer sexual relations. On the other hand, sex education in schools is poor and parents usually do not discuss issues of sex and reproduction with their children. In addition to this, knowledge of contraception is limited; therefore there is a high incidence of unwanted pregnancies and adolescents resort to abortion.

The provision of abortion services as part of the package of sexual and reproductive health is essential to improve the health outcomes of women in southern Africa.

Women and HIV and AIDS

Southern Africa has the highest HIV prevalence rates in the world. Estimates of adult prevalence rates for example show that about 20 percent of the entire adult population aged 15 - 49 is currently infected in nine southern African countries, Botswana, Lesotho, Malawi, Mozambique, Namibia, South Africa, Swaziland, Zambia, and Zimbabwe. Gender inequality is cited as one of the factors contributing to the spread of HIV as well as increases in poverty, intergenerational sex, illiteracy, stigma and discrimination, alcohol abuse and lack of communication about HIV and AIDS due to cultural barriers.

Below are some statistics detailing the extent of the epidemic in the region:

- Lesotho's prevalence rates are estimated at 31 percent with women constituting 55 percent of those infected in 2002. In 2003, there were an estimated 76,000 adults infected with HIV and of these 44,000 or 58 percent were women.
- in 2002, theHIV prevalence rate in Mozambique was 13.6 percent and 16.2 percent in 2004. Among the 15-24 year age groups, prevalence of the infection among women was three-higher than among men.
- Namibia is ranked seventh amongst the most infected countries in the world and women account for 53 percent of all new reported cases of HIV at health centres.[18]
- in Zambia, a Demographic Health Survey conducted between 2001 and 2002 found that the prevalence rates of HIV and AIDS of those between 15-49 years was 15.6 percent. Prevalence rates in urban areas are higher than those in rural areas at 23.1 percent and 10.8 percent respectively.[19]

Gender has been identified as critical in the fight against the pandemic. Women are more vulnerable to HIV due to biological, social, economic and cultural reasons. "Even where a woman knows she is at risk of contracting the disease from her husband, she is traditionally obliged to submit to her husband's advances. Tradition does not allow women to negotiate the use of condoms in marriage."[20] The consequences of gender inequality and patriarchy, gender based violence, poverty and women's lack of access to social and economic resources place women at particular risk of HIV infection.

Women and girls are also more vulnerable to HIV because of, among other things, sexual abuse and rape. Women and girls continue to suffer due to non-existent or weak law enforcement systems, ignorance by women, girls and society about the existence of protection acts, cumbersome court procedures for handling sexual offences and in some countries the non-recognition of sexual offences as criminal acts.

Gender violence in general is associated with significant adverse health outcomes for women, including acute physical injuries and emotional and behavioural problems. Violence and sexual violence in particular also impacts negatively on the reproductive health of girls and women including safe motherhood, vulnerability to STI infections and HIV and unwanted pregnancies. The increasing awareness of the intersection of sexual violence and HIV and AIDS has made the need to understand gender violence more urgent than ever.

Awareness of the impact of HIV and AIDS on food security, especially in subsistence farming communities is beginning to gain ground. As mortality among productive family members increases, the impact on labour and productivity is being felt. Household poverty as a result of expenses incurred caring for the sick and dying has a direct bearing on food security. The majority of farming households in most of the coun-

HIV and AIDS Prevalence Among Women and Men in SADC (2005)				Table 4.1
Country	Prevalence (%)		Adults Living with HIV	Women Living with HIV
	M	F		
Angola	3.4	4.4	240 000	130 000
Botswana	31.7	43.1	350 000	190 000
DRC	3.7	4.8	1.1 million	570 000
Lesotho	25.4	32.4	320 000	170,000
Malawi	12.4	16	900 000	460,000
Mozambique	10.6	13.8	1.3 million	670,000
Madagascar	1.4	1.9	-	-
Namibia	18.4	24.2	210 000	110,000
South Africa	18.1	23.5	5.3 million	2.9 million
Swaziland	35.7	41.7	220 000	110.000
Tanzania	7.6	9.9	1.6 million	840,000
Zambia	14.1	18.9	920 000	420,000
Zimbabwe	21	28.4	1.8 million	930,000

United Nations Population Fund (UNFPA), 2005.

tries of the region are subsistence. The food crisis in the region has not only worsened the vulnerability of farming households with HIV affected adults, but HIV and AIDS also has the effect of limiting the capacity and ability of such households to recover. Implementing long-term recovery efforts in the face of increasing mortality among the productive members of households is a critical challenge.

Data from Botswana and South Africa suggest that the number of women accessing Voluntary Counselling and Testing (VCT) and ARV public sector programmes is higher than of men accessing the same services. In South Africa for example, about 65 percent of patients enrolled in the public sector ARV program are women. A study of anti-retroviral treatment in Johannesburg conducted between April and June of 2004 reported that women accessing ARVs "outnumbered men by a ratio of 2 to 1."[21]

While it is a good sign that HIV positive women are accessing VCT and treatment for HIV and AIDS earlier, they need support in staying on treatment, especially if their current partner is not receiving treatment. Some public sector ARV programs insist on ensuring a treatment buddy for those who are enrolled, for many women the buddy is unlikely to be their spouse or sexual partner as women fear to disclose their HIV status to spouses or partners.

There is a clear need for a programmatic shift to get men to test and disclose to their partners and to take responsibility. Health workers and NGOs need to be sensitised to the challenges that testing poses for women in relationships when their male partners are not tested. Similarly, condom promotion programs need to target men more vigorously as they also need to take responsibility for disease and pregnancy prevention. Although many programs in the 1990s claimed success in empowering women to nego-

tiate condom use, current statistics on infection rates do not bear testimony to this. Programs targeting men specifically have only emerged in most countries since the late 90s.

Women as caregivers

The advent of home based care as a response to the AIDS pandemic has placed responsibility for the care of the sick and dying squarely in the hands of women. In sub-Saharan Africa, girls are more likely than boys to be withdrawn from school to care for sick family members and older women, who often have limited resources, become caregivers to adult children who fall ill and then surrogate parents to their orphaned grandchildren. A 2002 household survey conducted in South Africa by the Kaiser Foundation reports that, "in more than two thirds of households women or girls were the primary caregivers. Almost a quarter of caregivers were over the age of 60 and just less than three quarters of these were women."[22]

The Men as Partners program in South Africa asserts that not enough attention has been granted to ways in which gender roles also create the expectation that women will assume the burden of responsibility for taking care of family and community members weakened or made ill by HIV and AIDS. To date, little has been done to develop interventions that explicitly encourage men to play a more active role in care and support activities. It is imperative, then, that men begin to share this burden of care and support.[23]

While home based care is a necessary service, it perpetuates the undervaluing of women's work by relegating it to "volunteer" work where women are not paid for their services. Health systems also need to acknowledge and budget for the payment of caregivers who do back breaking work and risk contracting HIV infection themselves without provisions for post exposure prophylaxis that is provided to health workers. Although home based care kits for care givers are supposed to be standardised to include gloves, these are a luxury in many impoverished communities.

Nutrition

Micronutrient malnutrition is a serious public health problem in some of the countries in the region. Although all population groups are affected by micronutrient malnutrition, pre-school children and women of child bearing age have the highest prevalence of deficiencies of all the major micronutrients. Current information, although limited, suggests that vitamin A and Iron are likely to be the key micronutrients that are deficient among women in southern Africa. This is despite the distribution of iron supplements to pregnant women that has been practised for at least two decades in countries in the region, followed more recently by distribution of vitamin A capsules to children and mothers.

There has, however, been a decline in iodine deficiency disorders, especially goitre, most likely as a result of implementation of universal salt iodisation in most countries. In addition, micronutrient fortification of basic foodstuffs is gaining ground in most countries. The challenge, however, remains that of reaching subsistence farmers who consume their own foodstuffs with cost effective and affordable food fortification technologies. These are the households that will continue to be vulnerable to micronutrient deficiencies unless such interventions reach them.

Access to adequate micronutrients is particularly critical for women, especially during pregnancy and lactation as it affects delivery and the health of infants. For women who are vitamin and mineral deficient, improving micronutrient intake, especially iron, vitamin A, zinc, calcium, magnesium and iodine can be an important means of reducing maternal morbidity and mortality as well as reducing rates of premature births and increasing birth weights.

Conclusion

The SADC region is experiencing unprecedented development challenges including the realisation of commitments made at global and regional levels. Measures aimed at improving the overall health of the people of SADC as well as meeting specific targets that have not been met on women's health need to be put in place to:

- halt the high incidences of HIV and AIDS, especially amongst women and girls;
- reduce maternal mortality levels; and
- improve universal access to sexual and reproductive health services.

Resources to support regional bodies such as SADC to collect and disseminate information that will facilitate monitoring of progress in a timely manner are needed. Greater participation is needed by women as consumers of public health services in determining their own health needs as well as greater involvement of governments in addressing problems such as health worker migration, improving access to emergency obstetric services for women particularly in rural areas and improving quality of health care.

Characteristics of Countries in Southern Africa Affected by Food Shortages				Table 4.2
Country	Adults living with HIV (%)	Poverty[a] (%)	Children underweight[b] (%)	Population in need of food aid % (millions)
Malawi	14.2	76.1	25.0	29 (3.2)
Zambia	16.5	87.4	28.0	26 (2.9)
Zimbabwe	24.6	64.2	13.0	49 (6.7)
Lesotho	28.9	56.1	17.9	30 (0.65)
Swaziland	38.8	n/a	10.3	24 (0.26)

[a] living on less than $2 per day; [b] Weight for age <-2 Z-score.
Human Development Report 2004; Food aid: WFP assessment briefs

Endnotes

1   Statistics South Africa, *Mortality and causes of death in South Africa, 1997-2003: Findings from death notification*, Statistics South Africa, 2005

2   Global Fund to fight AIDS, Tuberculosis and Malaria, "The Status and Impact of the three diseases," The global fund to fight AIDS, Tuberculosis and Malaria, 2005

3   Human Development Indicators: Human Development Report 2004

4   SARIPS/SAPES databank, *SADC Regional Human Development Report 2000*, SAPES Books, 2000

5   Martin H.G, *A comparative analysis of the financing of HIV/AIDS programmes in Botswana, Lesotho, Mozambique, South Africa, Swaziland and Zimbabwe*, October 2003.

6   Dr. David Sanders, "Globalisation, health and health services in sub-Saharan Africa" *http://www.choike.org/nuevo_eng/informes/990.html*

7   Women's NGO Coalition and SARDC WIDSAA, *Beyond Inequalities 2005: Women in Botswana*, WNGOC/SARDC, Gaborone and Harare, 2005

8   UNAM and SARDC WIDSAA, *Beyond Inequalities 2005: Women in Namibia*, UNAM/SARDC, Windhoek and Harare, 2005

9   (http://bmj.bmjjournals.com/cgi/content/full/331/7519/709

10   http://www.africaaction.org/action#8

11   ttp://www.dfid.gov.uk/pubs/files/atm-factsheet0106.pdf

12   http://bmj.bmjjournals.com/cgi/content/full/331/7519/709

13   WLSA Malawi and SARDC WIDSAA, *Beyond Inequalities 2000: Women in southern Africa*, WLSA/SARDC, Limbe and Harare, 2005

14   UNAM and SARDC WIDSAA, *Beyond Inequalities 2005: Women in Namibia*, op. cit

15   http://www.unicef.org/mdg/maternal.html

16   Geloo Z, *Diverse Factors linked to maternal deaths in Zambia*, 2003

17   Horizons No 7, "HIV and partner violence: Implications for HIV Voluntary Counselling and Testing programs", Population Council, 2001 http://www.popcouncil.org/pdfs/horizons/vctviolence.pdf

18   UNAM and SARDC WIDSAA, *Beyond Inequalities 2005: Women in Namibia*, op cit

19   ZARD and SARDC WIDSAA, *Beyond Inequalities: Women in Zambia*, 2003

20   ZARD and SARDC WIDSAA, *Beyond Inequalities: Women in Zambia*, 2003, p 30

21   Henry Kaiser Family Foundation, "How households cope with the Impact of the HIV/AIDS Epidemic: A Survey of Households Affected by HIV/AIDS in South Africa," The Henry Kaiser Family Foundation, Social Surveys, Memory Box Project, 2002

22   Henry KeiserFamily Foundation

23   Manisha Mehta, Dean Peacock, LisettePernal, "Men as Partners:lessonsfrom engaging men in clinics and communities"

References

Ashford, L. S, "Women in 2005: Are they making progress?" Population Reference Bureau, 2005

British Medical Journal, "Medicines supply in Africa," in the *General Medical Journal*, 2005

Central Statistical Office, *Zambia Demographic Health Survey* 2001/2002, Lusaka, 2003

Sanders D, "Globalisation, health and health services in sub-Saharan Africa," Choike last accessed 28/03/06. http://www.choike.org/nuevo_eng/informes/990.html, 2006

DFID, "Access to medicines," in *DFID practice paper fact sheet*, January 2006, last accessed 28/03/06 http://www.dfid.gov.uk/pubs/files/atm-factsheet0106.pdf, 2006

Geloo Z, *Diverse Factors linked to maternal deaths in Zambia*, Population Reference Bureau, Lusaka, 2006

Gieco, M, *Maternal Mortality: Africa's burden, Toolkit on gender, transport and maternal mortality*, 2005

Henry Kaiser Family Foundation, "Hitting home, how households cope with the impact of the HIV/AIDS Epidemic: A Survey of households affected by HIV/AIDS in South Africa," *The Henry Kaiser Family Foundation, social surveys, memory box project*, Johannesburg, 2002

Human Rights Watch, *Suffering in silence: The links between human rights abuses and HIV transmission to girls in Zambia*, Human Rights Watch, New York, 2002

Martin, H.G, "A comparative analysis of the financing of HIV/AIDS programmes in Botswana, Lesotho, Mozambique, South Africa, Swaziland and Zimbabwe," Human Sciences Resource Council, Cape Town, 2003

Matambo J.R, *Nutrition needs and potential food vehicles for food fortification in the SADC region, draft report for the micronutrient initiative*, 2003

Maman S, [*et. al*], "HIV-positive women report more lifetime partner violence: findings from a Voluntary Counselling and Testing clinic in Dar es Salaam," in American Journal of Public Health Vol. 92; No. 8, 2002

SAPES, SADC, *Regional Human Development Report*, Harare, 2000

SARDC WIDSAA, *Beyond Inequalities: Women in Southern Africa*, Harare, Zimbabwe, 2000

SARDC WIDSAA and University of the Western Cape Gender Equity Unit, *Beyond Inequalities 2005: Women in South Africa*, Harare, 2005

SARDC WIDSAA and Women's NGO Coalition, *Beyond Inequalities 2005: Women in Botswana*, Gaborone, Harare, 2005

SARDC WIDSAA and Women and Law in Southern Africa and, *Beyond Inequalities 2005: Women in Malawi*, Lilongwe, Harare, 2005

SARDC WIDSAA and Zambia Association for Research and Development, *Beyond Inequalities2005: Women in Zambia*, Lusaka / Harare, 2005

SARDC WIDSAA and Zimbabwe Women's Resource Centre and Network, *Beyond Inequalities 2005: Women in Zimbabwe*, Harare, 2005

Smit, J [et. al], *Reproductive Health: the South African health review*, Health Systems Trust, South Africa, 2004

Statistics South Africa, *Mortality and causes of death in South Africa, 1997-2003: Findings from death notification*, Statistics South Africa, 2005

Suzanne, M [et. al], "HIV and Partner Violence: Implications for HIV Voluntary Counselling and Testing programs in Dar es Salaam," Horizons, Population Council, 2001

UN Secretary General's Task Force on Women, Girls and HIV/AIDS in Southern Africa, *Facing the future together: Report of the Secretary General's Task Force on Women, Girls and HIV/AIDS in Southern Africa*, UNAIDS, 2004

WOMEN, GOVERNANCE AND DECISION-MAKING

5

Introduction

Countries in southern Africa have made significant progress in increasing the number of women in politics and decision-making positions since 2000. In 2005, the average representation of women in parliaments in the region stood at 20 percent, but in line with a decision by the 2005 SADC Summit, Member States agreed to increase the target for women representation in politics and decision making from 30 percent by 2005 to 50 percent by 2015to align with the African Union target.

In the 1997 Declaration on Gender and Development, SADC Heads of State and Government expressed concern that "…disparities between women and men still exist in the areas of … power sharing and decision-making…" and as such committed themselves to "ensuring the equal representation of women and men in the decision-making of member states and SADC structures at all levels, and the achievement of at least 30 percent target of women in political and decision-making structures by year 2005."[1]

Gender parity is a crucial pillar for ongoing democratic processes and efforts for attaining good governance, and enabling economic and social reforms that are urgently needed in the SADC region. A greater presence of women in public office, consultation with women clients of public services to capture their voices, responding to their needs and demands and reforms to legal and policy frameworks and judicial systems are all key democratic factors that cannot be realised in the absence of women's participation in politics and governance.

The concept of democracy recognises that men and women decide upon political policies and national legislation jointly and women are best placed to articulate their own needs and concerns. For instance, because over three-quarters of women in Africa are engaged in food production, it follows that policy decisions in agriculture should not be made without the active involvement of women.

The Beijing Declaration and Platform for Action (BDPFA) argues, "Women's equal participation in decision-making is not only a demand for simple justice or democracy but can also be seen as a necessary condition for women's interests to be taken into account. Achieving the goal of equal participation of women and men in decision-making will provide a balance that more accurately reflects the composition of society and is needed in order to strengthen democracy and promote its proper functioning."[2]

Constraints to women's political participation

* socialisation, which entrenches perceptions that a woman's role is confined to the private (home) and the man's to the public domain;
* unwillingness of male colleagues to accept women as equals or superiors in the workplace;
* the way parliamentary candidates are selected, women may be lower down the party list;
* lack of resources, such as money to campaign;
* women are generally less educated than men;
* media that hound or ridicule women who dare to venture into the political sphere, focusing on their personal lives rather than their work for the parties and the electorate;

- inappropriate electoral systems that do not create space for women to participate on an equal basis; and
- constrained solidarity among women voters and candidates.

Policy framework

The analysis of the status of women in decision-making in the region is located within regional and international frameworks which include the BDPFA, the 1997 SADC Declaration on Gender and Development; the 1979 Convention on the Elimination of all forms of Discrimination Against Women

(CEDAW); the Protocol to the African Charter on Human and People's Rights and the Millennium Development Goals (MDGs).

The SADC Declaration on Gender and Development notes with concern that disparities between women and men still exist in the area of power sharing and decision-making. Upon the adoption of this declaration leaders committed themselves to ensuring the equal representation of women and men in the decision-making structures of member states and SADC structures at all levels, and the achievement of at least 30 percent target of women in political and decision-making structures by 2005.

The BDPFA (190 h) seeks to "encourage and, where appropriate, ensure that government-funded organisations adopt non-discriminatory policies and practices in order to increase the number and raise the position of women in their organisations." It also states that this equality should be noticed in non-governmental organisations, trade unions and the private sector (192 d) and recruitment and career development programmes should be restructured to "ensure that all women, especially young women, have equal access to managerial, entrepreneurial, technical and leadership training, including on-the-job training" (192 f).

Regarding the specific strategies for women elected to office, the BDPFA calls on states and governments to "review the differential impact of electoral systems on the political representation of women in elected bodies and consider, where appropriate the adjustment or reform of those systems" (190 d). The same instrument also encourages political parties to integrate women in elective and non-elective public positions in the same proportion and at the same levels as men. Party structures and procedures should also be examined to remove all barriers that directly or indirectly

---

SADC pushes for affirmative action to accelerate gender equality   Box 5.1

SADC is pressing for affirmative action to speed up progress towards substantive equality between women and men at all levels of decision-making.

The head of the SADC Gender Unit, Magdeline Mathiba-Madibela, said the region had experienced varied progress in implementation of commitments since leaders of the 14-member community adopted the SADC Declaration on Gender and Development in 1997.

On the key target of 30 percent women representation in positions of decision-making by 2005, progress has been significant, although the majority of member states are still below the mark in structures such as parliament and cabinet.

However, South Africa has surpassed the target for both parliament and cabinet, and Mozambique has more than 30 percent women in the legislature.

Now the stakes are higher since the SADC Summit of Heads of State and Government summit in Gaborone in 2005 elevated the 30 percent target to 50 percent in line with the African Union.

"To realise full implementation of this decision, member states must endeavour to adopt affirmative action to protect women and enshrine it in national constitutions," said Mathiba-Madibela who was speaking at a media briefing prior to the Council of Ministers that takes place in Gaborone this week.

Mathiba-Madibela said an analysis of recent trends in the amended constitutions of some member states shows that remarkable achievements have been made toward gender equality although huge gaps still remain.

The challenges faced by governments in the region include domesticating regional and international commitments into national laws.

A regional conference that took place in Botswana from 6 to 9 December 2005 proposed workable steps to the regional implementation framework on gender and development for the period 2006-2010.

Delegates to that conference called for regional and national consultations on elevation of the gender declaration of 1997 into a protocol to strengthen member states' commitments as contained in the declaration.

"The motivation behind the need to elevate the declaration arises from the reality that in legal terms, a declaration is a statement of intention and commitment, which has more of a moral rather than a binding effect," Mathiba-Madibela argued.

She said to upgrade the declaration would be a progressive step for SADC as the process would take on board existing commitments, and would also consolidate the commitments and "use the lessons from their implementation to design new strategies to accelerate progress towards gender equality."

The 2006-2010 implementation plan proposes the strengthening of institutional mechanisms, education, sexual and reproductive health rights, women's human rights, and media and information, which are critical in dealing with issues of gender irregularities.

Patson Phiri for SARDC, Harare 2006

discriminate against the participation of women.

The BDPFA also notes with concern that socialisation of women in most of our societies grooms them to fit into their subordinate position as wives and mothers and it "recognises that shared work and parental responsibilities between women and men promote women's increased participation in public life." (190i) Of significance to the promotion of women in decision-making positions as highlighted in the BDPFA are such things as leadership training, gender sensitivity training and mentoring.

As part of monitoring and evaluation, the BDPFA encourages states to implement mechanisms to monitor and evaluate progress in the representation of women through the regular collection, analysis and dissemination of quantitative and qualitative data on women and men at all levels in various decision-making positions in the public and private sectors. SADC member states have been monitoring and compiling data on the representation of women in parliament and cabinet positions, this should be extended to include data on other sectors.

Women in power and decision-making: what BDPFA proposes[3]

The Beijing Declaration and Platform for Action (BDPFA) proposes the following measures to be taken to ensure women's equal access to and full participation in power structures and decision-making.

By governments

Commit themselves to establishing the goal of gender balance in government bodies and committees, as well as in public administrative entities, and in the judiciary, including,

- set specific targets and implementing measures to sub stantially increase the number of women with a view to achieving equal representation of women and men, if necessary through positive action, in all governmental and public administration positions.
- take measures, including where appropriate in electoral systems, that encourage political parties to integrate women in elective and non-elective public positions in the same proportion and levels as men.
- protect and promote the equal rights of women and men to engage in political activities, to enjoy freedom of association, including membership in political parties and trade unions.
- review the differential impact of electoral systems on the political representation of women in elected bodies and consider, where appropriate, the adjustment or reform of those systems.
- monitor and evaluate progress on the representation of women through the regular collection, analysis and dissemination of quantitative and qualitative data on women and men at all levels in various decision-making positions in the public and private sectors, and disseminate data on the number of women and men employed at various levels in governments on a yearly basis.
- ensure that women and men have equal access to the full range of public appointments and set up mechanisms within governmental structures for monitoring progress in this field.
- support non-governmental organisations and research institutes that conduct studies on women's participation in and impact on decision-making and the decision-making environment.

⬩ encourage greater involvement of indigenous women in decision-making at all levels.

⬩ encourage and, where appropriate, ensure that government-funded organisations adopt non-discriminatory policies and practices in order to increase the number and raise the position of women in their organisations.

⬩ recognise that shared work and parental responsibilities between women and men promote women's increased participation in public life, and take appropriate measures to achieve this, including measures to reconcile family and professional life.

By political parties

⬩ consider examining party structures and procedures to remove all barriers that directly or indirectly discriminate against the participation of women.

⬩ consider developing initiatives that allow women to participate fully in all internal policy-making structures and appointive and electoral nominating processes.

⬩ consider incorporating gender issues in their political agenda taking measures to ensure that women can participate in the leadership of political parties on an equal basis with men.

By governments, national bodies, the private sector, political parties, trade unions, employers' organisations, research and academic institutions, sub regional and regional bodies, and non-governmental and international organisations

⬩ take positive action to build a critical mass of women leaders, executives and managers in strategic decision-making positions.

⬩ create or strengthen, as appropriate, mechanisms to monitor women's access to senior levels of decision- making.

⬩ review the criteria for recruitment and appointment to advisory and decision-making bodies and promotion to senior positions to ensure that such criteria are relevant and do not discriminate against women.

⬩ encourage efforts by non-governmental organisations, trade unions and the private sector to achieve equality between women and men in their ranks, including equal participation in their decision-making bodies and in negotiations in all areas and at all levels.

⬩ develop communications strategies to promote public debate on the new roles of men and women in society and in the family.

⬩ restructure recruitment and career development programmes to ensure that all women, especially young women, have equal access to managerial, entrepreneurial, technical and leadership training, including on-the-job training.

⬩ develop career advancement programmes for women of all ages that include career planning, tracking, mentoring, coaching, training, and re-training.

Citizen participation is regarded as important in the African Protocol and CEDAW. Article 9(1) of the African Protocol says that "State parties shall take specific positive action to promote participative governance and the equal participation of women in the political life of their countries through affirmative action, enabling national legislation and other measures to ensure that "women participate without any discrimination in all elections."

Article 9 (2) of the African Protocol, as part of setting targets for achieving gender equality, states that state parties shall ensure increased and effective representation and participation of women at all levels of decision-making. This is further reiterated by the MDGs under goal three whose intention is to promote gender equality and the empowerment of women.

The African Protocol also calls for affirmative action as a way of increasing the numbers of women in decision-making processes. This instrument says that state parties shall take specific positive action to promote participative governance and the equal participation of women in the political life of their countries through affirmative action, enabling national legislation and other measures to ensure that women are represented equally at all levels with men in all electoral processes.

Article seven of CEDAW reiterates this idea when it states that appropriate measures should be taken to ensure that women can "vote in all elections and public referenda and to be eligible for election to all publicly elected bodies." In article eight, state parties are called upon to take all appropriate measures to ensure women, on equal terms with men and without any discrimination, the opportunity to represent their governments at international level and to participate in the work of international organisations.

Status of women in politics in SADC

There has been an increase of women in decision-making in most SADC countries. Mozambique has a female Prime Minister, South Africa has a deputy president, Tanzania has a deputy speaker of national assembly and Zimbabwe has a female vice president though these high ranking positions remain largely a male domain. With the reintroduction of the Senate in Zimbabwe, a woman was elected as president of the Senate, thus increasing the number of women in political office. Statistics of women in local govern-

ment in southern Africa are incomplete and there are no comparable figures for the representation of women in local government. However, there are more women at this level as most men regard local government as a low profile office. Table 5.1 shows the trends of women in decision-making in SADC cabinets and parliaments.

The fact that women are underrepresented in parliament in proportion to their number in the total population of a country inhibits their participation in parliamentary committees. This in turn implies that there is little they can do in influenc-

Female Representation in Decision-Making in SADC from 1997-2008						Table 5.1
Country	Women MPs 1997 (%)	Women MPs 2000 (%)	Women MPs 2008 (%)	Women in Cabinet 2000 (%)	Women in Cabinet 2005 (%)	Next Elections
Angola	9.5	15.4	12.7	11(2002)	14.3	2008
Botswana	9	18.2	11.5	23.5 (2002)	28.6	2009
DRC	-	-	6.2	-	2.5 Senate	2011
Lesotho	12	10.3	25	12.5 (2002)	23.3	2012
Malawi	5.2	8.3	13.6	17.3	20	2009
Mauritius	7.6	7.6	17	8.0	4	2010
Mozambique	28.4	28.6	37.0	12.5	7.1	2009
Namibia	19.4	19.2	31.0	14.2	18.5	2009
South Africa	27.8	29.8	32.7	33	42.8	2009
Swaziland	19	7.3	19.0	13.3	18.8	2008
Tanzania	16.3	16.3	41.1	13.0	25	2005
Zambia	18.1	10.0	15.0	8.3	23.8	2006
Zimbabwe	14	10.7	16.0	24.0	13.0	2008

Information compiled by SARDC WIDSAA.

Gender Composition in Parliamentary Committees in Malawi, 2002				Table 5.2
Committee	Total	Men	Women	% Women
Agriculture and Natural Resources	17	15	2	11.8
Budget and Finance	12	12	0	0
Commerce and Industry	13	13	0	0
Defence and Security	13	12	1	7.7
Education, Science and Human Resources	19	17	2	10.5
Health and Population	14	12	2	14.3
International Relations	16	14	2	12.5
Legal Affairs	13	12	1	7.7
Media and Communication	13	12	1	7.7
Public Appointment and Declaration of Assets	17	15	2	11.8
Public Accounts	20	19	1	5
Social and Community Affairs	13	11	1	7.7
Transport and Public Works	13	13	0	0

The Malawi National Assembly, 2002

65

In what will definitely be a major boost for the political empowerment of women in Zimbabwe, the election of 20 women into the reintroduced Senate represented a plus 30 percent quota for women in the Upper House as per the SADC protocol requiring one-third of decision-making positions to be filled by females.

Zimbabwe's two legislative chambers have 150 and 66 members including non-constituency representatives, traditional chiefs and presidential appointees. The latest development in the senate signalled a new era as Zimbabweans surpassed, though by a slight margin, the SADC Declaration on Gender and Development target.

Women legislators drawn from the country's political divide now make up 41 members in the joint Parliament.

Elsewhere, Zimbabwe has made landmark appointments, particularly in the corporate world with Pindie Nyandoro and Charity Jinya now occupying lofty positions in their respective banking institutions – Stanbic and Barclays – headquartered in Johannesburg and London.

The practice and values of promoting women to decision-making posts are gaining ground. [It is] not only within SADC, where Mozambique has a female Prime Minister, Zimbabwe has a woman vice-president and South Africa a female Deputy President, but across the globe as well where countries such as Uganda at one time had a female vice president and Bangladesh, Pakistan and Sri Lanka have had female leaders at some point in their history.

Excerpt from the *Daily Mirror*, Zimbabwe
3 December 2005

ing policy change especially in agriculture, education, health and in the financial administration of a country. As such, efforts should be made to educate all parliamentarians on the importance of gender mainstreaming in all development efforts.

In order to ensure equal participation of women in decision-making, the government of Botswana has put in place a policy of affirmative action in the selection of specially nominated councillors and members of parliament. Other efforts to encourage women's participation in politics and decision-making include workshops held by the inter-party Caucus of Women Politicians established in 1998 for women candidates in the 2004 election. The Women's Affairs Department has also initiated programmes to educate the public and mobilise women to participate in politics and decision-making. These efforts are complemented by initiatives of NGOs such as Emang Basadi who organise political education projects that target political parties and their women's wings.

Representation of women in political parties

Getting more women into politics and decision-making is not something that can be left to chance; it must have strong political backing. It is no coincidence that gender equality features in the manifestos of the ruling Frelimo in Mozambique, African National Congress in South Africa, Chama Cha Mapinduzi (CCM) in Tanzania, ZANU PF in Zimbabwe and South West Africa Peoples Organisation (SWAPO) in Namibia.

Political party commitments as well as electoral systems and quotas can translate into increased numbers of women in decision-making positions. Women stand a better chance of getting elected under the Proportional Representation (PR) system in con-

cert with the quota system. Political parties should therefore have quotas for women's representation in Parliament. Even within internal party structures, women should hold office, as these can be a training ground for local and national politics. If women are integrated at political party level, they can push for quotas to be implemented within political parties.

Women should also be fielded in those constituencies where a political party is sure to win. Women in all SADC countries make up the majority of supporters within political parties but are under-represented in party decision-making structures. Women's wings also play a very important role in pushing for more women to be put in decision-making positions. This is true of the appointment of Joice Mujuru (Zimbabwe) to the vice presidency in late 2004. The ruling party's women's league gave Mujuru unwavering support and this contributed to her appointment.

Role of political parties in promoting women's democratic rights

Most SADC countries have witnessed a change from one party to multiparty rule. Throughout their history, African political parties have tended to be sympathetic to women's rights and hence the existence of "women wings" as party affiliates to most of these parties even before the attainment of political independence.

In Namibia, the ruling party SWAPO has a Women's Council that works towards the advancement of women and envisions gender equality within the party and in the economic, cultural and social arena. Other (opposition) parties have similar structures and vision. SWAPO has progressively worked towards attaining its stated gender goals and has reached 47 percent of women local authority councillors.

However, within the regional councils and as mayors, women are underrepresented, but better represented as Deputy Mayors, showing that men continue to hold the higher positions.

In Malawi political parties are elusive on matters of support to women. Much as the parties recognise women's rights in the electorate, the number of women chosen by their parties at party primaries is small. Sometimes women feel intimidated by their former party leaders and fellow male contestants and are thus forced to contest as independent candidates. Only one party committed itself to advancing women by choosing a woman to contest for the vice presidency in the May 2004 elections. Some parties ignored women during presentation of nomination certificates to the electoral commission, forcing them to contest as independent candidates. The media is not supportive either because although journalists continue to write on issues affecting women, they often do it using language that reinforces stereotypes of women as mothers, wives, victims, beauty and sex objects and not as professionals and leaders.

The political system in Malawi confines women to the local branch and district levels. Women's role is largely perceived as that of casting votes during election time, and providing entertainment at political rallies to mainly male political leaders.[4] The disproportionate representation of female MPs gravely affects their representation in the 13 parliamentary committees in the Malawi parliament.

In Tanzania, women leadership in political parties resembles that of parliament and government where they are underrepresented both in terms of aspirants for political posts and actual elected/appointed leaders in parliament and other positions of power as indicated in table five.

Much as electoral laws in most SADC countries give adequate attention to gender issues, democracy within parties leaves much to be desired both in terms of nomination criteria and distribution of the necessary resources for the campaigning, to the extent that very few women are elected despite the fact that women form the majority of voters in all SADC countries.

Electoral systems, quotas and affirmative action

Most SADC constitutions outlaw gender discrimination. Constitutions are not static and this has seen Malawi and Tanzania incorporating gender considerations into their constitutions, including, in the case of Tanzania, a quota of 30 percent minimum for women representation in parliament. There is therefore scope for strong gender provisions to be incorporated into the constitutions of all SADC countries. The SADC Plan of Action on Women in Politics and Decision-Making requires that all SADC countries include unequivocal commitment to the attainment, promotion and protection of gender equality in their constitutions.

The newly adopted Democratic Republic of Congo constitution, passed in 2005, includes key gender equality principles among other fundamental principles. The strength of the female vote and the increased participation of women in DRC during the constitutional process points to the importance of taking into account the specific needs of women during electoral and constitutional processes. UNIFEM for example worked with Congolese women by supporting a critical mass of women and men parliamentarians, and supporting women's mobilising and advocacy activities with the media and the public. It also assisted women in preparing to participate as candidates, voters, mobilisers, and observers in the 2006 elections.

Countries in the region operate under two main electoral systems, proportional representation, were parties are allocated seats in parliament according to the percentage of votes received, and the "First Past the Post" system were citizens vote for a candidate who represents the party in a geographically defined constituency.

Angola, Mozambique, Namibia and South Africa have different types of proportional representation (PR) systems except at the local level in South Africa (in which there is a combination of the PR and constituency-based system). Tanzania has a constituency-based system except that there are seats reserved by the constitution for women, which are contested on a PR basis. There is overwhelming evidence internationally to suggest that women stand a better chance of getting elected under the proportional representation, as opposed to the constituency based system. The chance of women getting elected is even higher when the PR system works in concert with a party or legislated quota. The United Republic of Tanzania, for example, now has 30.3 percent of women in Parliament.

The voluntary party quota, combined with the PR system is seen at work in South Africa and Mozambique and it is no coincidence that these two have the highest representation of women in parliament in SADC. ANC and Frelimo have their own voluntarily adopted 30 percent quotas. Because of the PR system, every third person on their list of candidates was a woman in the last elections in 2004. The Tanzanian constitution stipulates that 75 seats of the 324 seats are reserved for women.

In addition to quotas, the electoral systems of many countries allow the Head of State to make appointments to parliament for example Zimbabwe, Botswana and Swaziland. Such a measure can also be utilised to ensure that the thirty percent target is met.

Challenges

Major strides have been made towards gender mainstreaming in the political arena in the region during the last decade. Yet there is still low-level policy intervention to close the most serious gender gaps in decision-making in political structures, public and private institutions. Where there is political intervention, the few initiatives which do address women's concerns tend to be sensitive to practical gender needs as opposed to strategic gender needs. Because of this situation, the removal of gender gaps mostly remains in theory and is not practiced. For instance, the increase in the number of women in politics does not correspond with their ability to effect change in the parliament.

Most female parliamentarians are not adequately empowered to challenge the system and provide their views when decisions are made, especially those that impact negatively on women. Having more women political leaders does not necessarily lead to increased gender sensitivity. Despite the increase in women's participation quantitatively, the increase in level of political influence and quality of life for women has remained minimal, even where activists and strong champions of women's rights have had opportunities to hold public office. One explanation is that once in leadership, the representatives who usually gain public office through their political parties give more allegiance to their parties and uphold the party stance, rather than that of the electorate.

In addition to this, parties are still male-dominated and continue to maintain male patriarchy. Statutory and customary laws and practices are also still inherently dis-

Countries	Quota	Electoral system
Angola	No	PR
Botswana	No	FPTP
DRC	No	FPTP
Lesotho	Yes – LG	M
Malawi	No	FPTP
Mauritius	No	FPTP
Mozambique	Yes	PR
Namibia	Yes – LG	PR
South Africa	Yes	PR; M
Swaziland	No	FPTP
Tanzania	Yes	FPTP
Zambia	No	FPTP
Zimbabwe	No	FPTP

Quotas and Electoral Systems in SADC Countries Table 5.3

Adapted from Audit of the SADC Declaration on Gender and Development, Women in decision-making, 2005
Key: PR – Proportional Representation
FPTP – First Past the Post
M – Mixed
LG – Local Government

criminatory and continue to marginalise women, regardless of the international and regional instruments such countries signed and ratified which discourage such practices.

It is further observed that women tend to be more involved in local level politics than national level processes in power sharing. It is asserted that local level government is seen less as sites of power, as such, people are less resistant to women's participation at this level. Yet, it is true that strong local level leadership contributes to better performance of national level leadership. The challenges that remain point to the need to convince the populace that local level politics is as influential as national level politics.

Another challenge regards domesticating international and regional instruments that are already in place. This necessarily calls for an assessment of the bureaucratic bottlenecks involved in reforming the structures that hinder women's participation in politics and decision making. Where international and regional instruments are in place, for instance, governments have taken too long to domesticate them leading to very negligible application of the instruments by the courts although some progress is being made in constitutional reforms, establishment of human rights institutions/ commissions and review of laws relevant to the current democratic framework and respect for human rights.

The general low representation of women in established (formal) structures like parliament also calls for the building of strong networks for the advancement of women's agendas, hence the need to solicit support from lobbying civil society organisations to ensure a reliable lobbying force on gender issues.

Women in the corporate sector

Women often have lower educational levels and this limits their active participation in the formal segment of the economy. The SADC 2004 progress report on the Implementation of the Beijing Platform for Action by the region reports that 24 percent of women are formally employed compared to 71 percent men. A majority of these women are concentrated in low-paying middle-management positions.

To ensure that gender issues are addressed within the public sector employment framework, gender has been mainstreamed in the human rights provisions and guidelines that have been developed to address issues of recruitment, promotion, postings and sexual harassment among others. For example, Malawi, Zambia and Zimbabwe provide 90 days maternity leave for working women to breastfeed their babies and recover before returning to work. The maternity leave has assisted many women to continue with their employment while performing their reproductive roles.

The following tables depict the representation of women in decision-making positions in the public sphere in Botswana.

In the public sector, most of the managerial positions are occupied by women but very few advance to the top position of permanent secretary. There are many women who qualify for top management positions but it is very difficult for them to break the glass ceiling. There is need to change the mindsets of managers, as they still believe in male leadership, which is the major obstacle to the promotion of women.

The representation of women as Chief Executives in the private/parastatals sector has not changed significantly as organisations in these sectors are predominantly led by male Chief Executive Officers. Further, a limited number of women participate in private sector boards, as it is still a male

Women and Men in Decision-Making Positions in the Public Sector in Botswana			Table 5.4
Grade	Women	Men	Total
FO	0	4	4
F1	11	13	24
F2	10	36	46
E1	5	37	42
E2	53	122	175
D1	73	146	219

Botswana Women's Affairs Department 2003
Key
FO- F2 are salary levels that are for top chief executives in the public sector.
E1 - E2 are deputy level positions.
D1 – is middle management positions.

Gender Composition in Table 5.5 Decision-Making in the Private Sector in Botswana			
Position	**Women**	**Men**	**Total**
Board Member	20	122	142
Heads of Company	5	32	37
Heads of Department	119	320	439

Botswana Women Affairs Department 2002

domain and an exclusive elitist arena that is difficult to enter for both women and men that have limited power and economic wealth. *Beyond Inequalities 2005: Women in Namibia* reports that "women are severely underrepresented in parastatals, with only one of the 12 parastatals in the country having a woman Chief Executive Officer (CEO)."[5]

Barclays Bank, an international private financial institution now has its first Zambian female Managing Director after many years of the position being held by foreign directors.[6] Linah Mohohlo is the Governor of the Bank of Botswana.

Conclusion

There have been significant changes in terms of power relations between men and women in the domestic, community, public and private spheres. Some policies have attempted to address gender needs such as influencing sex stereotypes, sensitisation on gender issues and power sharing although some policies and programs are still limiting women's empowerment.

Whether it is by election or appointment to leadership positions, it is a pre-requisite that women should have attained an education. Illiterate people, the majority of who are women, in most countries would find it difficult to get into leadership while at the same time appointments to higher leadership positions require higher levels of educational attainment.

This implies that women's participation has to be enhanced through a supportive policy and legal environment and increased capacity building as well as raising of public awareness on gender issues. It is through education and training that men and women acquire knowledge and skills relevant for effective and well-informed political decision-making. Without basic and higher education, one cannot access relevant information nor appropriately articulate the political issues for which decision making and timely and appropriately proposed solutions are required to redress the concerns.

Empowerment of women must be accompanied by nationwide and region-wide campaigns whose aim is to shift mindsets so that a stage is reached when we can close our eyes and see power in both feminine and masculine moulds. These campaigns have to be able to challenge the status quo.

Gender considerations need to be built into existing and ongoing debates on electoral systems such as the First Past the Post (FPTP) system that up to now has been gender blind. Explicit constitutional provisions for gender equality as found in South Africa, Tanzania and Namibia are also powerful tools for ensuring transformation.

The subject of women in decision-making must be approached from the three perspectives of access, participation and transformation. Participation concerns where women are located within decision-making bodies and the institutional barriers to their effective contribution. Transformation is about what difference women make – to the institutional culture and exercise of power as well as to the making of laws and delivery of services.

Endnotes

1 SADC, The SADC Declaration on Gender and Development, SADC, Gaborone, 1997.
2 United Nations (1995) "The Beijing Platform for Action" paragraph 181, UN.
3 The GAD Exchange, SARDC, 2005.
4 ZARD and SARDC WIDSAA, *Beyond Inequalities 2005: Women in Malawi*, ZARD/ SARDC, Lusaka and Harare, 2005.
5 UNAM and SARDC WIDSAA, *Beyond Inequalities 2005: Women in Namibia*, UNAM/ SARDC, Windhoek and Harare, 2005.
6 ZARD and SARDC WIDSAA, *Beyond Inequalities 2005: Women in Zambia*, ZARD/ SARDC, Lusaka and Harare, 2005.

References

Gender Links, *Gender in Southern African Politics: Ringing up the change*, Gender Links, Johannesburg, South Africa, 2004.

Gender Links, *Missing the mark? Audit of the SADC Declaration on Gender and Development Women in Decision Making*, Johannesburg, South Africa, 2005.

Open Society Initiative for Southern Africa, *Open space*, Open Society Initiative for Southern Africa, Johannesburg, South Africa, Volume 1 Issue 1, April, 2005.

SADC, *Implementation of the Beijing Platform for Action, SADC region 2004 Progress Report*, SADC Gender Unit, Gaborone, Botswana, 2004.

SADC Gender Unit, *SADC Gender Resource Kit Supplementary Reading Material*, The Gender Unit, Gaborone, Botswana, 2004.

SADC GU, *Women in Politics and Decision Making in SADC: Beyond 30% in 2005*, Southern African Development Community Gender Unit, Gaborone, Botswana, 1999.

SARDC, *SANF 06 No 16, February 2006*, SARDC, Harare, 2006.

SARDC WIDSAA, *Beyond Inequalities: Women in Southern Africa*, SARDC, Harare, 2000.

SARDC WIDSAA, The *Gad Exchange Newsletter Issue 36*, SARDC-WIDSAA, Harare, 2005.

Southern African Development Community Parliamentary Forum, The *SADC MPs Companion on Gender and Development in Southern Africa*, Southern African Development Community Parliamentary Forum, Windhoek, Namibia, 2002.

Southern African Institute of International Affairs, *SADC Barometer*, Southern African Institute of International Affairs, Braamfontein, South Africa, Issue 6 August 2004.

UNAM and SARDC WIDSAA, *Beyond Inequalities2005: Women in Namibia*, UNAM/ SARDC, Windhoek and Harare, 2005.

Women in Action, *Beijing: A decade under scrutiny*, Women in Action, Quezon City, Philippines, 2005.

Women in Politics Support Unit, *Taking up the Challenge: Advancing Women's Involvement in Politics, Annual Report 2003/4*, Women in Politics Support Unit, 2004.

Women's NGO Coalition and SARDC WIDSAA, *Beyond Inequalities 2005: Women in Botswana*, WNGOC/ SARDC, Gaborone and Harare, 2005.

WLSA Malawi and SARDC WIDSAA, *Beyond Inequalities 2005: Women in Malawi*, WLSA/ SARDC, Limbe and Harare, 2005.

SARDC and ZARD , *Beyond Inequalities 2005: Women in Zambia*, Lusaka and Harare, 2005.

SARDC WIDSAA and ZWRCN , *Beyond Inequalities 2005: Women in Zimbabwe*, ZWRCN/ SARDC, Harare, 2005.

WOMEN, LAW AND LEGAL RIGHTS

6

Introduction

Advancing and realising women's legal and human rights through instituting new policies and laws has been a priority for countries in southern Africa from the time they ratified and acceded to the Convention on the Elimination of all forms of Discrimination Against Women (CEDAW) in 1979, which calls on governments to incorporate the principle of equality of men and women in their legal system, abolish all discriminatory laws and adopt appropriate ones prohibiting discrimination against women. The SADC Declaration on Gender and Development and its Addendum on the Prevention and Eradication of Violence Against Women and Children, and the Beijing Declaration and Platform for Action (BDPFA) also emphasise the importance of promoting women's legal and human rights.

Since 2000, there has been a shift from the needs-based approach to women's development to one which emphasises a human rights-based approach. The needs-based approach focused on women's marginalisation in an attempt to meet their practical needs. The approach did not challenge those structures which fundamentally impede on women's participation in human society on an equal basis with men. The recent emphasis on the human rights-based approach, which involves mainstreaming human rights in diverse areas, is caused in part by the approach's recognition of the existence of rights.

The rights-based approach focuses on those who are most vulnerable, excluded and discriminated against and reinforces the capacity of duty bearers (usually governments) to respect, protect and guarantee their rights. The approach thus requires institutional reform to allow for effective monitoring of development goals that have been set using human rights instruments. The rights-based approach has provided a fundamental shift in needs-based assessments, livelihood analyses as well as gender-based analyses. Rights are indivisible, interdependent and interrelated.

The approach considers the three fundamental aspects of change; participation, equity and protection. Participation focuses on enhancing the involvement of the vulnerable in society as rights holders to contribute to decision-making on issues that directly affect them. Equity addresses issues of power relations between rights holders and duty bearers, with special emphasis on relations between women and men, governments, minorities and others suffering from social exclusion while protection refers to securing the rights and interests of the most vulnerable in society by addressing the various injustices they experience through, among other actions, advocacy work at various levels. The human rights-based approach allows an identification of the relationship between claim and duty.

Policy framework

Southern Africa has seen the emergence of new policies and laws relating to gender equality and the advancement of women since the year 2000, at both regional and national levels. The following policies address law and legal rights of women in SADC.

Objectives of the SADC Box 6.1
**Protocol on Gender
and Development**

- To bring together in one legally binding regional instrument all the commitments to gender equality that have been made through, among others, the Beijing Declaration and Platform for Action, the SADC Declaration on Gender and Development and its Addendum, the Convention on the Elimination of all forms of Discrimination Against Women, the Protocol to the African Charter on Human and People's Rights on the Rights of Women in Africa, and the Millennium Development Goals;
- To address emerging gender issues and concerns; set realistic, measurable targets, time frames and indicators, and allocate resources for achieving the goals that will be set;
- To strengthen, monitor and evaluate the progress made by Member States towards reaching the targets and goals set in the protocol;
- To create a fora for involving all stakeholders and sharing best practices in the implementation of the protocol; and
- To deepen regional integration, sustainable development, and community building.

SARDC, *GAD Exchange* Issue 40, October-December, 2006

Draft SADC Protocol on Gender and Development

A comprehensive document, the draft Protocol on Gender addresses a wide range of issues that affect women in the region, including constitutional and legal rights, governance, education, productive resources, harmful traditional practices, health and HIV and AIDS in a number of targets; some to be achieved by 2010 and the majority by 2015.

If adopted, the draft Protocol will provide concrete, time-bound commitments to achieving key strategic objectives and will mark the end of an era of commitments to an era of implementation. The draft Protocol not only incorporates gender commitments from all existing regional, global and continental instruments but also enhances these by taking account of gaps that have been identified in the existing instruments and in their implementation. Such instruments include the SADC Declaration on Gender and Development and its Addendum on the Prevention and Eradication of Violence Against Women and Children, the Beijing Platform for Action, the Convention on the Elimination of all forms of Discrimination Against Women, the Millennium Development Goals, and the African Union Charter on Human and Peoples Rights and the Rights of Women in Africa.

Among others, provisions in the draft Protocol focus on the legal and institutional frameworks necessary to stimulate the region into accelerating implementation of commitments to achieve gender equality and the empowerment of women in the region by 2015. Towards this end, if unchanged by the proposed time of signing in late 2008, the Protocol will commit member states to ensure that gender equality and equity is enshrined in national constitutions and that these provisions take precedence over customary, religious and other laws by 2015.

SADC Declaration on Gender and Development and Addendum

In the 1997 Declaration, Member States committed themselves to repeal and reform all laws, amend constitutions and change social practices that still subject women to discrimination, and enact empowering gender-sensitive laws.

In the Addendum to the Declaration on Gender and Development on the Prevention and Eradication of Violence Against Women and Children, SADC Heads of State resolved to take the following legal measures against issues of abuse:

- enacting laws such as sexual offences and domestic violence legislation making various forms of violence against women clearly defined crimes, and taking appropriate measures to impose penalties, punishment and other enforcement mechanisms for the prevention and eradication of violence against women and children;
- adopting legislative measures to ensure the protection and removal of all forms of discrimination against women, and providing for the empowerment of women with disabilities, the girl-child, the aged, women in armed conflict and other women whose circumstances make them especially vulnerable to violence;
- reviewing and reforming criminal laws and procedures applicable to cases of sexual offences, to eliminate gender bias and ensure justice and fairness to both the victim and the accused;
- introducing, as a matter of priority, legal and administrative mechanisms for women and children subjected to violence, effective access to counselling, restitution, reparation and other just forms of dispute resolution;

◆ adopting such other legislative and administrative measures as may be necessary to ensure the prevention and eradication of all forms of violence against women and children.[1]

Monitoring the implementation of CEDAW

In December 2000, the optional protocol to CEDAW that enables groups of women to submit complaints to the CEDAW Committee was adopted. In 2004, Swaziland, the only country in SADC that had not ratified CEDAW, did so without reservations. The process of ratifying the optional protocol to CEDAW is ongoing. At the time of writing, half the countries in the region had either signed or ratified the CEDAW optional protocol (1999); these are Lesotho, Madagascar, Malawi, Mauritius, Namibia, South Africa and Tanzania, while some countries have initiated measures aimed at domesticating provisions of CEDAW.

In most countries, the CEDAW has triggered the creation of Law Reform Commissions, Human Rights Commissions, the Commission on Gender Equality in South Africa and the review of national legislation in specific areas such as violence against women, inheritance, citizenship, workers' rights, family law, rights to land, equal employment opportunities, marriage as well as encouraging affirmative action.

State parties to CEDAW must report to the United Nations (UN) CEDAW Committee every four years. The UN Committee of Experts on CEDAW holds twice-yearly sessions at which they review reports from governments' own assessments of progress and challenges in achieving gender equality. The government reports are also assessed in light of alternate information about the country situation provided by civil society organisations in the form of shadow reports.

The review of the country reports includes dialogue between the Committee of Experts and the national government in question. This dialogue culminates in concluding comments; identifying where the greatest shortcomings lie and what forms of action the government should consider taking.

For the SADC countries however, there have been no specific indicators to monitor their implementation of CEDAW beyond state reporting and the reporting process is fraught with challenges since most governments have inadequate resources and expertise to prepare the reports. Late reporting is a common feature for most SADC states, coupled with sending inadequate delegations whose leaders are unable to make commitments on behalf of their respective governments. However, the biggest challenge for SADC countries has been their failure to domesticate CEDAW. The lack of self-executing clauses in constitutions for automatic domestication of international instruments is also a major drawback. This is further complicated by the lack of serious law reform and the integration of CEDAW principles, as well as the failure to repeal laws that discriminate against women.

Protocol to the African Charter on Human and People's Rights

At their annual summit in 2003, the African Heads of State and Government adopted the Protocol to the African Charter on Human and People's Rights on the Rights of Women in Africa. The protocol came into force on 25 November 2005, with four southern African countries, Lesotho, Malawi, Namibia and South Africa having ratified it. The signing was an important step in recognising the rights of women and in governments' shows of commitment to a legal and rights framework through which these rights could be realised. The protocol complements the African Charter in ensuring the promotion and protection of human rights of women in Africa. Further, through this protocol, African Heads of State and Government committed themselves to taking concrete steps to give greater attention to the human rights of women in order to eliminate all forms of discrimination and gender based violence against women.

The 32 articles of the protocol address many sensitive and important issues which are deeply anchored in African societies and are not being sufficiently tackled at national level.[2] For example, the protocol:

- reflects specific violations against women and affirms the principles of equality and non-discrimination, while guaranteeing women's rights to life, integrity, security, elimination of all harmful practices, and access to justice and equal protection before the law;
- provides for and recognises women's economic rights, including the right to social protection, including protections for economic independence, the right to own and manage land, and the right to be equal partners in making decisions about property, regardless of marital status;
- offers special protections to women in situations of distress, for example pregnant and lactating mothers in prison, while the rights of widows are also secured;
- for the first time in international law, it explicitly sets forth the reproductive rights of women to medical abortion when pregnancy results from rape or incest or when the continuation of a pregnancy endangers the health or life of the mother;
- contains provisions seeking responses to specific problems such as multiple violations of rights in marital relations, violence and grave risks to the life of women and girls in war situations;
- recognises the importance of gender parity and notes that women should have equal opportunities with men in decision-making processes and on policy formulation;
- stresses the importance of the place of rights of women in the socio-political priorities of Africa and re-enforced through the challenge to move from commitments to actions in order to ensure visibility and access by women to organs of power and decision-making processes. One example is the decision by Heads of State and Government to share, on a 50/50 basis between women and men, the top echelons of the African Commission on Human and People's Rights (ACHPR);
- takes a stance on personal law, for example Article 6 on marriage seeks to encourage monogamy as the preferred form of marriage while the rights of women in marriage and in the family, including in polygamous marital relationships, will be promoted and protected. According to the protocol, a married woman shall have the right to retain her maiden name and to use it as she pleases, jointly or separately with her husband's surname. Further, a woman shall have the right to retain her nationality or adopt that of her husband. Other provisions catered for include women's access to justice and equal protection before the law.[3]

The need for practical application runs through the entire protocol. To be effective, the protocol will largely depend on national governments' review of their national laws and policies to reflect the spirit and rights articulated under the protocol.

African Court on Human and Peoples' Rights

Article 32 of the Protocol on the Rights of Women in Africa reaffirms the need for the African Court as it provides that pending the establishment of the African Court on Human and Peoples' Rights, the African Commission on Human and Peoples' Rights shall be concerned with matters of interpretation arising from the application and implementation of the protocol. The Protocol to the African Charter on Human and People's Rights on the establishment of an African Court on Human and People's Rights entered into force on 25 January 2004. One of the main reasons for the establishment of the African Court of Justice is to strengthen the regional human rights system under the African Charter, which has often been criticised as a weak system lacking judicial "teeth".

A comparative analysis of constitutions in SADC

In the period 2000-2008, countries in the region have made constitutional reforms to ensure gender equality. In some countries, constitutional reforms are still ongoing, with constitutional debates revolving around issues such as people-driven approaches, a justifiable bill of rights, including socio-economic and cultural rights and responses to HIV and AIDS, separation of powers, clear protection of women and children's rights and other minority groups, more representative electoral systems, including affirmative action provisions for women's entry into political positions.[4]

Most national constitutions in the region recognise formal equality of men and women before the law, requiring that men and women be treated on the same terms without special barriers or favours on account of their sex. Many of these constitutions however fail to make the distinction between equality and substantive equality or to pronounce themselves on the issue of customary law. Due to significant differences in the characteristics and circumstances of women and men, simply looking at 'equality' does not produce equal results. Substantive equality demands that laws take into account these differences to avoid gender-related outcomes that are considered unfair.

In Zambia, the 2005 draft Constitution has expanded protection from discrimination to include the right to non-discrimination on the basis of sex, pregnancy, health, marital status, race, ethnic tribe, social or economic status, origin, colour, disability, religion, conscience, belief, culture, language or birth. In addition, the draft Constitution now contains a clause on the equality of women and men and it also includes economic, social and cultural rights.

Table 6.1 shows a mixed picture of national constitutions that explicitly outlaw discrimination on the basis of sex, those that make no mention of the issue, and those that implicitly include the issue.

Gender machineries in SADC

Gender machineries are institutional mechanisms with the mandate to design, monitor, evaluate, advocate and coordinate the implementation of national or regional gender policies that promote the advancement of women. In the region, gender machineries include ministries responsible for gender or women's affairs, gender focal persons in government ministries and departments, and the Gender Unit at the SADC Secretariat.

National gender machineries have been established in all of the SADC countries; however where there is stronger partnership with the non-government sector such as in Botswana, Mauritius, Namibia and South Africa, the environment for promotion of gender equality is enhanced.

Constitutional Provisions for Gender Equality in SADC countries   Table 6.1

Country	Gender Sensitivity of Constitution	Issues
Angola	**Article 18 (1,2)** provides for equality irrespective of sex and sexual discrimination is prohibited. **Article 29** provides for equality between men and women in the family, with the same rights and duties.	◆ Falls short of providing for non-discrimination in all matters of personal law, an area where women encounter many disadvantages. ◆ Omits discrimination on the grounds of age, marital status, pregnancy and culture.
Botswana	**Section 15** protects against discrimination, but excludes protection from discrimination on the basis of sex. Aspects of customary law relating to matters of personal law such as marriage, divorce, inheritance and custody of children are exempt from this discriminatory clause.	◆ There is lack of protection from sexual discrimination. However, the highest court has interpreted another section of the constitution as prohibiting sex-based discrimination. ◆ Protection from discrimination does not extend to matters of personal and customary law, where women face many disadvantages.
*DRC	-	-
Lesotho	**Section 18** protects from discrimination based on sex.	◆ Protection from discrimination does not extend to personal and customary law, for example, issues of marriage, divorce, custody and inheritance.
Mauritius	**Section 16** excludes protection from discrimination on the basis of sex.	◆ There is lack of protection from sexual discrimination. Protection from discrimination does not extend to matters of personal law, where women face many disadvantages.
Namibia	**Article 10** provides for protection from discrimination on the basis of sex. **Article 14** provides for equal rights between men and women in, during, and at the dissolution of a marriage. ◆ The constitution recognises the right to practice and enjoy one's culture, but this is subject to other provisions of the constitution, therefore discrimination on the basis of sex is unconstitutional.	◆ Falls short of providing equal rights in all matters pertaining to personal and customary law where women face many disadvantages.
Malawi	**Section 20** protects against discrimination on the basis of sex. **Section 22** provides for full and equal respect of individuals within the family. **Section 24** provides for the rights of women to equal protection of the law, non-discrimination in marriage, capacity to enter into legally binding agreements, individual property, custody and guardianship of children, to acquire and retain citizenship and nationality, equal rights on the dissolution of marriage, protection from violence, discrimination at work, and deprivation of property, elimination of harmful/discriminatory customs and practices.	◆ Though progressive at the level of formal equality and equity, it remains problematic at the level of substantive equality.
Mozambique	**Article 66/67** provides for equality of rights between men and women in all spheres of political, economic, social and cultural affairs. It also spells out the need for motherhood to be protected, therefore impacting on pre and post-natal care. Emphasis however is on the protection of tradition and culture.	◆ There is no explicit provision protecting women's rights, given their historically disadvantaged position. ◆ Emphasis on the protection of culture may work against the interests of women.
Swaziland	-	-
South Africa	**Section 1** provides for democratic values of non-sexism, human dignity, equality and advancement of human rights and freedoms. **Section 9** prohibits discrimination on the grounds of sex and gender, pregnancy, marital status and sexual orientation. **Section 12 (2)** provides for the right to bodily and psychological integrity, including decisions on reproduction, security in and control over one's body.	◆ Makes no specific reference to the equal rights of women in matters of personal and customary law, where women face many disadvantages.

continued.....

Constitutional provisions for gender equality in SADC countries   Table 6.1

Country	Gender Sensitivity of Constitution	Issues
	✦ The constitution recognises affirmative action for previously disadvantaged groups.	
Tanzania	**Articles 12 and 13** provide for equality of persons and equality before the law. **Article 13 (5)** prohibits discrimination based on sex.	✦ There is no provision that explicitly protects women's rights, given their historical and contemporary disadvantages.
Zambia	**Article 23** protects individuals from discrimination irrespective of sex or marital status. It recognises that a person may enjoy their culture, tradition, custom and language but this should not be in contradiction to the constitution. However, customary law is protected from this clause.	✦ Protection from discrimination does not extend to matters of personal and customary law, areas in which women are most disadvantaged, for example, laws relating to marriage, divorce, custody, guardianship and inheritance.
Zimbabwe	Discrimination through law or through acts of public officials is prohibited and this includes discrimination by sex.	✦ Customary law in the area of personal laws are protected from this discriminatory clause. ✦ International instruments do not automatically form part of ✦ Zimbabwean laws unless incorporated by an Act of Parliament, therefore CEDAW only acts as a guiding tool, but courts are not bound by it.

Location of Gender Machineries in SADC Government Structures 2005   Table 6.2

SADC Member State	Full Ministerial position	Department /Unit in a Ministry
Angola	Ministério de Família e Promoção da Mulher	
Botswana		Ministry of Labour and Home Affairs-Women Affairs Department
DRC	Ministere du Genre, de la Famille et de l'Enfant	
Lesotho	Ministry of Gender, Youth, Sports and Recreation	
Malawi	Ministry of Gender, Child Welfare and Community Services, Women and Child Development	
Madagascar		Ministere de la Sante, du Planning Familial et de la Protection Sociale
Mauritius	Ministry for Women's Rights, Child Development, Family Welfare and Consumer Protection	
Mozambique	Ministry of Women and Social Action	
Namibia	Ministry of Gender Equality and Child Welfare	
South Africa		Office on the Status of Women –President's Office
Swaziland		Ministry of Home Affairs-Gender Coordination Unit
Tanzania	Ministry of Community Development, Gender and Children	
Zambia		Cabinet Office- Gender in Development Division
Zimbabwe	Ministry of Women's Affairs, Gender and Community Development	

Compiled by SARDC WIDSAA based on information from national gender machineries, 2005

Access to justice

A study conducted by Women and Law in Southern Africa (WLSA) titled "Women and the Administration of Justice Delivery: Problems and Constraints" revealed the various legal obstacles that prevent women's access to legal and judicial services in SADC. The legal obstacles fall into several areas, which are interrelated and tend to be mutually reinforcing such as:

+ laws that appear to be neutral at face value but are subject to different interpretations;
+ laws that have the potential of being discriminatory because of what is left out;
+ in the application of the law when people act on the contrary; and
+ the administering of laws being ineffective because the institutions or individuals who apply the law refuse or are unable to apply it.

WLSA research on the study of maintenance[5] revealed that throughout the region, most maintenance laws suffer from administrative problems because officials hesitate to apply a law which seems to run contrary to customary law or simply because administrative "red tape" slows down the process of receiving maintenance payments.

Laws may be ineffective in practice because they have not been communicated to people. Women in particular suffer from lack of knowledge of the laws that affect their lives. Because of their subordinate status, poverty, lack of education, and the fact that many women live in the rural areas, women have less access to information and material on the law. In some instances the women may know their rights, but may not be able to afford the travel expenses to the civil courts, let alone lawyer's fees.

SADC countries still operate under a dual system of law, general law and customary law. The duality of the legal system within most SADC countries still poses a hindrance to women's ability to access justice because of contradictions inherent in the two systems. For example, where rules of inheritance have changed, women are still at the mercy of judges, their interpretation of case law and their understanding of rules of equity. In the case Magaya vs Magaya,[6] the ruling by the Supreme Court of Zimbabwe that denied women the right to inherit under customary law has fuelled a review of the interface between customary and general law with respect to its treatment of women. In the judgment delivered by Muchechetere J A, the Supreme Court concluded that the appointment of male heirs to the estates of deceased African males remained unaffected by the Legal Age of Majority Act 15/1982.

The surviving spouse of a male deceased person similarly could not inherit as she was considered to be an 'outsider' to the family. The ruling set a retrogressive precedent and eroded years of progress made in advocating for the rights of women; it also heightened the contradictions in Zimbabwe's internal laws.

Traditional attitudes, socio-cultural myths as well as the patriarchal nature of societies in the region affect the way the law is interpreted where women are involved. In Zambia, WLSA Zambia documented the case of Chrystal Alyson Denn[7] to bring to light the shortcomings in the law.

Women and the administration of justice delivery systems

The WLSA study on problems and challenges in the administration of justice delivery systems[8] by WLSA reveals that even when women know their legal rights and are prepared to use the formal court system to exercise them, there are still inhibiting and interrelated factors preventing or discouraging them from doing so. These factors include:

- inaccessibility of courts;
- cumbersome administrative procedures;
- language used in the court;
- insensitivity of court personnel and other enforcement agents;
- conflicting laws; and
- inadequate and limited knowledge of legal aid facilities for economically disadvantaged people.

Even when the phrasing of the law is gender-sensitive, women know of their legal rights and are prepared to use the formal court system, the full benefits of these laws will not be realised if the structures that administer such laws are, for some reason, inadequate and ineffective. Over the years, WLSA studies have confirmed that general law does not have a monopoly over people's sense of justice. In the region, national justice delivery systems in many countries reflect the colonial legacy, and it seems within the interests of the elite in power for them to remain so.

The pluralistic justice and legal systems contribute to the inaccessibility of judicial services as they create practical problems on the ground for litigants and adjudicators. Women's lower socio-economic status often causes them to be dependant on either their husbands or families. For women, the possibility of withdrawal of emotional and material support by family members is a real threat that prevents them from suing husbands and other family members. The poor, who are mostly women, are caught up in a double bind situation; on the one hand they may be ignorant about their rights and how to exercise them, while on the other hand, due to their poor economic circumstances, they are unable to afford the cost of judicial and legal services. Further, women's minority status in some countries, where they have to appear in court assisted by their

(male) guardians does not auger well for women's ability to exercise their individual rights and to effectively use the justice delivery system.

Also, the high cost involved in the judicial process is prohibitive in most cases. Legal charges and lawyers' fees are beyond the average person's means, especially those of women. Generally in most SADC countries, the law is often discriminatory and legal processes are expensive, slow and complex. The result is that people, particu-

---

Zambian court sentences woman to life in prison 6.2

Allegations are that, Chrystal Denn, a 26 year-old woman married to Trevor Denn; a 34 year-old footballer had a turbulent marriage spanning a period of five years. During this period, it was reported that Chrystal had been battered and assaulted by her husband and had been treated for injuries ranging from bruises and cuts to haemorrhage and sprains.

Trevor Denn was also reported to have attempted to inspect her private parts for evidence of sexual intercourse with other men. This was done even in the presence of their domestic helper. Chrystal Denn made eight reports to the police of these incidents of assault and battery. On the night of 20 June 1999, the couple went out separately. Chrystal alleged that she arrived home after Trevor and he accosted her on her way to the toilet. She tried to avoid him but he grabbed her by the neck and struck her on the face. He went into a tirade of insults and after pinning her to the wall tried to strip her naked so as to examine her private parts to see whether she had had sexual intercourse with another man.

In the heat of the moment, it is reported that Chrystal picked up a knife, freed herself and stabbed him in the back. Upon seeing the blood, Chrystal tried to administer first aid to stop the bleeding but Trevor lost consciousness and died. In giving evidence, Chrystal explained that she did not intend to kill her husband but to scare him so that he would back off.

In her defence, Chrystal pleaded self-defence and provocation. The High Court rejected her defence and convicted her of murder. She was sentenced to life imprisonment. Chrystal appealed to the Supreme Court. In deciding the appeal before it in 2002, the court stated that the inspection of private parts by a partner in marriage would not amount to dehumanising conduct.

The Court acknowledged that although there had been tension and mistrust between the couple and evidence of serious assaults requiring medical treatment, it viewed Chrystal's use of a knife as not constituting self-defence. The Court also held that Chrystal was not provoked in any way on the night in question, and therefore this defence could not be relied upon.

On the issue of sentence, the Supreme Court accepted that the history of the marriage and the actual fight on the night in question was such as to establish evidence of extenuating circumstances. The Court accepted that Chrystal was not the aggressor on the night and she tried to fight off her husband.

In view of the evidence, the Court allowed the appeal against sentence of life imprisonment and substituted it with 15 years imprisonment.

The reason for trivialising the battering that went on for years and the humiliation Chrystal felt at having her private parts checked is rooted in socio-cultural myths and misunderstandings, as well as in the patriarchal nature of our societies. Patriarchy makes violent marriage relationships seem normal and morally just. Generally, we all share a natural horror of homicide and consider it the most heinous of crimes; however, there is a tendency to accommodate it in cases of spousal homicide, but only when the victim is the female spouse.

WLSA, *Justice for All* p1-5, 2002

---

larly women, have inadequate and unequal access to justice through the formal legal system. For these reasons, they tend to rely much more on customary justice systems, although these can be discriminatory. Improving access to justice requires that both formal and customary systems be made to work justly and equitably. It also requires efforts to not only reform legal procedures, but to make courts more user friendly.

Rights within marriage and changes in marriage laws

Women suffer discrimination due to non-uniform marriage and divorce laws, the application of customary property laws that still favour men's ownership of land, violence against women and lack of equal access to education. In SADC countries, marriage and divorces are governed by parallel legal regimes of statutory, customary and in some instances religious laws. Usually, customary and religious laws are not written, resulting in ambiguity and ambivalence in interpretation and application. Most of the marriages in SADC countries continue to be solemnised under customary law, in some cases as a first step, thereafter the practice is to register marriages under civil or statutory law.

Customary and Islamic marriages are potentially polygamous and permit some negative practices that have the effect of discriminating against women. Some of the practices relate to forced or arranged marriages, especially for young girls; leverot or widow inheritance; and the extensive marital power given to men in matters of property and women's reproductive rights. The employment of both customary and civil law in most countries in the region makes it difficult to harmonise the various marriage systems; customary, religious and statutory and come up with one unified system.

Most customary practices related to child custody favouring the father's custody in patrilineal groups and the mother's custody in matrilineal groups have given way to statutes mandating that custody decisions be made on the basis of the child's best interest. With regards to personal property, customary laws vary, but women may usually retain personal property brought into the marriage. However, anything acquired after marriage is considered part of the husband's estate in case of death. Restrictions on women, which may have their historical basis in custom rather than law, are legal restrictions when the courts enforce them. Under customary law as interpreted by the colonial courts, women were perpetual minors without contractual and proprietary capacity.

Women married under customary law are under the total guardianship of their husbands so any property they acquire is automatically vested in the husband. Judgments in courts have been passed to that effect. In a case heard in Zimbabwe (1986), former Chief Justice Gubbay summed it by stating in Jena vs Nyemba[9] that, "property acquired during a marriage becomes a husband's property whether acquired by him or his wife." In Zimbabwe the exception to this rule is the *mombe yeumai/inkomo yohlanga* (a cow given to a mother during negotiations for her daughter's bride price). In 2000, WLSA Mozambique found that most marriages in Mozambique were not legally valid under the law. As a consequence, the majority of women do not take up their cases through the formal court system. However, the Family Law (2003) contains important provisions that, among others, recognise customary unions and allow Mozambican women married under customary law to claim property and custody rights.

There are some significant changes that have occurred in marriage laws, for example the fact that in South Africa, the General Law Fourth Amendment Act of 1993 finally abolished marital power in all civil marriages. In Lesotho, the Married Persons Equality Bill (2000) which advocates for a change in the law on the legal status of married women, aiming to ensure legal equality between men and women in marriage was presented to Parliament. The Law Reform Commission was subsequently tasked with drawing up a proposal and issuing a paper to discuss the problems that are in the country's marriage laws, especially in the context of the dualistic nature of the legal system. Unfortunately, although it has been debated for years, the Bill has been pending enactment since 2000.

In December 2003, Mozambique passed the Family Law which secures a broad range of rights previously denied to Mozambican women. Among other provisions, the law ensures:

- that the head of the family may be either a man or a woman;
- that 18 years is the marriageable age for both boys and girls;
- that women can inherit property in the case of divorce;
- the non-recognition of polygamy; and
- the recognition of *de facto* unions and traditional marriages.

In Botswana, the Marital Power Act was passed in 2004. The Act was intended to abolish marital power in the laws of Botswana and to ensure the equality of spouses married in community of property. The Act has fuelled amendments to the Deeds and Registry Act which allow women to now register immovable property in their own names. Similarly, a wife now has to give her consent in property transactions undertaken by her husband, while the law also allows for sharing of property by co-habiting couples. Traditional chiefs have also been given power and authority to share the property for couples.

In Zambia, the Subordinate Court passed a judgment in a divorce matter that came on appeal from the local court. The local court had made a decision that all the household property acquired by the two parties during the existence of the marriage be shared equally. This prompted the man to appeal against the decision of the Local Court, citing a High Court decision in which the High Court held that Lozi custom cannot compel a husband to share property acquired during existence of the marriage with the wife. The Subordinate Court however observed that notwithstanding that the parties in the matter were married under customary law, justice demands that when a marriage has broken down the parties should be put in an equal position to avoid either one of them falling into destitution. The court affirmed the decision of the local court that all household property acquired by the two parties during the existence of the marriage be shared equally.[10]

Maintenance

The Namibian Maintenance Act 3 of 2003, which confers equal rights and obligations to couples with respect to the support of children, presents a best practice since it seeks to create legal obligations on persons or institutions to support children and on spouses to support each other. Emphasis is placed on parents' responsibilities to give support that is adequate for the child's or children's upbringing, irrespective of whether the child was born in or out of wedlock or whether the parents are subject to any customary law that does not recognise the duty of the parents to maintain their offspring. The procedures on accessing child and spousal maintenance have also been clarified and simplified.

Education

Favourable policies in the region have paved the way for a significant rise in school enrolment rates for girls. Most countries in SADC have put in place various policies to ensure gender parity and equality in education, for example the 50/50 enrolment policy at primary level, removal of stereotyping in school curriculum, revision of national education policies to allow re-entry for school dropouts due to pregnancy and free primary education for girls and boys.[11] In Zambia, the Education Minister is pushing for a bill in Parliament that would jail men who father children with or marry female pupils and students without the option for a fine.

Other developments include the establishment of day-care centres for women of low and middle income to support these women to attend school or training. There are also provisions to provide training and gender mainstreaming for middle management in ministries, removing gender stereotypes in careers, instituting affirmative action at tertiary level in the fields of medicine, law and accounting and revision of the agricultural curricula and bursaries given to girls.

In addition, a sub-regional counselling programme has been set up to serve countries in southern and eastern Africa. The programme is aimed at counteracting the pressures and special obstacles that girls face, whether in or outside of schools. Through a regional centre located in Malawi, these programmes help local teachers and social workers develop guidance skills needed to make a difference. The training modules that have been produced cover gender issues, adolescent reproductive health, teenage pregnancies, drug abuse, HIV and AIDS and civic education. The policy on reduction of the direct and indirect costs of girl education was introduced in Lesotho and Malawi, among measures implemented is the removal of primary school fees. There has also been increased advocacy by women's groups, both by the regional and national chapters of the Forum of African Women Educationalists (FAWE) on a variety of issues impeding girl's education.[12]

Right to physical integrity

During the period under review, Botswana, Lesotho, Malawi and Zimbabwe passed Sexual Offences Acts. South Africa and Swaziland have in place Draft Sexual Offences Bills while the Democratic Republic of the Congo passed a draft Law Against Sexual Violence in 2006. The Sexual Offences Acts, especially the one in Zimbabwe, also criminalise wilful transmission of HIV and AIDS while Zimbabwe, Namibia and South Africa have clarified that rape within marriage carries the criminal offence of rape. All jurisdictions in the region are engaged, at various stages, with the development of legislative or judicial interventions on the question of wilful transmission.

Most SADC countries do not criminalise marital rape. A wife's consent to the sexual act is presumed. However, in South Africa, the Prevention of Family Violence Act which provides for the conviction of a husband for the rape of his wife was enacted in 1993.

In the Chrystal Alyson Denn case in Zambia already mentioned earlier in this chapter, Denn had asked the Court to rule on her late husband's persistent marital rape every time he abused her. The Court, however, stated that the concept of marital rape has not been explored or discussed in Zambia. The Court's refusal to explore the issue of marital rape shows lack of activism on the part of the bench, who should explore this issue, even in passing.

Botswana has launched Police Service Sexual Assault and

Evidence Collection kits and revised the BP73 form which is used by medical personnel to record details of physical injuries suffered by victims of physical and sexual assault. The Botswana Police Commissioner also issued a directive outlawing the withdrawal of cases involving gender-based violence and sexual assault which was immediately incorporated into the police operational system.

Malawi and Zambia have instituted gender desks in the police service. In Zambia, Police Victim Support Units were introduced throughout all police stations in the country, while human rights programmes ensuring that knowledge by the police in the domain of human rights focusing on ethical values that will ensure that the police's conduct will be guided by the principle of the respect of the human rights of citizens were introduced in Botswana, Lesotho, Malawi, Mozambique, Swaziland and Zambia.

However, violence against women, including rape, wife battery and defilement of young girls remains a significant problem. Abuses generally go unreported and seldom come before the courts. Police still tend not to intervene in domestic disputes, while the withdrawal of cases by victims is rampant due to various reasons, the most common being women's economic and material dependence on the perpetrators.

Health

Generally, health standards have deteriorated in most countries due to economic malaise and the impact of HIV and AIDS. In the recent past, African countries have promulgated numerous laws and policies and have established high-level institutional frameworks to coordinate the national response to HIV and AIDS. A large number of African countries have passed legislation or policies that prevent dis-

crimination against people living with HIV and AIDS. At the continental level, the African Union held a Summit on HIV and AIDS, tuberculosis and other related infectious diseases in Abuja, Nigeria in 2001 during which HIV and AIDS was declared a state of emergency. More recently, African leaders adopted the Maseru Declaration on HIV and AIDS, malaria and other infectious diseases in July 2003. HIV and AIDS have also been included as a cross-cutting issue in the New Partnership for Africa's Development (NEPAD).

In addition to the HIV and AIDS pandemic, maternal and reproductive health is now a priority for all countries, and almost all countries have developed HIV and AIDS policies. Some countries have produced draft reproductive health policies. Other key policies include the creation of entry sites through the national programme for the fight against AIDS; voluntary tracking of HIV and AIDS, reproductive health and adolescent health programmes to prevent mother to child transmission and ensure universal access to Anti-Retroviral Therapy (ART) for all expectant mothers and free HIV testing centres for young adults. Other countries have introduced an AIDS levy and trained traditional midwives to work in rural areas where health facilities do not exist. South Africa, Namibia and Zambia have developed HIV and AIDS Human Rights Charters.[13]
However, the HIV and AIDS policies being put in place are not tackling the issue of the sexual autonomy of women. Women in SADC do not have full control over their bodies. Sexual autonomy means changing the perception of marriage as a contractual relationship in which one consents to give up their sexual and reproductive autonomy. This is important because the mode of transmission

in SADC is mostly through heterosexual intercourse. Because HIV and AIDS is a condition among human beings driven by human behaviour, it is a condition driven by the nature of power relationships among groups in society. Policies and intended legislation should thus tackle the issue of minimising infection rates among women and girls. Thus, addressing gender concerns and how they influence sexuality is very crucial for effective prevention and control of the epidemic, as opposed to only focusing on managing it through treatment alone.

Citizenship

According to Article 9 of CEDAW, state parties shall grant women equal rights with men to acquire, change or retain their nationality. The state's parties shall ensure in particular that neither marriage to an alien nor change of nationality by the husband during marriage shall automatically change the nationality of the wife, render her stateless or force upon her the nationality of the husband. It also requires state's parties to grant women equal rights with men with respect to the nationality of their children.

Discrimination against women in access to citizenship is a part of the tradition whereby wives were seen as appendages of their husbands and dependent members of the family follow the citizenship, domicile and residence of the head of the family. National constitutions typically envisage the possibility of a woman marrying a foreigner, moving to his country and acquiring his citizenship. The possibility of a man marrying a foreigner and moving to her country and obtaining her citizenship is rarely envisaged. For example, the 1990 Constitution of Mozambique states that a woman who has married a Mozambican citizen may acquire Mozambican citizenship by establishing domicile in Mozambique and renouncing her previous citizenship. A foreign man who marries a Mozambican woman in Mozambique would not have similar access to his wife's citizenship.

The issue of citizenship hinges on constitutionalism. Generally in SADC, the constitutions have perpetuated the denial of women's constitutional rights, such as the right to freedom of movement, and the right to pass one's citizenship to one's husband, inhibiting women's political development and their ability to play a role as full citizens within civil society. However, there has been a movement towards recognition of equal rights with regard to citizenship. There have also been cases like the 1991 Unity Dow vs. Attorney General (Botswana) case which challenged discriminatory citizenship laws in Botswana.

Electoral reforms

CEDAW states that state parties shall take all appropriate measures to eliminate discrimination against women in the political and public life of the country and in particular, shall ensure to women, on equal terms with men the right:

- to vote in all elections and public referenda and to be eligible for elections to all publicly elected bodies;
- to participate in the formation of government policy and the implementation thereof and to hold public office and perform all public functions at all levels of government; and
- to participate in non-governmental organisations and associations concerned with the public and political life of the country.

The period under review has witnessed SADC countries passing policies to enhance the achievement of at least 30 percent women's representation in all areas of decision-making by the end of

2005. The Tanzanian Constitution for example reserves 30 percent Parliamentary seats for women distributed on a Proportional Representation (PR) basis, while local government elections in Namibia are run entirely on a Proportional Representation basis. The electoral law in Namibia also provides that each party should field at least 30 percent women candidates, distributed equally on their lists. The ruling party South West Africa People's Organisation (SWAPO) adopted a 50 percent quota for women in local government elections. However, Namibia has only used this formula at local government level. South Africa and Mozambique also have electoral systems that provide for Proportional Representation though the proportion of women is not legislated.

Conclusion

Laws relating to women's legal status are important because they reflect societal attitudes that impact on women. The legal context of family life, access to education, laws and policies affect women's economic status and can contribute to the promotion or prohibition of women's access to justice. The fact that SADC countries are characterised by plural legal systems can be a hindrance to the advancement of women because this pluralism results in conflicts of laws and portrays a very unclear picture of what the actual status of women is under these circumstances.

While most of the countries in SADC have signed and ratified regional and international instruments which seek to give women more rights, there has been reluctance by many nation states to translate these commitments into action by domesticating them and adding them into their national constitutions.

The minority status of women, perpetuated by law and customary practices, is a major gender justice issue which SADC countries need to conclusively deal with. Not only do laws reflect societal attitudes, but unresponsive laws have a direct impact on women's ability to exercise their rights. The legal context of family life, women's access to education and laws and policies affecting women's economic status can also contribute to the promotion or prohibition of women's access to rights and their ability to make informed choices about their lives.

There are also challenges around the lack of knowledge of laws and international instruments by women, which is a drawback to ensuring gender justice. Therefore, the issue of legal education is key to women's emancipation and governments need to support the work of civil society in promoting the rights of women as they play a complementary role to government's efforts to ensure women's equality in the law. The need to strengthen gender machineries financially, technically and politically is also key to the realisation of women's empowerment, coupled with gender sensitive constitutions and laws and domestication of international instruments which have high standards. Equal access to legal services and courts should also be a priority area for governments to fulfil. Until governments take positive steps to move from rhetoric to action and as long as women's rights remain on paper, the gender justice gap will continue to widen.

Endnotes

1   Excerpt from SADC Gender and Development Declaration, SADC 1997
2   African Union, Protocol to the African Charter on Human and People's Rights on the Rights of women in Africa
3 Rights of women in Africa; not yet a force for freedom Pg 14
4   OSISA, Constitutions + Constitutionalism – protecting the RIGHTS of all citizens, Edition 4 – issue 3 2004, p1 and 7
5   WLSA, Maintenance Laws (1992)
6   WLSA, Venia Magaya's sacrifice A case of custom Gone Awry, 2001
7   WLSA, Justice For All p1-5 2002
8   WLSA, Women and the Administration for

All Justice Delivery Systems: Problems and constraints, 2001
9   Source: Jena vs Nyemba
10 Martha Kembo Mwanamwalye and Collins Mwanamwalye 2002/SPB LCA/15
11 Economic Commission for Africa Southern Africa Office, Report of the sub-regional Decade Review Meeting on the implementation of the Beijing Platform for Action in Southern Africa, 2004 p6
12 African Union, The Road to Gender Equality in Africa - An overview, 2004 p12 - 13
13 African Union Commission, The Road to Gender Equality in Africa: An overview

References

African Union Commission, *The Road to Gender Equality in Africa: An overview,* 2004, p 20 and 21, 12 and 13

Government of Namibia, in The Constitution of the Republic of Namibia "International Law" Article 144 Constitution of Namibia

Centre for Reproductive Law and Policy Women of the World: *Law and Policies Affecting their Reproductive Lives Anglophone Africa,* Progress Report, 2001

DfID – *Justice and Poverty Reduction,* Pg 12 Safety, Security and Access to Justice for All

Economic Commission for Africa Southern Africa Office: *Report of the sub-regional Decade Review Meeting on the implementation of the Beijing Platform for Action in Southern Africa,* UNECA, Lusaka, Zambia, 2004

Gender Links, Gender Justice Barometer, *Audit of the SADC Declaration on Gender Development, Addendum on the Eradication of Violence Against Women and Children,* Gender Links, 2005

Gender Links, *Missing the Mark? Audit of the SADC Declaration on Gender Development Women in Decision Making,* Gender Links, 2005

Open Society Initiative for Southern Africa. Constitutions + Constitutionalism – Protecting the Rights of all Citizens, Edition 4 – Issue 3 2004, p1 and 7

Report of the Evaluation of the Women and Law in Southern Africa Research and Educational Trust (WLSA) Prepared for the Open Society Initiative for Southern Africa, September, 2002

Swedish Ministry for Foreign Affairs, *A handbook on CEDAW – The Convention on the Elimination of All forms of Discrimination Against Women,* 1999

SADC, SADC Declaration on Gender and Development, Gaborone, Botswana, 1997

SARDC WIDSAA, *Beyond Inequalities:Women in Southern Africa,* SARDC, 2000

UNAIDS, *Where there is a will there is a way, Nursing and Midwifery champions in HIV/AIDS care in Southern Africa Best Practices collection,* 2003

UNIFEM, Pathway to Gender Equality: CEDAW, Beijing and the MDGs, UNIFEM, New York, 2004

WiLDAF, Protocol to the African Charter on Human and People's Rights on the Rights of Women in Africa, 2004

WiLDAF Zambia, Minimum *standards relating to women and children's rights to be incorporated in the republican constitution,* 2004

WLSA, *Justice For All,* WLSA, 2002

WLSA, *Maintenance Laws,* WLSA, 1992

WLSA, *Venia Magaya's sacrifice: A Case of Custom Gone Awry,* WLSA, 2001

WLSA, *Women and the Administration for All Justice Delivery Systems: Problems and constraints,* WLSA, 2001

WOMEN AND GENDER-BASED VIOLENCE

7

Southern Africa has recorded notable achievements in combating gender-based violence since 2000. A report by SADC women's NGOs in 2005 acknowledged that, "...there has been progress in legislating against gender violence, in particular domestic violence and sexual offences. A number of countries in SADC have now widened the concept of rape to include the rape of men and boys and recognition of marital rape as a criminal offence. It also provides for stiffer penalties, including higher minimum penalties for perpetrators of crimes against women and provides a broad definition of domestic violence, including the concept of family to protect the rights of men, women and children.

"Some countries now provide supportive structures for counselling crime survivors and have instituted victim-friendly support units in police stations and courts. There is now provision in some countries in the region for post-sexual violence medical therapies and counselling, including anti-retroviral drugs to reduce the risk of contracting HIV. Penalties are now in place that specifically relate to perpetrators of incest, aimed at protecting the rights of the girl child."[1]

Despite all these positive changes, southern Africa still has the highest rate of gender-based violence (GBV) in comparison with other regions of the world. For instance, Interpol reports that South Africa has the world's highest rate of rape. In Namibia, women's organisations have noted that despite positive legislative changes, gender based violence remains an issue. Veronica de Klerk, Executive Director of Women's Action for Development commented that, "the gender order appears in many communities to remain unaffected by the various reforms and violence against women continues unabated." Namibia's Prime Minister also noted that violence against women and children had reached "crisis point."[2]

Gender-based violence in the region is deeply embedded in the history of the sub-region, in poverty, political instability, in the legacy of civil unrest, racial and ethnic divisions and patriarchal structures.[3]

Violence that is "gender-based" involves abuse that takes place because of a woman's subordinate status in society. It encompasses violent acts committed by and against women and acknowledges that women can be perpetrators as well as victims in an intimate social setting.[4] The term "gender-based violence" reminds one that the violence that occurs takes place primarily because people have been "gendered" to act in a specific way. This analysis goes beyond an analysis that women are vulnerable to men and suggests that both men and women are vulnerable to the way dominant norms of gender relations within their context are working. This does not remove responsibility however from the perpetrator of this form of violence.[5]

SADC Addendum on the Eradication of Violence against Women and Children

The Addendum to the SADC Gender and Development Declaration on the Eradication of Violence against Women and

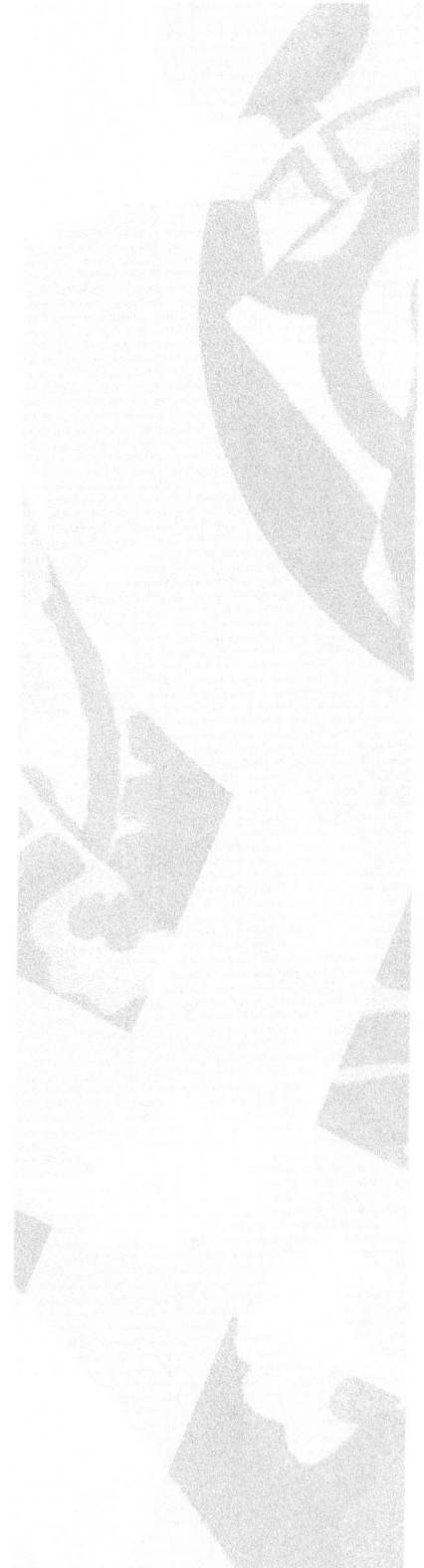

Children (1998) has served as an agenda-setting document for the region that articulates a set of standards and guidelines as well as adherence mechanisms for member states to ensure compliance. The addendum suggests reporting and peer review mechanisms that guide compliance and implementation. It spells out measures that SADC member states are urged to adopt in order to eradicate violence against women and children.

The addendum shows commitment by member states to reverse the culture of violence and abuse of women and children as it spells out clear, concise and directive policy guidelines for member states to follow in developing national policies and implementation of programs. It also sets the stage for member states to eradicate, rather than contain gender-based violence. Whilst eradication of violence against women has proved to be an ambitious goal to achieve within a short space of time, given the extent and prevalence of gender-based violence in southern Africa, the region has however set the stage for 'high standard' management of this form of abuse.

Section 26 of the Addendum foresaw the need to have a protocol on gender. In the document, SADC Heads of State and Government resolved that, "urgent consideration be given to the adoption of legally binding SADC instruments on preventing violence against women and children, and to ensure that these commitments are translated into tangible action." The draft SADC Protocol on Gender and Development, which is currently under consideration and which will be presented to SADC Heads of State and Government 2008 Summit, was drafted with this in mind. A Protocol was identified as the most binding of SADC legal instruments which could accelerate the implementation of gender commitments. The draft Protocol

carries a section on gender violence and is expected to address challenges faced in ending gender-based violence.

African Union Protocol on the Rights of Women in Africa

The Protocol to the African Charter on Human and People's Rights on the Rights of Women in Africa is another important policy document in the fight against domestic violence. The protocol complements other international agreements signed at the UN level but the agreement has an African focus.

Articles 2, 3, 4, 5, 8, 10, 11 and 13 of the Protocol are dedicated to outlining concrete actions that state parties can take against gender-based violence. The articles focus on:

- the elimination of discrimination against women;
- rights to dignity, the rights to life, integrity and security of the person;
- rights to peace, justice and equal protection before the law;
- protection of women in armed conflict;
- economic and social welfare rights, and
- elimination of harmful practices.

Thus the Protocol offers member states of the AU a comprehensive mechanism to implement legal and policy actions to eliminate gender-based violence according to regional and international human rights instruments they have already acceded to.

The Beijing Declaration and Platform for Action

Among its objectives, the BDPFA seeks to take integrated measures to prevent and eliminate violence against women. To achieve this objective, the BDPFA calls on governments to enact or reinforce legislation to punish and redress violence against women and girls in the home, workplace, community and society.

Governments are also called upon to promote an active and visible policy of mainstreaming a gender perspective in all policies and programmes related to violence against women; actively encourage, support and implement measures and programmes aimed at increasing the knowledge and understanding of the causes, consequences and mechanisms of violence against women among those responsible for implementing these policies, such as law enforcement officers, police personnel and judicial, medical and social workers, as well as those who deal with minority, migration and refugee issues.

The BDPFA also calls on governments, regional organisations, the United Nations, research institutions, women and youth's organisations and non-governmental organisations to study the causes and consequences of violence against women and the effectiveness of preventative measures.

In its third strategic objective to eliminate gender violence, the BDPFA calls for the elimination of trafficking in women and assistance for victims of violence due to prostitution and trafficking.

A historical perspective on gender violence

Women in the region occupy comparatively lower social, political, cultural and economic status to that occupied by men. This state of affairs has been described by the BDPFA as both a cause and a consequence of violence against women.[6] Women's position in society has been a result of most countries in the region embracing and upholding patriarchal values whose interpretation has emphasised inequality in power relations and authority between men and women. Different cultural interpretations and justifications of abusive behaviour by society have also contributed to displays of tolerance, condoning of gender violence

and failure to take action against injustices and perpetrators.

Most countries in southern Africa to a large extent share a common colonial heritage, which has resulted in duality and parallelism of social systems in areas of governance, law and religion. These systems have influenced the current subordinate situation of women as characterised by social inequality, legal minority status (e.g. Botswana and Swaziland) and women's general gross underrepresentation in decision-making positions.

According to the BDPFA, "...violence against women is a manifestation of the historically unequal power-relations between men and women, which have led to domination over and discrimination against women and to the prevention of women's full advancement. Violence against women throughout the life cycle derives essentially from cultural patterns, in particular the harmful effects of certain traditional and customary practices and all acts of extremism linked to race, sex, language or religion that perpetuate the lower status accorded to women in the family, workplace, community and society."[7]

Southern African countries are members of the SADC and UN. Through reporting to these bodies, women's groups in the region have worked to put gender-based violence on the regional and international agenda.

Forms of gender violence

Violence against women is multi-dimensional and takes various forms, as illustrated by the UN definition below. Its scope in southern Africa remains wide as it occurs at family, community and state level.[8] Violence in the family takes many forms, ranging from spousal abuse, incest, marital rape, emotional and psychological abuse and failure to provide economic support to dependent members. Violence

91

Forms of violence against women in southern Africa follow those outlined in the UN definition, which encompasses but are not limited to the following:

- physical, sexual and psychological violence occurring in the family including battering, sexual abuse of female children in the household, dowry-related violence, marital rape, female genital mutilation and other traditional practices harmful to women;
- physical, sexual and psychological violence occurring within the general community, including rape, sexual abuse, sexual harassment and intimidation at work, in educational institutions and elsewhere, trafficking in women, forced prostitution, forced sterilisation, forced abortion, forced use of contraceptives, female infanticide and prenatal selection;
- physical, sexual and psychological violence perpetrated or condoned by the state wherever it occurs; and
- violation of the human rights of women in situations of armed conflict, in particular murder, systematic rape, sexual slavery and forced pregnancy.

Platform for Action and the Beijing Declaration, September 1995

against women can take a singular or a combination of the different forms. The demarcation between the various forms is hazy as more than one form of violence is often present in any given situation.

Physical violence is the most visible form of violence mostly because of its tangible effects. Reports indicating how widespread this form of abuse is are derived from hospitals and police charge offices. In South Africa, studies indicate that about 25 percent of women have experienced physical violence from an intimate partner.[9] Domestic violence reports in the region confirm this percentage as similar in all SADC countries.

Status update

Since the last *Beyond Inequalities: Women in Southern Africa* was published in 2000, some milestones have been achieved, albeit slowly, in addressing violence against women in the form of consciousness raising, research and advocacy work, putting in place institutional mechanisms as well as developing frameworks for policy and legislative reforms and enacting progressive legislation to protect women. There are also noted moves to conflate protection of children with that of women from gender-based violence. This has thus far had a positive spin-off for women who have stood to benefit from empathetic moves by member states to protect children from abuse.

Despite these achievements, violence against women has persisted and has mutated as the region succumbs to challenges brought about by HIV and AIDS, persistent poverty, declining economic opportunities and trafficking of women and girl children. GBV has managed to outlive the 'ten-year-tenure' post-Beijing conference as the region is now firefighting and grappling with the consequences of this form of violence.

Developments towards the protection of women and girl children are slow as indicated by slow provision of services like counselling and safe halfway housing. In some respects, this protection is almost non-existent as in the case of provision of life-saving and critical services like Post-Exposure Prophylaxis (PEP) anti-retroviral treatment to survivors, development of policies and laws to avail timely and speedy assistance to survivors and setting up structures and institutions that offer 'one-stop-shop' services to women who have been abused.

The magnitude of each form of violence in the different countries remains an estimate based on the cases that are reported to the formal structures, especially to police charge offices. For instance, there are on average 2,000 cases of domestic violence reported to the Namibian police each year, of these, 86 percent of the survivors are female and 14 percent male. Conversely, men commit 93 percent of these crimes while women commit seven percent.[11] These figures indicate that domestic violence is usually a gender-based crime where men are perpetrators and women are the survivors.

In addition to reports submitted to the police, there is reporting of gender-based violence outside of the formal judicial structures to structures such as the family, traditional leaders (chief's court) and other recognised leadership structures. However, these reports often do not end up informing the national reports (for bulletins and for planning purposes) that in turn determine prevalence estimates. As a result, gender-based violence in most countries remains grossly under-reported and facilities under-resourced.

Other factors contributing to lack of reporting of gender violence include feelings of inadequacy among victims, and helplessness due to justice delivery systems that are slow, insensitive and non-responsive. Reporting is also affected by the secrecy surrounding gender-based violence, shame, sense of family loyalty, negative perception of gender violence, self-blame and internalisation of a sense of guilt by survivors.

Southern Africa is also grappling with emerging forms of gender-based violence in the form of trafficking of young women and children, child prostitution and pornography. The findings of an audit commissioned by the SADC Gender Unit and the SADC Parliamentary Forum in 2005 on the extent to which the provisions of gender equality in regional and international instruments for gender equality have been implemented noted, "...new forms of gender violence, such as trafficking, are on the rise." Trafficking is increasingly being acknowledged in policy documents such as the draft SADC Protocol on Gender and Development. Mozambique has enacted legislation on human trafficking and countries such as South Africa and Zambia are in the process of having such pieces of legislation in place.

Most countries in the region are affected by trafficking, but the International Organisation for Migration (IOM) has cited Mozambique as one of the key source countries for women and children trafficked to South Africa.[12] Other source countries include Malawi, Namibia, Swaziland, Zambia and Zimbabwe.

In Mozambique, the age range of victims of sexual trafficking is fourteen to twenty-four years. These girls are transported to Johannesburg in South Africa where they are engaged in domestic work or prostitution. Reports from Lesotho show that truck drivers transport young girls from all over the region and dump them on

the border between Lesotho and South Africa or abandon them far away from their country of origin.[13]

Policy and legislation
Countries in the region have made major strides in legislating against gender violence. The SADC Gender-Based Regional Integration Plan: Strategic Implementation Framework (SIF) 2006-2010 has set a target to have all member states enact laws against gender violence, domestic violence and sexual offences by 2008. Gender violence legislation in the region covers a whole range of issues, for example, the Zimbabwe Sexual Offences Act (2001) covers sexual exploitation of young persons and persons with disability; seeks to combat commercial sex work; punishes the deliberate transmission of HIV; provides compulsory testing for HIV and AIDS of sexual offenders; and removes discriminatory aspects against women. In addition to this, Zimbabwe has a Domestic Violence Act, passed into

Gender Violence Legislation	Table 7.1
Country	**Gender Violence Legal Provisions**
Angola	No Specific Law
Botswana	Sexual Offences Act (2001)
DRC	Draft New Law Against Sexual Violence (2006)
Lesotho	Sexual offences Act (2003)
Malawi	✦ Prevention of Domestic Violence Act (2006)
	✦ Rape included in general Penal Code
Madagascar	No specific legislation but addressed in general Penal Code
Mauritius	Domestic Violence Act (1997)
Mozambique	Addressed in the Family Law (2004)
Namibia	✦ Combating of Rape Act (1999)
	✦ Domestic Violence and Child Maintenance Act (1999)
	✦ Combating of Domestic Violence Act (2003)
South Africa	✦ Domestic Violence Act (1998)
	✦ Draft Sexual Offences Bill (2003)
Swaziland	✦ Draft Sexual Offences Bill (2006)
	✦ Draft Domestic Violence Bill (2006)
Tanzania	Sexual Offences Special Provision Act (1998)
Zambia	No specific legislation but addressed in general Penal Code
Zimbabwe	✦ Sexual Offences Act (2001)
	✦ Domestic Violence Act (2006)

Compiled by SARDC WIDSAA

law in 2006. The majority of countries in the region now have gender violence legislation in place as shown in Table 7.1.

Domestic violence

Domestic violence is the biggest form of violence against women in the region and it can take the following forms; physical, sexual, emotional, economic and social violence.

Domestic violence accounts for a higher proportion of all forms of violence committed against women. Because it takes place within the sanctity of the family it usually remains concealed to the outside world. Communities often deny its existence mainly due to privacy accorded to the family. Like all forms of gender-based violence, the true extent of this type of violence is not known. Family members resort to all extents to conceal this type of violence and will very seldom actively assist the victim to seek outside help.

Despite laws that have been passed, southern Africa still has a high incidence of domestic violence. In South Africa, researchers for the Medical Research Council estimated in 2004 that a male partner kills his girlfriend or spouse every six hours, and in Harare, Zimbabwe, a 2004 United Nations report noted that domestic violence accounts for six out of 10 murder cases in courts in the country.[14]

Implementation of gender violence legislation also affects effectiveness in combating gender violence. In South Africa, despite the existence of a Domestic Violence Act, the legacy of apartheid and under-resourcing of rural areas obstructs rural women's access to justice. In a research carried out in the Southern Cape (South Africa), it was noted that women faced problems in seeking help for domestic violence. Some reasons cited revealed that, there were limited bus or taxi services, and where they were available, they were too expensive; the response time for police and ambulance services was slow; there were poor telecommunication services; few support services for abused women; no safe accommodation if the woman had to leave home and there was a high rate of unemployment or under-employment which made the payment of the above expenses difficult.

Other issues that compound these problems include courts' inability to cope with the administrative requirements of the Act. Courts also revealed that although there are 11 official languages in South Africa, application forms for a protection order are available in only two languages, presenting a big challenge when women's lower literacy levels are considered.[15]

In countries such as Angola, which does not have specific laws for domestic violence or marital rape, women are not offered protection against gender violence. This problem is compounded by the fact that in the provinces of Angola there is an almost non-existent judiciary system, a legacy of the war.

Culture, tradition and domestic violence

Research undertaken by WLSA in seven countries of southern Africa provides an insight into how communities in southern Africa perceive domestic violence. It shows that contrary to a commonly held notion that southern African countries condone violence against women under the guise of culture and tradition, this has never been a correct interpretation of custom.

It has been shown that in the different countries of southern Africa, customarily, excessive beating and resultant injury inflicted by a husband on his wife has never been accepted nor condoned. Moreover, traditional societies have always had forums and mechanisms of redress to deal with 'delinquent' men who beat up their wives. For instance, in forums held with traditional leaders in Lesotho, WLSA researchers were informed that traditionally Basotho society exercised different deterrent mechanisms on men who were abusive to their spouses. These included being beaten up with whips and fighting sticks by other men at a *khotla* (community court). The man who committed the crime was summoned to a tribunal of old ladies who would use their skirts (*thethana*) to discipline him. This information points to some level of misinterpretation and misinformation by abusive people who in defence of their actions use culture and tradition as a justification.

However, despite recourse that was provided (traditionally) for excessive beating, there is evidence to the fact that not all forms of abuse were addressed or brought to these structures. Communities generally turned a blind eye to what was perceived to be 'chastisement' or 'moderate beating'. In Botswana, for example, under customary law and in practice, men have the right to chastise their wives. Marital rape in that country is also not addressed in the law. In August 2003, a magistrate dismissed a case of marital rape on the grounds that the marriage contract implies consent, making rape impossible unless a husband and wife are legally separated.[16] In a fact sheet produced by the United Nations in 2004, it was noted that 51 percent of women believe that their husbands have the right to beat them.

This interpretation is reinforced by common law's definition of assault, which emphasises the presence of bruises, cuts and injuries. In countries where there are no Domestic Violence laws, unless there are injuries, perpetra-

tors get away with light sentences (if any) for most acts, which constitute domestic violence. This acceptance of abuse has contributed to reluctance and fear on the part of women who are being abused to disclose and take legal action for acts like pushing, shoving and slapping. These debates and insufficient action have led to continued widespread of domestic violence in southern Africa today.

Domestic violence also takes place in a context where there is a broad definition given to what constitutes a family. Southern Africa (like the rest of the continent) is characterised by broad or expanded family networks that recognise family membership beyond a nuclear unit. While this extended family is potentially protective against an abusive member, women at times endure abuse from other members who claim to have a sense of right over them as a member of that family. This sense of right may take the form of maintenance; claim for sexual relations (in the form of ritual cleansing or the levirate system) and as a pretext of deliverance of disciplinary measures.

WIDSAA notes that the extended family can have a role in instigating domestic violence (by encouraging the husband to beat up his wife), perpetrating violence against women (by a member other than the partner to beat up the woman) or advising her to endure the violence.[17] While there is an increase in awareness about domestic violence as a gross violation of human rights and its effects on society as a whole, there is still persistent silence and inaction from the wider family network when a woman is battered and abused. There are still generally held beliefs that a woman who gets abused is somehow to blame.

Domestic violence is not just a women's rights violation, given the impact it has on women's dignity and self-worth, health and well

Traditional norms condemned domestic violence — Box 7.2

Traditional norms and values in various countries in southern Africa had manageable mechanisms of fighting domestic violence.

Research by the Women and Law in Southern Africa (WLSA) in seven southern African countries reveals that traditionally, stern measures were taken against perpetrators of domestic violence.

The research conducted in Botswana, Lesotho, Malawi, Mozambique, Swaziland, Zambia and Zimbabwe on how communities in southern Africa perceive domestic violence shows that customarily, excessive beating and resultant injury inflicted on the victim (of domestic violence) has never been condoned.

Traditional societies had methods of redress to deal with perpetrators of domestic violence.

In the past, the WLSA research notes, elders used proverbs and folktales as a means of educating young people about the evils of domestic violence.

In Lesotho, for example, WLSA researchers were informed that traditionally, Basotho society exercised different deterrence mechanisms to men who were abusive to their spouses including being beaten up (with whips and fighting sticks) by other men at a *khotla* (community court).

According to the Centre for the Study of Violence and Reconciliation in South Africa, perpetrators of domestic violence were tried in *makgotla*, which were formed to meet the needs of the communities with regard to domestic disputes.

In rural Namibia, domestic disputes were primarily reported to relatives, neighbours, headmen or chiefs. Customary laws from the courts' roles appeared to differ not only from culture to culture but also from headman to headman. Women found the proceedings at customary courts more sympathetic to victims of violence and the period between the crime and trial much shorter.

With increased urbanisation and the destruction of traditional societies, society changed and so did gender relations that saw the manifestation of domestic violence as an endemic problem.

Sekuru Tapera Dzviti, the Deputy Secretary of Administration at Zimbabwe Traditional Healers' Association (ZINATHA), an organisation that is involved in traditional health care with a cultural approach to HIV and AIDS education, prevention, counselling and palliative care holds the opinion that traditional courts were more prominent than police stations and the judiciary system in dealing with cases of violence and thus play an important part in seeing the eradication of domestic violence among African families.

Catherine Butai for SARDC 2006

being, but it is a developmental concern in the different countries in the region.

Sexual violence

Sexual violence against women and girls is still widespread in southern Africa, a fact which presents a challenge to a region struggling with the HIV and AIDS pandemic and its devastating effects.

This region currently has the highest proportion of HIV and AIDS and still faces the challenges brought about by poverty, food insecurity and economic recession.

The United Nations Programme on HIV and AIDS (UNAIDS) (2004)[18] reports that women and girl children are disproportionately affected by HIV and AIDS as a result of unequal gender relations and sexually related violence.

Sexual violence presents a particular risk to women given that heterosexual relations account for the highest mode of HIV transmission in Sub-Saharan Africa. Moreover, the highest per capita reporting of rape in the world is in South Africa. Like other forms of gender-based violence, sexual violence is broad but is not limited to use of force in having sexual relations with women and young girls.

Sexual violence can take the form of rape (including marital rape and defilement), sexual harassment at places of work, sexual exposure, attempted rape, having sexual relations with under-age children and mentally challenged women, abduction of girls, and insertion of objects and degrading sexual treatment of women. Sexual violence also includes incest, forced marriage and forced cleansing of widows.[19] Sexual violence can be instilled by way of singular or a combination of intimidation, threats and physical harm directed at victims and their families members.

Rape is the most reported form of violence and tends to be regarded as the the most serious form of sexual violence. Rape is a capital offence in countries such as Botswana, Lesotho and Swaziland but there is no record of a rape perpetrator who has been sentenced to death for this crime. Sexual violence is a manifestation of social control subjected on women in the region and is a reflection of an expression of inequality that makes it difficult for women to turn down unwanted sex. In order to deal with the high rates of sexual violence in southern Africa, efforts undertaken by stakeholders should deal with sexual violence as a form of gender-based violence and point to the link between vulnerability to HIV and AIDS and sexual violence.

Sexual assault of young girls is one of the manifestations of sexual violence in the region. *Beyond Inequalities 2005: Women in South Africa* for example shows that in 2000, rape of children accounted for 40 percent of all the rape cases reported in the country. It has also noted that teenagers and young women are the highest risk group for sexual assault. There are some specific forms of abuse of young girls, for example forced marriages and abduction that continue to expose young girls to HIV and AIDS and affect their chances of improving their lives. In Angola, unmarried victims in rural areas are often expected to marry the perpetrator as it is believed they would otherwise not find a husband.[20] These forms of violence may lead to girl-children dropping out of school, having unwanted pregnancies, getting into commercial sex work and participating in risky sexual practices.

Gender-based violence related to economic rights

Studies have broadened the concept of gender-based violence to property dispossession of women, especially those who are widowed.[21] This form of violence takes many forms inclusive of grabbing, seizing, diverting or disposing of a deceased person's property in a manner that disadvantages widows and their children.

Property dispossession as a form of violence has increased in the last ten years as a result of deepening poverty and high death rates as a result of HIV and AIDS. For example, UNECA (2003) reports that in Lesotho, Malawi and South Africa, the HIV epidemic has increased the vulnerability of women, children and poor households to land dispossession by patrilineal kin on the death of a male household head.

In addition, the economic form of violence is exacerbated by discrimination in the customary and statutory laws that exclude women's ownership and control over productive resources. The report of the United Nations Secretary General Task Force on Women, Girls and HIV and AIDS in Southern Africa highlights that as the death toll rises and poverty deepens in many countries of southern Africa, women and girls face dispossession and destitution.

Property dispossession gives rise to psychological problems like anxiety, depression and fear. It has been justified by cultural practices that restrict women's access to immovable property. Further, the problem is compounded by laws and customs that are patriarchal and thus define ownership and control of resources in a manner that justifies the exclusion of women.

Conclusion

On the whole, southern Africa still faces challenges of high rates of violence against women, especially taking into account the effects of HIV and AIDS and endemic poverty that the region is battling with. Needless to say, unless drastic changes are made to improve the situation of women socially, culturally, economically and politically, efforts made to contain and eradicate violence against women will be futile.

Violence is a political struggle that must be approached with caution. The reality in the region is the presence of organised and orchestrated resistance to maintain the status quo. Efforts to improve women's lives originated with and are being driven by women themselves, from influencing the definition of gender-based violence to how it should be approached and eradicated. Southern Africa has high rates of abuse against women but there is also evidence that this region is showing leadership and innovative strategies to address specific needs of women.

Endnotes

1 Information in a communiqué from the Southern African Development Community (SADC) gender and women's empowerment Non-Governmental Organisations (NGOs) to the sub-regional Decade Review Meeting on Implementation of the Beijing Declaration and Platform for Action in SADC, UNECA in Pambazuka News, *"Africa: Reviewing the Beijing Declaration,"* Pambazuka, 2004 last accessed 28/03/06, http://www.pambazuka.org/index.php?id=21940
2 IRIN News.org, *"Namibia: Rising demands for action against gender-based violence."* http://www.irinnews.org/report.asp?ReportID=49559SelectRegion=Southern_Africa
3 Gender Links, *Amalungelo journal -Gender Justice Barometer for Southern Africa: Volume 5,* South Africa, March - April 2004
4 WLSA Swaziland and SARDC WIDSAA, Beyond Inequalities: Women in Swaziland, WLSA/ SARDC, Mbambane and Harare, 1998.
5 Bennet. J, *"Gender-based violence in South Africa,"* http://web.uct.ac.za/org/agi/pubs,newsletters/vol6/gbvsa.htm
6 Beijing Conference Report: 1995
7 UN Department of Information, *Fourth World Conference on Women,* 1995
8 SARDC WIDSAA, *Beyond Inequalities: Women in Southern Africa,* SARDC WIDSAA, Harare, 2000, p155
9 South Africa Demographic and Health Survey, 1998
10 Platform for Action and the Beijing Declaration, September 1995

11 UNAM and SARDC WIDSAA, *Beyond Inequalities 2005: Women in Namibia,* UNAM/SARDC, Windhoek and Harare, 2005.
12 International Organisation for Migration (IOM), "Seduction, Sale and Slavery: Trafficking in Women and Children for Sexual Exploitation in southern Africa", IOM, 2003
13 Gender Links Workshop Proceedings, "Reporting Gender and HIV", Maseru, 2004.
14 LaFraniere S, "Entrenched Epidemic: Wife Beatings in Africa," The New York Times 11/08/05, http://www.nytimes.com/2005/08/11/international/Africa/11women.htm
15 LaFraniere S, "Entrenched Epidemic: Wife Beatings in Africa," The New York Times 11/08/05,
16Botswana, http://www.state.gov/g/drl/rls/hrrpt/2003/27713.htm
17 Beyond Inequalities: Women in Southern Africa: SARDC WIDSAA, 2000.
18 Beyond Inequalities: Women in Southern Africa: SARDC WIDSAA, 2000 & www.rapecrisis.org.za
19 Women and Law in Southern Africa Research and Education Trust-Zambia, *Gender Violence: the Invisible Struggle,* WLSA 2001.
20 Human Rights Watch, 31-12-04, "Essential Background: Overview of human rights issues in Angola," http://www.hrw.org/english/docs/2005/01/13/angola9892.htm
21 Women and Law in Southern Africa Research and Education Trust- Malawi, *Dispossessing the Widow; Gender Based Violence in Malawi, WLSA 2002*

References

African Union, Protocol to the African Charter on Human and People's Rights on the Rights of Women in Africa, Maputo, 2003

Bennet. J, *"Gender-based violence in South Africa",* http://web.uct.ac.za/org/agi/pubs,newsletters/vol6/gbvsa.htm

Gender Links, *Amalungelo -Gender Justice Barometer for Southern Africa: Volume 5,* South Africa, March - April 2004

International Organisation for Migration (IOM), "Seduction, Sale and Slavery: Trafficking in Women and Children for Sexual Exploitation in southern Africa", IOM, 2003

LaFraniere S, *"Entrenched Epidemic: Wife Beatings in Africa",* The New York Times 11/08/05, http://www.nytimes.com/2005/08/11/international/Africa/11women.htm

Pambazuka News, *"Africa: Reviewing the Beijing Declaration",* Pambazuka, 2004 last accessed 28/03/06

SADC, Addendum to the SADC Gender and Development Declaration on the Eradication of Violence Against Women and Children, SADC, 1998

SARDC WIDSAA and WLSA Swaziland, *Beyond Inequalities: Women in Swaziland,* WLSA/ SARDC, Mbambane and Harare, 1998

SARDC WIDSAA, *Beyond Inequalities: Women in Southern Africa,* SARDC, Harare, 2000

UNAM and SARDC WIDSAA, *Beyond Inequalities 2005: Women in Namibia,* UNAM/SARDC, Windhoek and Harare, 2005

UN Department of Information, Beijing Declaration and Platform for Action, *Strategy and Objectives: Violence Against Women;* Beijing Declaration and Platform for Action, Beijing, 1995

WLSA, Research and Education Trust-Zambia, *Gender Violence: the Invisible Struggle,* WLSA, 2001

WLSA, Research and Education Trust- Malawi, *Dispossessing the Widow; Gender Based Violence in Malawi,* WLSA, 2002

THE GIRL CHILD

Introduction

Since 2000, different countries in the region have made strides towards developing the needs of the girl child through the development of policies that ensure that the girl child is legally protected from sexual assault and has improved access to education and health services. Despite these positive changes, the girl child remains particularly vulnerable in various situations and some traditional attitudes ensure that girls are discriminated against and remain vulnerable to abuse. As a result girls, in comparison to boys, continue to have unequal access to education, health care and other services, and face violence in the form of female genital mutilation, forced and early marriages and sexual exploitation. Interventions need to continue in order to protect girls from gender-based discrimination, oppression and exploitation.

The difficulties that girl children already face have been worsened by the additional burden placed on them by the HIV and AIDS pandemic. Sixty percent of those living with HIV in the region are women and girls. In many countries in sub-Saharan Africa, HIV prevalence among girls under 18 is four to seven times higher than among boys the same age. In addition, girls have a lower average age of death from AIDS.[1] Women and girls also bear the increasing burden of care, through home-based care of those infected with the virus, caring for orphans and seeking forms of income to sustain households. It can also be noted that increasing numbers of children and in particular young girls are withdrawn, drop out of school or have lower attendance rates as a result of HIV and AIDS. This is partly because of the inability of an AIDS affected household to pay school fees and buy uniforms. The trauma related to illness and death due to HIV and AIDS, and the discrimination and stigma experienced by children affected may result in fewer children being able to complete their education.

Former United Nations Secretary General Kofi Annan commented on the need to place HIV and AIDS on the agenda when looking at issues to do with the girl child, "We must make sure that girls, who run a particular risk of infection, have all the skills, services and self confidence to protect themselves. Across all levels of society, we need to see a deep social revolution that transforms relationships between women and men, so that women will be able to take greater control of their lives, financially as well as physically."[2]

Policy framework

Southern Africa has seen the emergence of new policies and laws relating to gender equality and the advancement of women since the year 2000, at both regional and international levels. A number of these regional and international commitments and targets contain prescriptions that specifically seek to ensure the protection of the girl child.

Beijing Declaration and Platform for Action

The Beijing Declaration and Platform for Action lays out recommendations for the elimination of all forms of discrimination against the girl child, including discrimination in inheritance, education, health, nutrition and elimination of nega-

99

tive cultural practises and attitudes against girls. These issues feed into Millennium Development Goals, two and three which focus on provision of a full course of primary education for all children regardless of their sex and the elimination of gender disparity in primary and secondary education.

Convention on the Rights of the Child

On 20 November 1989, the General Assembly of the United Nations adopted the Convention on the Rights of the Child (CRC). The Convention is a code of the rights of the child which applies to all people below the age of 18 years, unless according to national law, majority is attained earlier. The Convention is an instrument of advocacy on behalf of children and a point of reference in respect to the health, development and welfare of children.[3] The preamble to the CRC reaffirms the fact that because of their vulnerability, children need special care and protection; and places special emphasis on the primary caring and protective responsibility of the family, the need for legal and other protection of the child before and after birth, the importance of respect for the cultural values of the child's community, and the vital role of international co-operation in achieving the realisation of children's rights.[4]

All countries in southern Africa have ratified the CRC and accepted in principle the framework of the CRC as the model by which children's rights should be implemented in their countries. However, some problems have been faced in integrating CRC provisions into the national laws that are already in existence. Though most countries in southern Africa have begun the process of integrating the CRC into their local legislation, the process has been slow and impeded by social and resource problems.[5]

African Charter on the Rights and Welfare of the Child

In 1990, member states of the Organisation of African Unity (OAU) adopted a charter on the Rights and Welfare of the African Child (ACRWC).[6] The charter emerges out of the social and cultural values of Africa, including those relating to family, community and society. It takes into account "the virtues of their cultural heritage, historical background and values of the African civilization which should inspire and characterise their reflections on the concept of the rights and welfare of the child."[7] The African Charter was seen as a means of complimenting the CRC and was noted for especially mentioning the plight of the girl child. The Charter, which came into force in 1999, has been ratified by nine countries in SADC, namely Angola, Lesotho, Malawi, Mauritius, Mozambique, South Africa, Swaziland, Zambia and Zimbabwe.

The SADC Gender and Development Declaration

The SADC Declaration on Gender and Development places special emphasis on children in issues of violence, access to education and removal of gender stereotyping in the curriculum, career choices and professions. Special mention is made of the need to recognise, protect and promote the reproductive and sexual rights of women and the girl child.

All the instruments discussed above adhere to the same basic principles of equality, justice and non-discrimination. The available policies point to the commitment of, and attempts by the international and regional community to protect and uphold the rights of children, with special emphasis placed on the protection of the girl child. However, these instruments are only the beginning, until such a time as there is full government commitment and resource allocation to the issue of children's rights, there will remain problems in implementation.

Reproductive health and HIV and AIDS

Women and girls face risks and vulnerabilities with regards to HIV and AIDS that men and boys do not. Statistics reveal that women and girls make up to 57 percent of adults living with HIV in sub-Saharan Africa. Prevalence rates among young girls are much higher than those of boys. Within the 15-24 years age group for example, it is estimated that young women are three to six times more likely to be infected with HIV than young men of the same age group.[8] Young girls are at a higher risk of contracting HIV than are older women because the vagina and the cervix are less mature and less resistant to HIV and other Sexually Transmitted Infections (STIs). This is because tissue within the reproductive tract is more susceptible to HIV and young girls produce less vaginal secretions that help to provide a barrier to HIV than older women. In southern Africa, women and girls often get infected with HIV almost as soon as they start engaging in sexual intercourse. In a study in Zambia, 18 percent of women who said they had been virgins a year before being tested for HIV were found to be HIV-positive, while in South Africa, 21 percent of sexually active girls 16–18 years of age tested HIV-positive.[9]

As well as biological factors, girls are more vulnerable to HIV because of socio-cultural and economic factors. The 2001 Zimbabwe Young Adult Survey, a national representative population based survey of the HIV risk behaviours and prevalence among young adults aged 15-29 years found a prevalence of 22 percent among young women and 10 percent among young men.[10] The report cites lack of knowledge about sex and risks of HIV and AIDS, espe-cially among young women and girls, as one of the gender related factors contributing to the rapid spread of the virus, along with poverty, lack of control and access to resources, stigmatisation, sexual exploitation and rape, the low status of women and inadequate reproductive health services.

There is a strong link between HIV and AIDS and poverty. Reports from Zambia for example show that families that are affected by AIDS suffer severe financial strain related to illness and death among breadwinners and the requirements of dealing with orphans. Financial difficulties due to the effects of HIV and AIDS can propel girls into risky sexual behaviour and make girls more vulnerable.[11] Many girls who are forced to drop out of school due to poverty seek survival strategies such as having multiple partners in exchange for "gifts". In such situations, women and girls find themselves using sex as a commodity in exchange for goods, services, money, accommodation and other basic necessities. Often such "transactional sex" involves older partners who have superior economic positions and access to resources and women who have difficulties in meeting their basic needs.[12] Further, "The tendency to form transactional sexual relationships has also been heightened by the penetration of makeup, clothing, cellular phones and cars and so on – into impoverished communities throughout southern Africa."[13] A qualitative research study conducted in Maputo, Mozambique among young women aged 16-25 years found similar patterns.[14] The study found that young women were involved in multiple sexual partnerships, which are classified into a range of different types of relationships:
- *namorados* (same age boyfriends, with whom there is a perceived relationship of trust);

- *pitos* (partners for sexual pleasure and with whom there is no economic exchange);
- *sengue* (older married men); and
- *amante* (lovers).

The latter two are both transactional relationships with the primary motive being for economic gain and the young women state that they have no emotional attachments or expectations beyond exchange of sex for money.

These young women perceive themselves as active agents, rather than victims, involved in a continuing process of defining their social and sexual identity and making choices about the risks they are engaged in. The women see it as a strategy by which they are able to reverse the existing balance of gender and power-relations. This group of women found it difficult to access their aspirations through traditional and socially acceptable means such as studying, professional employment and securing a good marriage. Obstacles faced by the girls included lack of employment opportunities; lack of access to education; corruption; low wages and poor communication between men and women.

The research found that the young women had very high knowledge of HIV and AIDS, but the risk of losing the immediate economic resource of the *sengue* and thus social status is perceived to far outweigh the longer term risk of contracting HIV and AIDS. The group surveyed also rationalised the risk of contracting the virus by suggesting that AIDS is a myth or western phenomena aimed at controlling their sexual freedom. In addition, a fatalistic attitude was prevalent whereby there was the consideration that since dying was inevitable; the cost of losing social and economic gain was greater.

Inter-generational sex between older men and younger women plays a part in increasing the vulner-ability of young women to HIV. In a review of more than 45 quantitative and qualitative studies[15] in 2003, it was suggested that relationships between young women and older partners, which involve economic transactions, are common in many parts of sub-Saharan Africa. Unfortunately, these asymmetries are often associated with unsafe sexual behaviour, low condom use and increased risk of HIV infection. There is evidence that the age gap between partners affects the chances that young women will become infected with HIV. In rural Zimbabwe, reported HIV prevalence was approximately 16 percent amongst teenage girls (15–19 years) whose last partner was less than five years older than themselves, but among girls with partners 10 or more years older, HIV prevalence was twice as high.[16]

Because of the vulnerability of women and young girls, policy responses by governments in the region have noted the important link between gender and HIV and AIDS. In response to the pandemic, the Government of Zimbabwe adopted a National HIV and AIDS Policy in 1999 and launched it in 2004. The national policy recognises the importance of addressing the gender dimensions of the pandemic.[17] In Zambia, the National AIDS Council emphasised the threat to young girls especially due to socio-cultural factors, some of which include, "initiation ceremonies that prepare the girl child for marriage, that are common and widespread in both rural and urban Zambia. Some of these practices may increase risks associated with STI and HIV transmission. For example, among the Tonga and Bemba people, instructions include lessons on how to use corrosive herbs and ingredients to dry out the vagina in order to increase sexual pleasure (dry sex)...."[18] The Malawi National Gender Policy 2000-2005 noted that women are at great risk of contracting HIV because of their disadvantaged and subordinate positions.[19]

The National Reproductive Health Policy for the Kingdom of Lesotho (2002) noted that women (in particular, young women), the majority of whom are housewives (75 percent) are more affected by HIV and AIDS than men. A survey revealed that 80 percent of female teenagers with primary or secondary education have had sexual intercourse, but only 10 percent of males and 6 percent of females used condoms when they had sex for the first time.[20]

It is increasingly acknowledged that providing appropriate information and dissemination strategies around HIV and AIDS to adolescents is essential in preventing the spread of HIV. Messages sent out that centre around the ABC (Abstain, Be faithful, use Condoms) have proved ineffective in most countries. This is because these messages assume that girls are free to make empowered choices, opt to abstain from sex, stay faithful to one partner and use condoms consistently.[21] A summary of surveys conducted by the Zimbabwe National Family Planning Council and other organisations indicate a lack of knowledge amongst adolescents pertaining to sexuality. For example, a 1999 survey found that 25 per cent of youth think that a girl could not get pregnant the first time she has sex and 46 per cent believe that a girl cannot get pregnant if she has sex standing up.[22] In addition, national level laws and policies generally uphold parental consent requirements for adolescents below the age of 18 to access services and information on contraception and prevention of sexually transmitted infections.[23]

There is an increasing burden on women and girls in taking care of people who are infected or affected by the virus. Generally, women and girls provide most home-based care and are more likely to look after orphans, cultivate crops and seek other forms of income to sustain households. In South Africa for example, a survey showed that three-quarters of AIDS-infected households were female-headed and a large number of infected women were taking care of themselves.

Other issues that affect the girl child with regard to HIV and AIDS indicate the need to look strongly at beliefs and interventions around the pandemic.

Early onset of sexual activity

Studies have shown that the onset of sexual activity amongst the youth in Zimbabwe is in early adolescence, with an average age of 14 years.[24] Interviews with adolescents indicate that just over 50 percent of both boys and girls had their first sexual encounter when they were twelve years old and almost 85 percent had already had their first sexual encounter by age fourteen. This finding was supported by the opinion of stakeholders who also found that often adolescents had their first sexual encounter by the time they were 12 years old.

Namibian women experience sexual intercourse in their teens, often without any contraceptives. According to *Beyond Inequalities 2005: Women in Namibia*, a study conducted among school students in urban Namibia shows that 73.1 percent of respondents in Grade 12, and almost 50 percent of those in Grade eight have had sexual intercourse, while 64 percent of respondents consider having sexual intercourse before the age of 20 years as inappropriate.

Early and unwanted pregnancy

The Zimbabwe National Family Planning Council reports that there are an estimated 60,000-70,000 unsafe abortions performed every year in the country. Most individuals who have illegal abortions are adolescents.[25] However, adolescents report that most of them use abortion as a family planning method due to the difficulties encountered in accessing family planning services.

Exposure to Sexually Transmitted Infections

The prevalence rate of HIV and AIDS amongst adolescents has increased despite interventions during the past decade. The risk to adolescent girls is exacerbated by the "sugar daddy" phenomenon where girls develop sexual relations with older men for economic reasons. Also, adolescents involved in the sex trade do not routinely carry condoms for use by their clientele; rather they depend on their clientele to provide them and will circumvent the use of condoms if paid more for their services.[26]

In Namibia, lack of information on and knowledge about sexual and reproductive health pose challenges. Health officers often refuse to provide young people with sexual and reproductive health information or treatment for sexually transmitted infections, often criticising these young people for "bad behaviour." There is a need for youth-friendly programmes and teachers who are confident to discuss these issues as part of planned curriculum.

Sexual abuse of children

The region has made significant legal achievements with regards to the sexual abuse of children. Despite these changes children, women and girls are still abused sexually because of:
- non-existent or weak enforcement mechanisms;
- ignorance about the existence of protection acts and laws;
- cumbersome procedures in handling sexual offences;
- insensitivity to the effect of sexual offences on humanity and the society at large; and
- lack of recognition of sexual offences as criminal acts.

The World Health Organisation (WHO) defines child sexual abuse as the involvement of a child in sexual activity that he or she does not fully comprehend, is unable to give informed consent to, or which the child is not developmentally prepared and cannot give consent to, or that violates the laws or social taboos of society.[27] Behaviours that are defined as sexual abuse would include fondling of a child's sexual parts (including genitals, breasts and buttocks), attempted or actual penetrative sex with a child, whether vaginal or anal, exposing an adults genitals to a child, exposing a child's sexual parts for the gratification of an adult and oral sex with a child.

One of the worst forms of sexual abuse is rape. Within the region, one worrying trend is the myth that sexual intercourse with a female virgin will cure AIDS. This belief is widespread in southern Africa and research carried out in South Africa noted that 25 percent of young South Africans do not recognise that this is a myth.[28] Moreover, rapists may also be targeting young girls in the belief that being less sexually active, young girls are less likely to have HIV or AIDS. Human Rights Watch and Amnesty International noted that child rape as a phenomenon is becoming more common. In South Africa, data suggests that 40 percent of rape survivors are girls under the age of eighteen.[29]

Issues around sexual abuse have traditionally been underreported and so interventions have been difficult, as the extent of this problem has always been underrated. Interpol reported that in a comparison of 89 member countries, South Africa had the highest ratio of reported rape cases per 100,000 although only eight percent of cases were ever reported.[30] Similarly, in the United Republic of

Tanzania, it was also reported that the great majority of rape goes unreported.[31] Similar trends on non-reporting are apparent in Zimbabwe. The reasons for not reporting are the same wherever one may look; the system forces the complainant to prove that she or he was raped. The experience within the legal system is so unsupportive that families do not bother to look for help, rather the two families of the complainant and the accused often come to an agreement to pay money, livestock or other commodities as compensation for the damage caused to the victims' family.

Another reason why families do not report sexual abuse to the criminal justice system is the lack of knowledge about child abuse among police, public prosecutors and even doctors and nurses. Families complain that they perceive barriers in seeking recourse through the legal system or are unaware of the correct procedures for reporting, may delay the report until it is too late to obtain forensic evidence or become so confused by the procedures that they withdraw the report before the case reaches the courts.[32] Communities also indicate that they are treated harshly at police stations, are not interviewed in a private environment and there is inadequate explanation of the procedures being followed.[33]

There is also mythology that surrounds the issue of sexual violence. This mythology invades the whole system that exists to protect children and instead blames the victims. Such myths include the concept that women say "no" when they actually mean "yes". Another myth with serious repercussions is with regards to sexual offenders where legal judgments are littered with the ideas that men who commit sexual offences against children or women did so "on impulse" or had "a sudden violent mental lapse". Other rea-

sons move the burden to the victim whereby the child would be described as "sexually aggressive" or the fact that the defendant was "so beautiful and well developed" as to have incited the perpetrator to commit the crime.[34]

With the increased realisation of the widespread assault on young girls, governments in the region have made attempts to curb the trend through various sexual offences acts. By 2006, only Angola, Madagascar, Mozambique and Zambia did not have specific laws on sexual offences, although in Zambia, sexual offences are addressed in the general penal code. Lesotho enacted the Sexual Offences Act in 2003 and Zimbabwe in 2001. Namibia introduced the Combating Rape Act in 1999 and the United Republic of Tanzania passed the Sexual Offences Special Provision Act in 1998.

The Democratic Republic of the Congo has a draft Law Against Sexual Violence Bill (2006) while South Africa has a Draft Sexual Offences Bill (2003). Swaziland's proposed Sexual Offences and the Domestic Violence Bills (both 2006), provide for stiffer penalties for sexual crimes, after the increasing incidence of sexual abuse of young children who subsequently contracted HIV was noted. The bill states that "any person who is convicted of rape under this bill is liable to the death penalty if the victim is below the age of 14 years, or to the death penalty if HIV and AIDS are an aggravating factor, and where such person has parental power over the child."[35] News reports from Zambia in 2005 also showed that Parliament in that country is increasingly leaning towards stiffer penalties for rape. A news report in 2005 noted that the Zambian parliament was discussing the issue of castration of child rapists. The Zambian Parliamentary Select Committee on Legal Affairs, Governance, Human Rights and Gender matters recommended this move.[36]

Also in Zambia, new legislation provides for a broader definition of rape, which regards rape as penetration of any orifice by any object. This replaces the traditional concept of male on female vaginal rape being rated the worst crime and other crimes such as sodomy being considered lesser crimes whereas the trauma experienced in both offences is the same.

Besides review on laws around sexual offences, countries have put in place measures such as the introduction of special courts for children and other vulnerable witnesses to give evidence on camera.

Child-friendly courts in Zimbabwe and South Africa　　　Box 8.1

In 1992, the Ministry of Justice, Legal and Parliamentary Affairs in Zimbabwe set up a committee composed of regional magistrates, prosecutors and police officers to investigate the problems faced by "vulnerable witnesses" such as women and children in court. Court officials reported that children cried or did not speak in the presence of the perpetrators. Simultaneously, gender groups and non-governmental organisations petitioned the Minister of Justice, Legal and Parliamentary Affairs to make legislative changes to procedural law to accommodate women and children's needs within court rooms. The committee investigated and outlined changes required in the *Vulnerable Witness Report*. The changes were very much influenced by the Wynberg Sexual Offences Courts in South Africa where committee members had been on a study visit.

In 1994, the National Victim-Friendly Courts Committee was established. Its mandate was to set in place victim-friendly courts for children to prepare the courts for legislative change. The committee was composed of line ministries including health, social welfare, police and justice. It also included non-governmental organisations with expertise in children's rights. Thus began a plan of work, which included the training of staff within a multi-sectoral framework. Two pilot courts were set up in the main centres of Harare and Bulawayo. Hospitals also set up victim-friendly procedures to deal with children quickly and in a counselling framework without invasive examining procedures. The police too began setting up victim-friendly units around the country so that children, women and their families could report with privacy and confidentiality. Although the procedures were already in place, the Criminal Procedure and Evidence Act 8/97 was only amended in 1997. It provided definitions of vulnerable witnesses and measures to be adopted in handling such witnesses. The measures included appointing an intermediary and support person to assist the child. The child or vulnerable witness must be placed in a separate room or behind a screen and uses anatomically correct dolls to avoid being handicapped by a lack of language.

The success of the programme may be largely attributed to cooperation between government and non-governmental organisations. The role of the non-governmental organisations has been to co-ordinate administrative issues, source resources, ensure their safekeeping and conduct research. In addition, non-governmental organisations focused on legislative change, public and community education, and training of professionals in the area of child sexual abuse. At present, there are 11 such courts based at regional courts in Zimbabwe. In South Africa, the Wynberg Sexual offences Courts are being expanded to establish an additional 20 courts in the nine provinces, bringing the total up to 26.

Centre for Reproductive Law and Policy and the Child and Law Foundation, 2002

The disabled girl child

In the 1940s and 1950s, the UN focused on promoting the rights of persons with physical disabilities through a range of social and welfare approaches. In the 1960's, initiatives within the disability community, coupled with the adoption of the International Covenant on Civil and Political Rights and its sister instrument the International Covenant on Economic, Social and Cultural Rights resulted in a fundamental revaluation of the rights of individuals with disabilities within disability politics.

The World Programme of Action concerning disabled persons was adopted by the General Assembly at its thirty-seventh session in 1982. The World Programme of Action is a comprehensive global strategy that utilises "equalisation of opportunities" as its guiding principle for the achievement of full participation of persons with disabilities, on the basis of equality, in all aspects of social and economic life and development. The World Programme of Action transformed the disability issue from a "social welfare" issue to that of integrating the human rights of persons with disabilities in all aspects of life. However, women, let alone the girl-child with disabilities, are not enjoying the full benefits of the programme in question.

Poverty conditions such as inadequate natal care, poor nutrition and lack of health services cause a majority of disabilities in children. Further, the socio-economic conditions and lack of capacities to develop children with disabilities are main causes of the poor conditions they face. Rural populations experience higher degrees of deprivation due to resource and access constraints.

The general attitude of families and the community towards children with disabilities is negative. Feelings of pity, shame and denial are commonplace along with superstitious beliefs that pervade many communities. Many children with disabilities are hidden and their families forbid social interaction with members of the community.

Extreme poverty faced by most disabled persons in southern Africa may lead to the practise of unsafe transactional sex by the girl child, making them more vulnerable to HIV and AIDS. Some HIV positive men are abusing disabled girl children and albinos, as they strongly believe in myths, which claim that HIV positive individuals can rid themselves of the virus by having sex with virgins. Assumed to be virgins, women and girls with disabilities are specifically targeted for purposes of fulfilling this mythical treatment. The disabled girl child is also subjected to abuse, as perpetrators of this form of violence believe that the chances of being brought to account are slimmer than when abusing a person without a disability. This belief points to the existence of frequent violation of the rights of disabled girls, as well as to the inadequate legal and social frameworks in place to the disabled in many countries in the region.

At national level, measures must be put in place to ensure equal educational opportunities at all levels for the girl child with disabilities. The region must strive to ensure that women with disabilities have access to rehabilitation and other independent living services and assistive technology to enable them to maximise their well being, independence and full participation in society. There is also an urgent need to educate society about the rights of women with disabilities as well as to educate women and girls with disabilities about their rights.

Child labour

Across Africa, there are an estimated 80 million child workers, a number that could rise to 100 million by 2015. Africa has the highest incidence of child labour in the world.[37] According to the International Labour Organisation (ILO), 41 percent of all African children between the ages of five and 14 are involved in some form of child labour. This is in comparison to 21 percent in Asia and 17 percent in Latin America. The picture is even bleaker for girls, as their rate of participation is 37 percent in Africa, 20 percent in Asia and 11 percent in Latin America. Since the problem of child labour is closely linked to the continents' poverty, and can only be eliminated with increases in family incomes and children's educational opportunities, most development organisations are focusing on the "worst forms" of child labour. These include forced labour and slavery, prostitution, employment in drug trafficking and other criminal activities, and occupations that are especially dangerous to children's health and security.

These "worst forms of child labour" are the ones where estimates of prevalence are difficult due to the nature of the crime. The ILO conducted two surveys in Zimbabwe and the United Republic of Tanzania and found that the majority, 88 percent, of economically active children came from households that earned less than US$36 a month in Zimbabwe. In Tanzania, they found that the introduction of school fees under the country's structural adjustment programme has contributed to higher drop-out and truancy rates. Enrolment has gone from 90 percent in 1980 to 77.8 percent in 1996, with 30 percent of children between 10-14 years not attending school. Another major contributing factor in southern Africa is HIV and AIDS. Many breadwinners have died and driven families into poverty, often forcing children into exploitative labour due to this dissolution of families.

Commercial sexual exploitation of children

The different forms of commercial sexual exploitation of children include child prostitution, child pornography, sex tourism and the sale and trafficking of children. These issues are intertwined but statistics as to the occurrence of these within the region are not readily available. These issues have however been highlighted at different meetings such as the UNICEF Congresses on the Sexual Exploitation of Children in 1996 and 2001. The report on the southern Africa consultation for the second congress noted that there is a prevalence of sexual exploitation of children in the region. This includes sex tourism where travellers employ the services of commercial sex workers, some of whom are children. There is also the issue of child prostitution in which children, both boys and girls are used in prostitution, which is in part caused by increased urbanisation and rural-urban migration which increases the numbers of children living on the streets, thus increasing their vulnerability to sexual abuse. Pornography involving young children is done in a clandestine manner which is difficult to detect due to the use of new technologies such as the Internet which is difficult to police.

Child trafficking particularly for purposes of sex has over the years failed to attract adequate attention from researchers despite the fact that many children and women have been victims of various forms of sexual exploitation through trafficking. The literature available is not comprehensive due to the nature of the activities: many researchers have encountered difficulties in trying to collect valid and reliable information.[38] The ILO has drawn attention to this phenomenon in their study in June 2005, which found that child trafficking in West, and Central Africa is on the rise. Most of the children are sent to other countries to do domestic work, work on plantations, in petty trade, begging or soliciting.

Trafficking involves all acts in the recruitment or transportation of people within a country or across borders and involves some elements of deception, coercion, force, debt bondage or fraud and the reasons for doing so are normally to put people under situations of abuse or exploitation involving pornography, prostitution and slavery. Commercial sexual exploitation of children is a violation of children's rights, which involves sexual abuse by adults where remuneration in cash or kind might be paid to the child and the child is taken as a commercial and sexual object.[39]

Research carried out by the International Organisation for Migration (IOM) from August 2002 to February 2003 on trafficking in women and children in southern Africa unearthed rampant activities of trafficking in human beings involving both foreigners and citizens. According to UNICEF, most of the victims are young girls whose ages range from four to 17 years. Civil unrest and the worsening economic environment were sighted as forcing women and children to migrate to South Africa or Europe as economic refugees.[40]

Trafficking takes more than one dimension in different countries of the region. Research shows that in Lesotho, children migrate to Maseru from rural areas, running away from domestic violence or the effects of HIV and AIDS where as street kids they are forcibly abducted and trafficked to border towns and farms in the Eastern Free State, South Africa. They are then taken to private homes where they are sexually assaulted and held captive. After this ordeal, the children are then returned to the border from where they will find their own way home.[41] The research found that street children are also trafficked by long distance truck drivers from Maseru to as far as Cape Town in South Africa, Zimbabwe and Zambia and are kept as sex slaves.

In Mozambique research revealed that victims whose ages range from 14-24 are offered employment as sex workers or waitresses in Johannesburg. The victims are said to pay their traffickers to smuggle them across the border in minibus taxis across the borders with South Africa and Swaziland. The victims spend nights in transit houses where they are sexually assaulted as part of their initiation into the sex trade. On arrival in Johannesburg, these women and girls are sold to brothels in the central business district (CBD). Others are sold as slaves on private order or shopped around to mine workers on the West Rand as "wives". The research by IOM estimates that at least 1,000 Mozambican victims are recruited, transported and exploited in this way every year, earning traffickers approximately 1 million South African Rand annually.

In Malawi, trafficking takes more than one dimension. Businesswomen lure children to Europe with the promise of finding employment or educational opportunities. On arrival in a country such as the Netherlands a victim might be sold to a Nigerian madam and forced to work as a sex worker to pay off a debt of up to US$40,000. The victim is threatened with death through a ritual, which is performed with magic if she is not co-operative. The victim is subsequently sold to Nigerian agents from Belgium, Germany and Italy or rented out to local brothels. Victims who do not perform sexually to the satisfaction of brothel owners are beaten and given sex lessons or resold.

Long distance truck drivers who travel to South Africa also recruit children from Malawi

where they are promised employment, marriage or educational opportunities. On arrival in Johannesburg, the victim is often held as the trafficker's sex slave in a flat. The trafficker will then bring clients who will pay him to have sex with the victim. Businessmen from Malawi also traffic children for the same purposes to brothels in Johannesburg, South Africa.

Along the shores and resorts of Lake Malawi, European sex tourists who promise educational opportunities in Europe and pay some money to parents of the victims may recruit both girls and boys. The victims are often used as actors in pornographic videos that are featured on the Internet giving details of the children, names and contact addresses.

In Eastern Europe, women are trafficked from Moscow and Bulgaria and by Russian mafias to brothels in South Africa on South African visas fraudulently obtained in Russia. The victims are promised jobs in South Africa as dancers, waitresses, strippers and hostesses. On arrival in South Africa, the victims are told that they have to pay a debt of US$2,000/month for six months and if they do not pay; their relatives back home are threatened with violence.

In Zimbabwe, children cross into South Africa with the assistance of the *Magumaguma* (these are persons who facilitate the crossing of people into South Africa illegally at a cost of 200 Rand per person). The *Magumaguma* is an organised syndicate operating on both sides of the border.[42]

The existence of organised crime syndicates makes it very difficult to uncover some practices that result in the trafficking of children for sexual and other forms of exploitation. As was reported by the Institute for Security Studies in 1999, there were 500 organised

Molo Songolo, a non-governmental child focused organisation carried out research on trafficking in South Africa in 2000. Their research focused on both in-country and cross border trafficking. The research uncovered that children are coerced into prostitution for the enrichment and economic survival of others. It also touched on the socio-economic factors prevailing in South Africa, which forced children into exploitative situations. According to the research report by *Molo-Songolo*, the most predominant phenomenon of trafficking in South Africa is in-country, where most children, girls being the majority of the victims, are trafficked within the vicinity of their places of origin. The primary traffickers are parents and local gangs, so trafficking according to *Molo Songolo* is predominantly done by locals. As regards the cross border trafficking, foreigners are the main perpetrators and they operate as individuals or organised crime syndicates from Thailand, Mozambique and Eastern Europe.

Molo Songolo, Cape Town, South Africa, 2003

criminal groups in South Africa, many with global networks, which arranged the trafficking of women and children. These are comprised of West African networks, Chinese triad groups, and Russian and Bulgarian Mafia groups. There are others, which are ethnically based and operate on a smaller scale, using their comparative advantage to traffic women and children across a particular border where they have developed a network of official and unofficial contacts.[43] Recently, with increased public awareness, African governments and stakeholders have begun to move towards systematically countering this trend. This has taken the form of legislation, cross border treaties, protocols for repatriation and public awareness programs.

Regional campaign against child trafficking

The Regional Campaign Against Child Trafficking in Mozambique is a network of organisations from Mozambique, South Africa and Zimbabwe who are working together to combat child trafficking in the southern African region. The Campaign was launched in 2002 and has as its patrons Graca Machel and Bishop Desmond Tutu. The aims of the project are the prevention, legal protection and rehabilitation of victims of child trafficking.[44] The specific aims of the project are:

- protection of victims from imminent deportation;
- obtaining legal and financial assistance for the victim from the trafficker;
- obtain reasonable restitution from the trafficker so that the victim may be reintegrated into society as smoothly as possible;
- voluntary and safe return of victims; and
- training for police officers, immigration officials, medical personnel and judicial officers on handling victims.

Reducing child labour in southern Africa

Since 2004, the Reducing Exploitative Child Labour in Southern Africa (RECLSA) Project has been working in the sub-region to reduce the number of children caught up in the worst forms of child labour while helping them to obtain access to education. There are 14 project activities, which help to raise awareness, improve educational opportunities, enhance social services and strengthen government policies in Botswana, Lesotho, Namibia, South Africa, and Swaziland. By 2008, the project hopes to have enrolled at least 10,000 children who are caught in or are at risk of child labour.

Education

Generally, there has been an increase in the number of girls who attend school within the region. This is largely due to gender equality objectives being integrated into policy initiatives in the different countries. However, there are still more girls in primary school than those that eventually go to secondary school, and even less in tertiary institutions. In Tanzania, since 1995, there have been an equal number of girls and boys enrolled in primary school. However, in secondary school, only 34 percent of all pupils enrolled are girls.[45] In Zambia in 2003, 71.7 percent of children attended primary school, 73.3 percent of boys and 60.1 percent of girls. However, although still low, these figures represent an increase from previous years. These changes have been due to initiatives such as the introduction of free basic education (Grade 1-7) under the Basic Education Sub-sector Investment Programme (BESSIP), introduced in 1999.[46]

According to the government of Zimbabwe, the net primary school enrolment ratio in 1994 was 81.8 percent males and 80 percent females, in 2000; this had risen to 96 percent for males and 90 percent for females. The aim of the government is to achieve gender parity by the year 2015. One of the policy initiatives which is set to improve the enrolment ratio of children is the Basic Education Assistance Model (BEAM) programme. Since its inception in 2001, the BEAM programme has managed to provide social protection to orphans and vulnerable children by assisting with tuition fees, levies and examination fees. Through these initiatives, BEAM has managed to reduce the number of children who drop out of school due to failure to pay fees. Under this programme, 50 percent of the beneficiaries should be female.

In Mozambique, the Mozambique report on the Millennium Development Goals (MDGs) (2002) showed that there were 78 girls for every 100 boys enrolled in school, which was an improvement from 71 in 1998. These positive changes have been attributed to the National Education Policy and Implementation Strategies (1995) and the "education for girls project," which was started in 1994.[47]

In an attempt to remove some of the costs that hamper education, several countries introduced policies of free education. Mozambique abolished school fees in 2005, Malawi has a free education policy, and Zambia introduced a free basic education (Grade 1-7) policy. Zimbabwe had a free education policy soon after independence and thus achieved a high literacy rate.

Countries in the region have also made initiatives towards allowing pregnant girls who have dropped out of school to go back to school after they deliver. In Malawi, for example, the Gender Policy states as one of its policy objectives the need to allow pregnant girls to go back to school. In 2001, the Ministry of Education, Sports and Culture in Zimbabwe released a policy document that allows pregnant girls to go back to school after delivery while in Namibia, learners are allowed to go back to school after their babies are a year old. The programme has its challenges, among which are issues of stigma and girls not always having support to look after their babies. These challenges are further outlined in this book, in the chapter on women and education.

Despite positive policy changes within the area of gender equality in education, there remain certain challenges that girls face within the region that hamper their access to education. Reports in Zambia indicate that despite positive policies, girls are still discriminated against in the school system, the curricula, in their access to educational materials, teachers' attitudes and classroom interaction. Most countries within the region face economic hardships and this affects the standards, infrastructure and quality of teaching. Although there is free education in some countries, dropout rates may remain high because other materials need to be bought such as textbooks, writing materials, school uniforms and transport costs. Other issues include sexual harassment by headmasters, teachers and male peers within the school system, early marriages and heavy workloads that girls bear at home.

Conclusion

The plight of children, and in particular the girl child in southern Africa has added another obstacle to development especially with the advent of HIV and AIDS. The pandemic has completely overwhelmed the gains of the last decade as children have become more and more vulnerable to sexual exploitation, less likely to get an education and more likely to die earlier than they did a decade ago.

Although extensive regional and international legislation exists to protect the rights of children, poverty and lack of resources are major impediments. This review has attempted to highlight how adults have exploited children sexually and by not empowering them with sufficient information to make informed decisions about their sexuality. The chapter also highlights how children's labour is exploited. It is also apparent that strategies to protect the girl child cannot succeed if there are no parallel strategies for boys. In order to stop the demand in trafficking of children there is need for research in the region to provide more information and to target men, women and organisations involved in trafficking.

As a region there is need to gain some clarity and understanding on how to intervene with information for adolescents on sexuality and reproductive health as these are the challenges facing children in the new millennium. Many of the parameters by which one assessed improvements in the lives of children are no longer valid as they have been eroded by the consequences of HIV and AIDS which has brought with it more complexities and fewer options. The new challenge is helping the many orphans who are left to look after themselves after one or both parents die from AIDS related illnesses. The immediate priority should be on how to prevent orphans from becoming infected. The stigma of having lost parents to the disease, trauma, and low self esteem all place children at risk from sexual predators who offer false comfort. Also due to resource limitations, many young girls and children are driven into prostitution as a last resort.

Trafficking and other forms of child labour are major obstacles to efforts to protect and ensure the rights of the girl child. Unfortunately, southern Africa has seen a rise in the abuse of the rights of the girl child as more and more children are left destitute and unprotected by the death of parents and caregivers.

Endnotes

1   *A Dose of Reality: Women's Rights in the fight against HIV/AIDS*. Human Rights Watch. http://hrw.org/english/docs/2005/03/21/africa10357.htm.

2   Ministry of Health and Child Welfare, *National Policy on HIV and AIDS, Republic of Zimbabwe*, Harare, 1999

3   WHO/AFRO, *Inter country Training Workshop for the prevention and management of child sexual abuse: A Multi- Sectoral and Participatory Approach*, WHO/ AFRO, Harare, 2000

4   DC Unofficial summary of *The main provisions of the Convention on the Rights of the Child Briefing Kit*, DCI/ UNICEF Briefing Kit, 1988

5   WHO/AFRO, *Inter country Training Workshop for the prevention and management of child sexual abuse: A Multi- Sectoral and Participatory Approach*, WHO/ AFRO, Harare, 2000

6   AHG/ST.Rev.1, adopted by the Assembly of Heads of State and Government of the OAU at its Sixteenth Ordinary Session in Monrovia, Liberia, from 17 to 20 July, 1997

7   AHG/ST.Rev.1

8   ÄIDS Epidemic Update: December 2004 http://www.unaids.org/wad2004/EP/update 2004_html_en/epi04_04_en.htm

9   "AIDS Epidemic Update: December 2004", http://womenandaids.unaids.org

10   CDC/UNAIDS (2003) cited in *Zimbabwe Country Report on the UN Secretary General's Task force on Women, Girls and HIV/AIDS in Southern Africa* (2004), UNAIDS and The Global Coalition on Women and AIDS.

11   http://www.hrw.org/reports/2003/zambia/zambia1202-04.htm

12   "AIDS Epidemic Update: December 2004," http://womenandaids.unaids.org

13   Centre for Reproductive Rights, *State of Denial: Adolescent Reproductive Rights in Zimbabwe*, Centre for Reproductive Rights and the Child and Law Foundation in Zimbabwe, New York, 2002

14   Population Services International, *Milking the Cow: A peer Research Study on Transitional and cross-generational sex in Maputo*, Options Consultancy Services and Population Services International, Mozambique, 2005

15   Luke, N, *Age and Economic Asymmetries in the Sexual Relationships of Adolescent girls in Sub-Saharan Africa: Studies in Family Planning*, (125-134)

16   "AIDS Epidemic Update: December 2004," http://womenandaids.unaids.org

17   Ministry of Health and Child Welfare, *National Policy on HIV and AIDS, Republic of Zimbabwe*, Harare, 1999.

18   http://www.hrw.org/reports/2003/zambia/zambia1202-04.htm

19   Malawi National Gender Policy 2000-2005, Government of Malawi.

20   National Reproductive Health Policy, Kingdom of Lesotho (draft), December 2002

21   AIDS Epidemic Update, 2002

22   AIDS Epidemic Update, 2002

23   AIDS Epidemic Update, 2002

24   AIDS Epidemic Update, 2002

25   Klofkorn, A, *Assesment of Adolescent Reproductive Health needs in Zimbabwe*, Ministry of Health and Child Welfare and the United Nations Population Fund, Harare, 1999

26   Klofkorn, A, *Assesment of Adolescent Reproductive Health needs in Zimbabwe*, Ministry of Health and Child Welfare and the United Nations Population Fund, Harare, 1999

27   Cited in: *Child Sexual Abuse: A Training Manual for Practitioners*. Child and Law Foundation and Save the Children Norway, 2003

28   http://www.sarpn.org.za/documents/d0000240/P204_HIV_Gender.pdf

29   http://www.hrw.org/reports/2003/zambia/zambia1202-04.htm

30   The Centre for Reproductive Law and Policy, *Women of the World; Laws and Policies Affecting their Reproductive Lives: Anglophone Africa*, The Centre for Reproductive Law and Policy, United States of America, 2001

31   The Centre for Reproductive Law and Policy, *Women of the World; Laws and Policies Affecting their Reproductive Lives: Anglophone Africa*, 2001

32   Loewenson R, *Sexual Abuse of Children: The Legal Issues in Zimbabwe*. Paper presented to the training program on victim-friendly courts, Judicial College, Harare, 1995

33   Loewenson R, *Sexual Abuse of Children: The Legal Issues in Zimbabwe*. Paper presented to the training program on victim-friendly courts, Judicial College, Harare, 1995

34   Khan, N, *Men who sexually assault children: Let's shatter some myths: Volume 10, Number 3*, Legal Resources Foundation, Harare, 1998

35   http://afroaidsinfo.org/public/Home/news221.htm

36   http://www.newsfromafrica.org/newsfromafrica/articles/art_2621.html

37   Harsch, E, *Child Labour rooted in Africa's poverty, Africa Recovery, Vol. 15, No.3*, 2001

38   Khan N, *Unearthing the Phenomena of Child Trafficking in Zimbabwe: A Report of an exploratory study in the Border Town of Beitbridge*. Child and Law Foundation, Harare, 2003.

39   Khan N, *Unearthing the Phenomena of Child Trafficking in Zimbabwe: A Report of an exploratory study in the Border Town of Beitbridge.*, 2003

40   International Organisation for Migration (IOM), Research study on Trafficking

41   IOM, Research study on Trafficking

42   IOM, Research study on Trafficking

43   IOM, Research Study on Trafficking

44   Child and Law Foundation, *Protecting the Sexuality of our Children, Report of a Regional Meeting*, Child and Law Foundation, 2002

45   http://www.minbuza.nl/default.asp?CMS_ITEM

46   SARDC-WIDSAA and ZARD and, *Beyond Inequalities 2005: Women in Zambia*, ZARD/ SARDC, Limbe and Harare, 2005

47   SARDC-WIDSAA and Forum Mulher and, *Beyond Inequalities 2005: Women in Mozambique (draft)*,

References

CDC/UNAIDS (2003), cited in *Zimbabwe Country Report on the UN Secretary General's Task force on Women, Girls and HIV/AIDS in Southern Africa*, UNAIDS and The Global Coalition on Women and AIDS, 2004

Centre for Reproductive Law and Policy, *Women of the World; Laws and Policies Affecting their Reproductive Lives: Anglophone Africa*, The Centre for Reproductive Law and Policy, United States of America, 2001

Centre for Reproductive Rights, *State of Denial: Adolescent Reproductive Rights in Zimbabwe*, Centre for Reproductive Rights and the Child and Law Foundation in Zimbabwe, New York, 2002

Child and Law Foundation, *Protecting the Sexuality of our Children, Report of a Regional Meeting*, Child and Law Foundation, 2002

Human Rights Watch, *A dose of reality: Women's Rights in the Fight against HIV and AIDS*, Human Rights Watch, New York, 2005

Klofkorn, A. *Assessment of Adolescent Reproductive Health needs in Zimbabwe*, Ministry of Health and Child Welfare and the United Nations Population Fund, Harare, 1999

Ministry of Health and Child Welfare, *National Policy on HIV and AIDS, Republic of Zimbabwe*, Harare, 1999

Molo Songololo, *The trafficking of children for purposes of sexual exploitation*, Molo Songololo, Cape Town, 2000

Population Services International, *Milking the Cow: A peer Research Study on Transitional and cross-generational sex in Maputo*, Options Consultancy Services and Population Services International, Mozambique, 2005

SADC, *Key Policy and Program Documents: Fact Sheets on HIV and AIDS and Education*, SADC, 2004

SARDC WIDSAA, *Beyond Inequalities: Women in Southern Africa*, SARDC, Harare, 2000

Tsanga, A. (et al), Children and Women's Rights in Zimbabwe, Theory and Practice, A critical analysis in relation to the women and children's conventions, UNICEF, 2004

WHO/AFRO, *Inter country Training Workshop for the prevention and management of child sexual abuse: A Multi- Sectoral and Participatory Approach*, WHO/ AFRO, Harare, 2000

World Bank and Oxford University Press, *World Development Report: Equity and Development*, World Bank and Oxford University Press, 2006

GENDER AND MEDIA

9

Southern Africa has been witnessing an unprecedented wave of gender and media activism in the period since the first *Beyond Inequalities: Women in Southern Africa* book was published in 2000. There is greater awareness of gender disparities in the region as well as a marked improvement in ensuring gender sensitivity of media content by media houses that have taken the initiative to introduce and implement gender policies.

In the first *Beyond Inequalities: Women in Southern Africa,* the lack of a framework or policy to ensure the integration of a gender perspective in all media policies, programmes and institutional and operational structures was cited among the major problems contributing to media coverage that excluded the voices of women, children and even a majority of men.[1]

Ownership and control of the media, in most cases by men, was noted as a key factor contributing to the invisibility of women in the media, the negative portrayal of women, as well as women's low representation in decision-making positions in media organisations and institutions.

The last decade has brought with it an awakening of the media in the region, with many new publications being established and some governments freeing the airwaves and liberalising the media industry, leading to new private, public and community radio stations. While the media is becoming a flourishing and vibrant industry in the region, achieving gender balance in media coverage in southern Africa is still a daunting challenge, with women's views and voices continuing to be under-represented. Even in states where the media is privately owned, the majority of the decision-makers are men, and women's access to and control of editorial issues is limited.

Freedom of expression is guaranteed in the constitutions of all southern African countries. However, none of the southern African countries specify that freedom of expression as including the right of men and women to be heard and to voice their concerns through the media. Women's access to the media and their representation in and control over the media is important insofar as the media has an important role to play in challenging all forms of discrimination and in contributing to policy development through keeping the public informed.

The media is one of the most powerful forces for shaping the way society thinks; hence it has a key role to play in foregrounding, monitoring and transforming gender relations. For this reason, national, regional, and international instruments aimed at addressing gender inequalities and advancing the status of women have incorporated provisions to address aspects of media and information in their development activities.

Policy Framework

The Beijing Declaration and Platform For Action (BDPFA) identifies women and media as a critical area of concern in addressing gender inequalities and women's empowerment. Section J of the BDPFA spells out two strategic objectives with regard to women and media that are aimed at promoting women's empowerment and development:

+ increase the participation and access of women to expression and decision-making in and through the media and new technologies of communication; and

+ promote a balanced and non-stereotyped portrayal of women in the media.

In order to ensure women's equitable access to and coverage in the media, the Beijing Declaration commits nation states to:

+ support women's education, training and employment to promote and ensure women's equal access to all areas and levels of the media;

+ support research into all aspects of women and the media so as to define areas needing attention and action and review existing media policies with a view to integrating a gender perspective;

+ promote women's full and equal participation in the media, including management, programming, education, training and research;

+ aim at gender balance in the appointment of women and men to all advisory, management, regulatory or monitoring bodies, including those connected to the private and State or public media;

+ encourage, to the extent consistent with freedom of expression, these bodies to increase the number of programmes for and by women to see to it that women's needs and concerns are properly addressed;

+ encourage and recognise women's media networks, including electronic networks and other new technologies of communication, as a means for the dissemination of information and the exchange of views, including at the international level, and support women's groups active in all media work and systems of communications to that end;

+ encourage and provide the means or incentives for the creative use of programmes in the national media for the dissemination of information on various cultural forms of indigenous people and the development of social and educational issues in this regard within the framework of national law; and

+ guarantee the freedom of the media and its subsequent protection within the framework of national law and encourage, consistent with freedom of expression, the positive involvement of the media in development and social issues.

An audit of the regional and international commitments to facilitate gender equality and advance the status of women reveals that media provisions are the weakest of all.[2]

While the BDPFA provides the most detailed analysis and action points on issues of gender and the media, the SADC Declaration on Gender and Development also identifies media as a key area in promoting women's empowerment and gender equality and equity in the region. Article H (x) of the SADC Gender Declaration, signed in 1997 in Blantyre, Malawi commits governments in southern Africa to "encourage the mass media to disseminate information and materials in respect of the human rights of women and children."

While various stakeholders in southern Africa are addressing the two strategic objectives outlined in the BDPFA as well as the provisions in the SADC Gender Declaration, a lot of work needs to be done to improve women's media access, representation and decision-making power in media organisations. To achieve this, sensitisation for both audiences and journalists on how women and men are portrayed, and to what extent, and on which issues they are quoted, or not given a voice, including how the lack of women in decision-making positions affects these portrayals, needs to be intensified.

The media in southern Africa has played a positive role in influencing public attitudes on many issues of governance, democracy, accountability, and human rights. The media can play a similar role in achieving gender equality. This role would involve influencing public attitudes and policy change towards narrowing the existing gender inequalities in the region.[36]

Portrayal and representation of women in the media

The portrayal and representation of women in the news has remained low although there is increasing awareness on gender issues in the region. A 2003 Gender and Media Baseline Survey (GMBS) by Gender Links and the Media Institute of Southern Africa (MISA) which monitored media across twelve southern African countries (Angola, Botswana, Lesotho, Malawi, Mauritius, Mozambique, Namibia, South Africa, Swaziland, Tanzania, Zambia and Zimbabwe) indicates that if unknown sources are excluded, women on average constitute 17 percent of news sources.[4] This figure is close to the global figure of 18 percent in the Gender and Media Monitoring Project. There are however, considerable differences between countries, ranging from women constituting 26 percent of news sources in Angola (the highest) to 11 percent in Malawi (the lowest).

The study found that women whose voices are more likely to be heard are in the 35-49 year bracket for both print and electronic media. Also, women are still more likely to be identified as a wife, daughter or mother, while men are often identified in their own right, not as a husband, son or father. The voices of older women are almost unheard, while most women are still described in terms of appearance rather than abilities.

Gender equality in the media and editorial content

The media has an important role to play in challenging all forms of discrimination if it is to truly be a champion of a democratic society based on the respect and enforcement of human rights for everyone regardless of race, sex, religion and ethnicity, among others. Media that only champions rights and entitlements of and for a few through gender-blind reporting perpetuates sexism. Some of the challenges faced in attempts to achieve equal representation of women in the media are related to the following:

- women television presenters constitute the highest proportion of women media practitioners in the region, but they have to be young. The heaviest concentration of women among electronic media practitioners is in the 20-34 year bracket. In essence, women stand their best chance in the electronic (and especially TV presenter category) of the media, but have a limited "shelf life". All this highlights the fact that the main determinant of women's success in the visual media is their looks rather than their ability;
- women are least represented in the print media where they constitute only 22 percent of those who write news stories. They are also under-represented in the critical images/cartoons and opinion and commentary categories; and
- women media practitioners predominate in the "soft beats". There is not a single news category in which women media practitioners dominate. Their absence is especially marked in the economics, politics and sports, mining and agriculture beats. The only beats that come close to achieving gender parity are health and HIV and AIDS, human rights, gender equality, gender violence, media and entertainment.

Women politicians constitute only 6 percent of news sources
Box 9.1

At the time of the 2003 GMBS study, women constituted an average of 18 percent of the members of parliament in the region yet women constituted only six percent of the sources in the political category. Countries that have the highest representation of women in parliament, Mozambique, South Africa and Tanzania also had some of the lowest proportions of women politicians being accessed as news sources. South Africa, for example, had 31 percent women in parliament and a similar proportion in cabinet. Yet women constituted only eight percent of the politicians quoted in the media monitored.

Excerpt from the GMBS, 2003

Further, the trend in the region is that gender equality issues are hardly considered newsworthy. For instance, gender specific news items accounted for a mere two percent of the total of the over 25,000 news items monitored, while about 25 percent related to politics and economics, and close to 20 percent were on sports.[5]

Barriers to women's access to the media and information

Recommendations on media made at the 1995 Fourth United Nations Conference on Women in Beijing show how necessary it is for women to occupy decision-making positions in media structures; to encourage change and to have access to communication technology to disseminate their views. However, barriers to women's access to expression in and through the media persist, often influenced by the following factors:

- women's absence in positions of formal authority or decision-making;
- women's lower literacy and educational levels;
- persisting traditional and cultural expectations;
- heavy workloads and lower purchasing power;
- patriarchal structures in media organisations; and
- women's continued treatment as minors.

In Malawi, the media presents a particularly challenging work environment for women. Irregular hours, the need to travel away from family, the strong "old boys network", perceptions of danger on certain beats, the technical nature of some media operations (especially in the electronic media), sexist attitudes and sexual harassment are mentioned as some of the factors that conspire against the effective participation and advancement of women in media professions.[6] A frequent constraint and frustration for women journalists is that they are assigned "soft beats" such as fashion, health, beauty and lifestyle that do not give them an opportunity to cover the beats that make top stories which usually determine access to training and promotion.

National surveys conducted in 2002 uncovered the continuing under-representation of women in media professions and especially in top editorial, decision-making and managerial positions in South Africa. According to a national skills audit commissioned by the South African National Editors' Forum (SANEF), newsrooms still display a gender imbalance. A general tendency was identified in print media that much more attention is given to achieving a racial balance as opposed to gender equity. In other instances it was however found that news organisations pay as much attention as possible to address the gender imbalance in line with the Labour Relations Act, to the extent that in some newsrooms, the staff component almost solely consisted of female employees, often under 30 years of age and in management positions. Some editors stressed that a number of female employees had been promoted to assignment editors in the immediate past, with the percentage of assignment editors being appointed in the regions also becoming more balanced in terms of gender equity.[7]

The Zimbabwe Gender and Media Baseline Study, as well as other studies, show that media in the country continue to be a male domain. The majority of reporters, those who gather and initially shape the stories, in both print and broadcast media are men. More importantly, those in positions of power and decision-making, who are able to decide what will be on the media's agenda and what moves through the media's gates to the public, are also predominantly men.

The situation in Zimbabwe is mirrored in Namibia where women are still under-represented in management positions within the media. As of 2002, the Namibia Broadcasting Corporation (NBC) had two women on the Board of Directors and only three out of the eight management level personnel were women, although the NBC mid-level management had a fair representation of women. Encouragingly, the Namibian media industry does employ a high percentage of women as reporters and presenters. Women constituted about half of television reporters (47 percent) and presenters (53 percent). Further, 21 percent of all radio and print reporters are women, which is only one percent less than the global average.[8]

Gender policies in the media

The BDPFA recognises the importance of "reviewing existing media policies with a view to integrating a gender perspective." Although all countries in the SADC region are signatory to the Convention on the Elimination of All Forms of Discrimination Against Women (CEDAW) and the SADC Declaration on Gender and Development, very few media houses have formulated a gender policy framework that spells out gender considerations in editorial content, programming, human resources and workplace issues, sexual harassment policy or staff composition.

An audit of gender and HIV and AIDS policies in the media undertaken as part of the Media Action Plan (MAP) on HIV and AIDS and gender to find out how many media houses in the SADC member states have policies on HIV and AIDS and gender show that out of 366 media houses surveyed, only 10 percent had HIV and AIDS policies and eight percent had gender policies.[9] However, these mostly related to workplace issues rather than editorial content.

Among the success stories in terms of the formulation and implementation of gender policies in media organisations, Times Printpak Zambia Ltd, producer of the *Times of Zambia* and its sister paper, the *Sunday Times* formulated a gender policy that addresses editorial content, employment and conditions of service. The 2003 policy, which has been commended as an example of best practice in gender mainstreaming in the region, provides guidelines for the implementation of aspects of the policy over a period of time, the evaluation of outcomes and undertaking any corrective actions as necessary. Times Printpak also has in place a Gender Policy, a Gender-Sensitive House Style Manual and an HIV and AIDS Policy.

In South Africa, the national broadcaster, the South Africa Broadcasting Corporation (SABC) does not have a stand-alone gender policy, although the corporation's editorial policies do include policy on discrimination and stereotypes. The SABC endeavours to ensure that its reporters do not use sexist language so as to avoid offending, or creating the impression – through repetition – that certain activities are associated with only one sex. In its policy, the SABC also undertakes to strive to ensure that its programming, when judged within context, does not promote violence against women, depict women as passive victims of violence or abuse, degrade women and undermine their role and position in society, promote sexism and gender inequality or reinforce gender oppression and stereotypes.

Some media houses in the region have also started developing and implementing gender policies based on their interpretation of their mandate.

In 2002 MISA, a regional media network adopted a gender policy.

The main aim of this policy is to ensure that implicit references to gender in freedom of expression discourse are made explicit. As a membership organisation with chapters in twelve southern African countries, MISA plays a key role in promoting professional policies and practices in the media.

Media Regulation

Nation states are encouraged to develop, consistent with freedom of expression, regulatory mechanisms, including voluntary ones, that promote balanced and diverse portrayals of women by the media and international communication systems and that promote increased participation by women and men in media production and decision-making. Regulatory authorities have a responsibility not only to incorporate gender considerations into ethical standards, but also to monitor that they are complied with. Unfortunately, evidence suggests that the existing media regulatory authorities in the region have made little effort in this regard.

The Media and Information Commission (MIC) in Zimbabwe which was established in 2002 only had one woman out of seven commissioners. The MIC carries out no campaigns to encourage gender-related complaints. The Advertising Media Association in that country will investigate any complaints it receives from the public about particular advertisements. Few gender-related complaints have been raised or investigated.

Zambia has in place a Code of Ethics, formulated and enforced by the Media Council of Zambia (MECOZ) established as a self-regulatory body by the media fraternity in July 2003. The membership of MECOZ is both individual and institutional. With the exception of the *Post* newspaper, all major media institutions now subscribe to MECOZ, having accepted the Code and its principles. Media organisations in Zambia are encouraged rather than required to

---

Media lags behind on HIV and AIDS and gender policies   Box 9.2

Less than ten percent of media houses in southern Africa have in place HIV and AIDS policies, and an even lower proportion have gender policies, according to a study conducted by Gender Links as part of the Media Action Plan (MAP) on HIV and AIDS and Gender.

The study, released at the annual general meeting of MISA covered 366 media houses in twelve SADC countries, or 91 percent of the total media houses in the region.

It found that of the 37 media houses with such policies, South Africa (18) and Zambia (12) had the highest number, although this is still relatively small compared to the media density in each country and especially in South Africa.

A number of media houses that said they had policies indicated that these are not in written form and only a few shared copies of their policies, citing confidentiality as the main reason for not doing so. Those that had not developed policies either cited resource constraints for not doing so, or said that they did not think that such policies are important for the media.

The study found that almost all the existing policies focus on workplace issues such as hiring practices, avoiding stigma and discrimination, but did not touch on how these link to editorial policies, including how HIV and AIDS and gender considerations should be integrated into codes of ethics and editorial style books.

The report indicates that the findings give "added urgency and impetus" to the MAP, a multi-sector initiative led by the Southern African Editor's Forum (SAEF) in partnership with several regional NGOs that work to promote diversity and professionalism in the media.

MAP aims to ensure that 80 percent of media houses in the region have HIV and AIDS and gender policies by 2008.

Gender Links press release, Media Lags Behind on HIV/AIDS and Gender Policies, issued on 23 August 2005

formulate and implement gender policies, and there is no requirement by any authority for media organisations to set targets for achieving diversity in ownership, employment and content to be consistent with the demographics of the country.

There have, however, been some positive steps taken and significant advances made with regard to gender mainstreaming and the promotion of equal participation of both sexes in the production process. There are no statistics available, but there appear to be more women than men working in the Zambian media today. The Head of the Zambian National Broadcasting Channel-TV is a woman, and women make up the great majority of newscasters and writers in the ZNBC newsroom. At the Zambia *Daily Mail*, the Editor-in-Chief is a woman, in addition to four other women who now sit on the nine-member editorial board. This is in contrast with only three women in top positions in 1999.

However, although more women now occupy top positions and have been brought into newsrooms in Zambia, their effect on content shows little impact to date. Coverage still does not reflect the wider issues of concern to women as it tends to concentrate on high-profile women such as ministers and civil society activists. Further, women sources are generally absent from media content, apparently because reporters prefer to quote "knowledgeable" sources, usually considered to be men.[10]

In November 1998, the Malawian parliament passed a new communications act, the Malawi Communications Regulatory Authority (MACRA), which for the first time established an independent regulatory body for broadcasting and telecommunications. An independent body, the MACRA, is charged with ensuring "reliable and affordable communication services"

throughout the country. It is required to be independent and impartial while doing so.

Like in Zambia, the regulatory authority in Malawi does not require, through licensing conditions, that media houses demonstrate or set targets for achieving diversity in ownership, employment and content consistent with the demographics of the country. However, for the electronic media, the licensing (through the Third Schedule of the Communications Act 1998) spells out the obligations for fairness, objectivity and extra care in order to accommodate various sensitivities in the audience. However, there is no explicit mention of gender considerations, although these need to be explicitly mentioned in the laws that govern regulatory authorities and to be publicised in their awareness campaigns. The regulatory authorities receive and encourage complaints for public and private media. So far, however, there have been no gender-specific complaints. On the other hand, a number of newspapers, on their own have carried articles against the abuse of females as objects in advertising.

Training

With the necessary will, support and expertise, gender can be mainstreamed into media training, with visible outcomes and improvements in the professionalism of media practitioners who undergo such training. This is of importance because of all the strategies to bring greater gender balance and sensitivity in the media, training remains one of the most important ways of opening the eyes of the media to the more professional reporting and fresh story ideas that gender awareness brings. The BPFA recognises the importance of "encouraging gender-sensitive training for media professionals, including media owners and managers, to encourage the creation

121

Small grant on gender reporting in southern Africa   Box 9.3

In early 2002, the Southern African Research and Documentation Centre's (SARDC) gender programme, Women in Development Southern Africa Awareness (WIDSAA), established a small grant scheme to enable journalists to research and write articles that reflect the range of perspectives related to gender policies and their effect among communities and governments in the region. With financial support from Sidaand later HIVOS.

WIDSAA's interest in undertaking gender and media activities is motivated by its objective - To enable the SADC region to effectively manage and process information in order to facilitate women's empowerment, gender mainstreaming and the achievement of gender equality in the southern African region.

The small grants for journalists aimed to:

◆ promote in-depth coverage of gender issues in the region using gender instruments like the BDPFA, Beijing + 5 commitments, and the 1997 SADC Gender and Development Declaration as points of reference;

◆ motivate journalists to contribute to the sustenance of the momentum and synergies gathered on regional gender issues in the SADC and as a result, stimulate meaningful contribution and participation of the region's citizens in the quest for gender equality and equity;

◆ strengthen the media's understanding of the available gender instruments; and

◆ encourage cross-boarder sharing of gender and development issues of concern in the SADC region.

This was with the understanding that the media has a role to play in the facilitation of women's empowerment, gender mainstreaming and the achievement of gender equality within the region. Gender is still a subject that until recent years, the mainstream media has often been reluctant to spend time and money on. Yet like any good reporting, gender reporting requires that journalists get out of their chairs and go out and report.

Thus the small grant on gender reporting in southern Africa enabled journalists to go out, research, and produce articles that reflected the range of perspectives related to the implementation of gender policies to determine the extent to which gender equality and equity was being realised.

The small grant facility on gender reporting is a unique, cost-effective, and action-oriented way of strengthening the media's capacity to report on gender and development issues in the SADC region.

Participating journalists in the gender and media activities under the small grant facility were empowered with additional research-writing skills and current information on the prevailing gender instruments to work with in their endeavours to write articles or produce broadcasts that are sensitive towards gender equality and equity.

Barbara Lopi for SARDC 2005

and use of non-stereotyped, balanced and diverse images of women in the media."

Skills development for improving journalistic skills and experience, which is offered and sponsored by various institutions, has increased in the region. From entry level and university media education, to on-the-job training for journalists already in the field, there have been a variety of strategies instituted for "mainstreaming" gender into media education in various countries in the region.

Mauritius has made significant progress towards achieving greater gender balance in the news and in newsrooms. This may be attributed in part to the three-year honours degree course in Communication Studies offered at the University of Mauritius which has gender mainstreamed in all learning processes and materials, although the course lacks a specific focus on gender in the media. However, the subject of gender in the media has been taught as part of the studies for the degree in social science at the university.

While more journalists have started writing about gender issues, there is still a lack of informed analysis and media reports focusing on gender issues. The SADC region still needs to do more to empower journalists with additional skills and current information on prevailing gender instruments to enhance their work as they endeavour to write articles and produce broadcasts that are sensitive to gender equality and equity. The media should be strengthened and capacitated in gender reporting so that media practitioners and media houses can reflect the facilitation of women's empowerment, gender mainstreaming and the achievement of gender equality in the region.

The Department of Media Technology at the Polytechnic of Namibia (PON) embarked on a three-year pilot project to systematically mainstream gender into entry-level journalism at the college. The pilot project, which was designed to cover the three full years of the programme, began in 2002 when the PON introduced its three-year diploma programme in Journalism and Communication Technology. The project included training activities and study materials focusing on gender and the media. Students were also assessed and encouraged to contribute articles to be published in the student newspaper.

Zambia Institute of Mass Communication (ZAMCOM) has a Gender and Media Training Manual to instil gender and ethical values in journalism students and the profession.

Women as sources in political and electoral coverage

In South Africa, women constitute almost 50 percent of representation in government at national level, 28 percent at provincial level and 28 percent at local level, yet research conducted on the 1999 and 2004 general elections in South Africa indicates a "very worrying" absence of women as sources of information in election-related news. In 1999, women constituted eight percent of the gender-specified sources used in election news and information, while 87 percent of news sources were male.[11]

A number of gender and media monitoring exercises have taken place around recent elections in the region. A study on gender, media, and the 2005 elections in Zimbabwe entitled "So Many Rivers to Cross" found that women constituted 17 percent of sources in election coverage and only nine percent of the "newsmakers". It also found that women were far more likely to be identified according to their personal rather than professional credentials.

Monitoring of election coverage in South Africa and Malawi showed a dramatic improvement in the representation and portrayal of women as voters, candidates, and citizens. Studies showed that women sources increased from eight percent in the 1999 elections to 25 percent in the 2004 elections. In some newspapers, this proportion was even higher, at 40 percent.

However, another study indicates that only 12 percent of all sources across media in Malawi are women compared to 88 percent men. Men predominate as sources in hard news; for example, the study revealed that in politics, men constitute about 75 percent of sources, 85 percent in sports, 71 percent in education and 81 percent in media and entertainment. Gender violence is the only topic where women were accessed more than men in the country. In general, women are seldom sourced or quoted in stories, even where they are obviously in the majority.[12] Research shows that the majority of stories covered in the Malawi media suffer from "gender-blindness" in that the coverage is still largely about men in positions of authority.

Legislative provisions for information technology

Getting gender issues placed on the table of Information and Communications Technologies (ICT) policy making has been gaining momentum. Chapter J of the Beijing Platform for Action states that "during the past decade, advances in information technology have facilitated a global communications network that transcends national boundaries and has an impact on public policy, private attitudes and behaviour, especially of children and young adults." One of the strategic objectives is to "increase the participation and access of women to expression and decision-making in and through the media and new technologies of communication."

While governments have not always taken a gender aware approach to ICTs, a number of women's organisations in the region have been active in promoting gender aware approaches to policy development; access, capacity building and to using the internet as a tool for advancing gender equality.

Several ICT policies that are emerging as countries clamour to become part of the new information and communication societies are gender blind. For example, in 2003, the Ministry of Communications and Transport in Tanzania published the National Information and Communications Technologies Policy that recognises the use of ICT in economic development. However, the policy makes no specific reference to women. Despite this oversight however, in October

2004, the WSIS Gender Caucus in collaboration with the Tanzanian Ministry of Communication and Transport and Advancing IT Knowledge in Africa (AITEC) Tanzania, organised the first "Road to Tunis" conference on Women and ICTs. The motivation and intention of the workshop was to discuss the issues hindering women's access, use, adoption and development of ICTs on the continent, and to provide a forum where examples of good practices could be showcased.

The goal of the conference was to amplify the opportunities available to, and discuss solutions for the effective participation in, and use of information communication technologies by women and to place a gendered agenda on the global ICT platform in the bid to create an inclusive information society and economy.

The Malawi Communications Policy Statement (1998) outlines the national policy for the development of the country's communications sector, covering broadcasting (both radio and television), telecommunications and postal services. The policy's aim is to ensure that a full range of modern services is accessible to all Malawians, although it does not specify access by women. In so far as it has increased business opportunities, women in Malawi have benefited from the liberalisation of the telecommunications sector, although more gain can be made if women's needs were directly mentioned and catered for in policy implementation.

Some gender awareness is apparent in Mauritius where the National Telecommunication Policy 2004 provides for universal access, with a view to expanding the availability of affordable telecommunications and ICT services to the public irrespective of gender, ethnicity, socio-economic level, or geographic location.

In South Africa, the Telecommunications Act (1996) provides for the "regulation and control of telecommunications matters in the public interest. Objects of the Act include the promotion of universal service. Other provisions include (g) the needs of local communities and (h) disabled people are duly taken into account. Access by women is also specifically recognised in the Objects of the Act in (q) where it commits to the empowerment and advancement of women in the telecommunications sector.

Conclusion

As the struggle for gender equality broadens from mere legislative reforms to the underlying mindsets without which change is impossible, the media has a key role to play. Dilemmas over how to balance the imperatives of gender equality and freedom of expression have led to weak provisions and strategies for addressing this key area of transformation. Policy makers both in government and the media have failed to see gender equality as intrinsic to freedom of expression.

The tools available to governments and regulatory authorities for advancing gender equality in and through the media, such as licensing agreements, are gender blind. With a few notable exceptions, gender awareness has not been integrated into information, communication and media laws in the region.

Much of the initiative on gender and the media in the region has been taken by civil society organisations who have conducted research, provided training, supported media houses in developing policies, worked with activists in becoming more strategic in their approaches to the media, sparked off consumer activism campaigns and monitored progress towards achieving greater gender balance and sensitivity in the media.

Endnotes

1   SARDC WIDSAA, *Beyond Inequalities: Women in Southern Africa*, SARDC WIDSAA, Harare, 2000
2   Lowe Morna, C and Mufune, J. *Media on the a-Gender,* Gender Links, MISA, GEMSA, 2005
3   Lopi. B, "Why Gender and Media?" A presentation to a gender and media workshop for SADC Journalists, organised by SARDC, Harare, Zimbabwe, 21 June 2004
4   MISA and Gender Links, "The Southern African Gender and Media Baseline Study" 2002
5   MISA and Gender Links, 2002
6   SARDC WIDSAA and WLSA Malawi, *Beyond Inequalities 2005: Women in Malawi,* Limbe & Harare, 2005

7   Steyn, E. and de Beer, A, SANEF's 2002 South African National Journalism Skills Audit Final Report, 20002, Noordburg, Unpublished.
8   SARDC WIDSAA and UNAM, *Beyond Inequalities 2005: Women in Namibia,* Limbe and Harare, 2005
9   Muriungi. A, "Report on audit of HIV-AIDS & gender policies," Gender Links, 2005
10   Banda, F et al. Panel Discussion of the African Media Barometer Zambia, Lusaka, 2005
11   SARDC WIDSAA and University of the Western Cape, *Beyond Inequalities 2005: Women in South Africa,* Cape Town & Harare, 2005.
12   SARDC WIDAA and WLSA Malawi
13   SARDC WIDSAA and ZWRCN, *Beyond Inequalities 2005: Women in Zimbabwe,* Harare, 2005.

References

Banda, F. et al. Panel Discussion of the African Media Barometer Zambia, Lusaka, 2005
http://www.fesmedia.org.na/power_presen/AFRICAN%20MEDIA%20BAROMETER%20ZAMBIA.doc

Gender Links and MISA, "The Southern African Gender and Media Baseline Study," Gender Links, South Africa, 2003

Lowe Morna, C. and Mufune. J, *Media on the a-Gender,* Gender Links, Media Institute of Southern Africa MISA, GEMSA, South Africa, 2005

Muriungi.A, "Report on audit of HIV-AIDS & gender policies," Gender Links, South Africa, 2005
SADC, "Gender and Development Declaration," SADC, Gaborone, 1997

SARDC WIDSAA, *Beyond Inequalities: Women in Southern Africa,* SARDC, Harare, 2000

SARDC WIDSAA and Forum Mulher, *Beyond Inequalities 2005: Women in Mozambique,* Maputo and Harare, 2005

SARDC WIDSAA and WLSA, *Beyond Inequalities 2005: Women in Malawi,* Limbe and Harare, 2005

SARDC WIDSAA and ZARD, *Beyond Inequalities 2005: Women in Zambia,* Lusaka and Harare, 2005

SARDC WIDSAA and ZWRCN, *Beyond Inequalities 2005: Women in Zimbabwe,* Harare, 2005

SARDC WIDSAA and UNAM, *Beyond Inequalities 2005: Women in Namibia,* Windhoek and Namibia, 2005

WOMEN AND THE ENVIRONMENT

10

Introduction

Current information on the environment in southern Africa is not disaggregated by sex and there is little mainstreaming of gender issues and concerns in environment issues. This points to research gaps and lack of capacities in gender analysis and discussions on environment in the region.

This chapter highlights the links between gender and environment and the importance of analysing the gender dimensions of environment issues. All countries in SADC are signatories to the Beijing Declaration and Platform for Action (BDFPA) in which gender inequalities and management of natural resources is one of the 12 critical areas of concern. Three countries (Angola, Botswana and Mozambique) have taken Women and Environment as a critical area of concern. Article 15 of the Protocol to the African Charter on Human and People's Rights on the Rights of Women in Africa notes that in order to ensure food security, there is need to provide for women's access to clean drinking water, sources of domestic fuel and means of producing nutritious food.

The natural environment includes land, water, minerals, all living organisms and life processes, the atmosphere, the climate, the polar icecaps, remote ocean depths and even outer space. An important shift over the years in defining the environment has been one that takes into account the relationship between human activities and natural environments and between poverty and environmental degradation.

The region's environment is suseptible to different processes of change resulting from:

- population growth and poverty, which are still the main causes of land degradation due to pressure on marginal lands;
- improper land husbandry, which causes erosion and a decrease in soil fertility;
- deforestation, which results in shortages of fuel wood, building materials and further soil erosion;
- overgrazing and improper range management, which leads to land degradation;
- neglect of soil conservation, which gives rise to high sediment loads in rivers and rapid siltation of water reservoirs; and
- insufficient institutional, organisational and human resources and inadequate marketing incentives for agriculture based activities in the rural areas which limit the possibilities of undertaking widespread conservation measures.[2]

127

Women and men's roles in society generally define how they relate to various aspects of the environment such as land, water, flora and fauna, wetlands, energy and forests. Women play various roles in food processing, agricultural management, household chores and family health which all impact on the environment. Their knowledge and skills therefore should be taken into account in the conservation of natural resources and in environmental policy and infrastructure development.

Besides the different gender-based roles and responsibilities of women and men in their households and communities, they also have different knowledge of, access to, and use of natural resources, as well as different opportunities to participate in decisions regarding natural resource use. Gender differences are evident in:

+ use and management of natural resources;
+ knowledge of the environment, specific resources, and of environmental problems;
+ responsibility for managing, owning or stewarding resources, and rights to resources;
+ encounters with the environment, perceptions of the environment, nature and severity of environmental problems; and
+ accountability, stewardship, and action for the environment.[3]

Poverty and the environment

Environmental and livelihood sustainability is dependent on improving the security of land and resource tenure of women particularly but not exclusive to rural areas. In southern Africa, women continue to be deprived of vital economic resources such as land, incomes, credit, agricultural inputs and technology.

Because of different social roles women have less income earning opportunities than men. In Zimbabwe for example, a comparison of tasks in rural areas reveal important differences. Men's work has seasonal peaks (ploughing and cattle herding) or is done once in many years (constructing houses and granaries). This gives men the ability to take seasonal or permanent employment elsewhere. In contrast women's tasks may be seasonal, for example weeding and harvesting, but social reproductive tasks are daily chores. These are not transferable to men due to cultural practices.[4]

In a community, rights and access to resources are often organised along lines of kingship, sex, and type of production. Men commonly have rights to resources such as land, water and fisheries. They even have the right to control and allocate certain amounts of women and children's labour to crops which they control and for which they retain revenue. In natural resources management, men commonly have full disposal rights while women have user rights.[5]

Water and sanitation

Because culture and tradition assigns women and girls the nurturing and caring roles in society, they are in touch with the environment on a daily basis through collection of water, wood and forest products. As managers of households, women play a major role in water use and collection and are therefore key in water management at both household and community level. Women and girls provide almost all water that is required for domestic use in rural areas, for drinking, cooking, cleaning and personal hygiene among other uses. Women therefore know where safe water can be collected, and how to use, manage, and dispose of wastewater.

Recurring droughts, low rainfall patterns and seasonal rainfall characteristic of the region makes it a challenge to provide accessible water supplies especially in rural areas that are dependent on rivers and wells. Because of frequent droughts or as water resources deteriorate, women and girls walk longer distances to secure water. Poor water access and quality increases the amount of labour that women endure to collect, store, protect and distribute water.

With regards to metered tap water, female-headed households have lower income levels than those headed by men and are less able to afford metered tap water. In Namibia, the 2000 National Gender Study found that for "urban areas, female-headed households are less likely than male-headed-households to have piped water inside the house, 20.8 percent compared to 33.7 percent, while for rural areas female-headed households are more likely to use free public water taps, 27.7 percent compared to 16.8 percent, and boreholes, 9,8 percent compared to 5.4 percent."

Although access to clean water is a challenge, there have been some improvements. The Malawi Population and Housing Census in 1998 found that only 48 percent of the population had access to clean water, 27 percent of households had access to boreholes as their main source of drinking water, 21 percent used piped water or communal taps as their main source of drinking water and 25 percent drew their drinking water from unprotected wells. By 2000, 65 percent of Malawian households had access to clean water sources, 23 percent from piped water and 42 percent from protected wells or boreholes.[7]

Besides its use in the home, water is important for economic production in agriculture, micro-enterprise and other income-generating activities. Women usually depend on small-scale or hand irrigation for crops that are grown all year round. Often however, technologies that are available to women do not respond to their needs, for example pumps with handles they cannot reach or manipulate or that they have not been trained to repair. A study done on irrigation in southern Africa (in South Africa, Zambia and Zimbabwe) revealed that women are the main users of small-scale irrigation, mostly growing vegetables, whereas men participate in irrigated farming on a part time basis or on a supervisory basis. Their main employment is either off-farm or in rain-fed and livestock enterprises.[8]

The majority of households in the region have no access to modern sanitation facilities, and the majority of these are in the rural areas. Over 50 percent of the people in the SADC region have no access to modern sanitation and over 40 percent are without access to safe drinking water. Since most female-headed households are to be found in rural areas, it can be assumed that they have less access to these facilities. In relation to modern sanitation facilities, 79 percent of all households in both urban and rural areas in Malawi use pit latrines while 19 percent of the households in Malawi do not have any toilet facilities. In addition, 21 percent of the rural households have no toilet facilities as compared with two percent of households in urban areas.[9] In

Access to Safe Water and Sanitation		Table 10.1
COUNTRY	**Population with access to safe water (2002)**	**Population with access to sanitation (2002)**
Angola	50	30
Botswana	95	41
DRC -	-	
Lesotho	76	37
Malawi	67	46
Madagascar	-	-
Mauritius	100	99
Mozambique	42	27
Namibia	80	30
South Africa	87	67
Swaziland	52	52
Tanzania	73	46
Zambia	55	45
Zimbabwe	83	57

Adapted from UNDP Human Development Report, 2005

Zambia, about 30 percent of rural households have access to safe water and just two percent have access to sanitation, compared to 40 percent in urban areas.

Energy sources and hazardous emissions

Most rural areas in southern Africa are not electrified therefore its inhabitants are dependent on wood fuel and charcoal as the main source of energy for lighting and cooking. The use of wood fuel and charcoal can potentially degrade the environment and can be hazardous to the health of women due to the fumes produced as women cook. In Zambia for example, only about 17 percent of households have access to electricity and between 2001 and 2002, electricity use decreased from 14.9 percent to 8.5 percent.[10]

In Namibia about 60 percent of households use traditional sources of energy such as wood, charcoal and animal waste.[11] Malawi and Tanzania derive over 90 percent of their energy from biomass whilst South Africa, Swaziland and Zimbabwe get below 50 percent each.[12] According to UNDP, UNDE-SA and World Energy Council, in 2000, over two billion people still relied on biomass fuels and traditional technologies for cooking and heating, and 1.5 to two billion have no access to electricity.

In spite of these challenges, there have been efforts to promote rural electrification programmes in countries such as Namibia, South Africa, Zambia and Zimbabwe. However, rural electrification proceeds very slowly and donor funding for it has decreased since it was ascertained that electricity in rural areas did not directly stimulate the establishment of small industries, as had been hoped and supposed, but is primarily used for lighting in houses and for household appliances such as televisions.[13]

An average rural woman is not likely to benefit from rural electrification at the expense of large-scale agricultural enterprises. Rural electrification projects therefore rarely aim at alleviating the burden on women. Of the "new and renewable" technologies, only biogas, and perhaps briquetting technology from various agricultural wastes, (besides improved stoves), are of immediate interest and benefit to women.

Nutrition levels can be compromised by overgrazing, soil erosion, lack of access to wood fuel and safe drinking water. For example, the shortage of biomass fuels such as wood fuel force families to economise on fuel by shifting to less nutritious foods which can either be eaten raw or partially cooked. There is also little likelihood of poor women being able to afford the extra calories for the

Mainstreaming gender in energy: The linkages	Box 10.3

1. Gender, energy and environmental degradation
   - Do national policies on energy match up with policies on rural livelihoods and sustainable development?
   - Within the household, who is responsible for collecting, transporting and/ or purchasing biomass energy supplies?
   - How much time do women, men and children spend on obtaining energy supplies?
   - How do men and women explain the causes of ecological degradation and scarcity of wild products?
   - How do men and women view their own behaviour in this context?
2. Energy needs and the gender division of labour
   - How much time do women and men spend on 'drudgery' activities, which could be eased by labour-saving activities?
   - Do energy-conserving projects take account of the priorities of men and women in overall household energy planning e.g. women's income earning opportunities?
   - Do energy-conserving projects take account of the constraints and choices made by women concerning energy usage?
3. Gender and energy-related decisions
   - Who makes decisions over energy usage?
   - Are energy usage and conservation messages gender disaggregated?
   - How do men and women use current sources of energy?
   - How are energy technologies gendered?
   - What strategies are in place to ensure that girls are not prevented from attending school by the need to obtain fuel?
4. Energy efficiency
   - Have new stove designs taken account of the different priorities of women?
   - How have women and men changed their cooking practices, selected types of food, quantity of food, number of meals etc?
   - Do both women and men participate and give their views in the field-testing of new technologies?
   - How are women and men likely to benefit from improved stove design?
   - DFID/SDD - Sectors: Natural Resources: Environment: Core Text, 2005

http://www.siyanda.org/docs_gem/index_sectors/natural/energy_coretext.htm

additional energy expended in fuel collection.

The primary source of air pollutants and hazardous gases in the home are biomass (wood and animal dung) and coal used by women mainly for heating and cooking. Rural areas in particular have a heavy reliance on wood fuel with poor households being more affected by these conditions, as they have no access to safer and cleaner sources of energy. This exposure of women and children may lead to eye infections and lung cancer. In South Africa for instance, considerable respiratory problems have been registered in townships where coal and wood fuel are used for cooking and heating.[14]

Access to land and technology

While women constitute the majority of the agricultural labour force and are responsible for most food production, their land rights are limited in the region. Land tenure systems vary across the region but women are generally not considered equally in land allocation. Women's ability to access land usually depends on their relationships with men. Whether married, single, widowed or divorced, women often have to depend on chiefs or headmen to make a decision about their rights of access and use.

In Zambia for example, 90 percent of land available for agriculture falls under traditional land controlled by chiefs who follow patriarchal principles in its allocation. Despite a clause in the 2002 Land Policy of Zambia to allocate 30 percent of land to women, there is no specific strategy to change customary law that places women in the position where they can only have use of land but not own it.

In South Africa, the legacy of apartheid and patriarchal attitudes and behaviour has resulted in women having unequal access to land. Land access and ownership have always been linked to race,

gender and class in South Africa. The post-apartheid South African government has made a constitutional commitment to redress land access inequalities and is particularly concerned about redressing the gender inequities in access and ownership. *Beyond Inequalities 2005: Women in South Africa* notes that, "women, especially in the rural areas, have historically been excluded from rights to land. The patriarchal culture of domination and inherited legislation on allocation of land resources prohibit women's claims to property, residential rights and land use. These laws and customs particularly affect black women in the rural areas where traditional authorities still largely control communal land. In addition, customs and customary practices still exclude women from the right to own, inherit, or profit from land."[15]

In recognition of women's unequal access to land the Zimbabwe government in 2002 committed to allocating a 20 percent quota for women to benefit from the fast track resettlement programme begun in the same year, but implementation of this provision is weak. By August 2002, the land quota for women had not been put into law and the number of women allocated land was low countrywide. In addition, policy documents and laws setting out the basis for the fast track programme make no mention of gender issues.[16]

Women's use of land is often limited by a lack of access to technology. Women in the region apply traditional environmental technologies to combat and address the low fertility and productivity of the land.[17] For example in agriculture, technological development has mainly focused on cash crops, which are grown by men to the exclusion of food crops grown by women. Extension services are also largely directed to cash crops grown by men.

131

In Zambia, where there has been the promotion of the use of treadle water pumps which are considered simple, cheap to manufacture, affordable, cheap to operate and maintain and for which spare parts are readily available, gender dynamics are starkly evident. This is because although the pumps are relatively cheap, they are still out of reach of average rural women who constitute less than one percent of the buyers. The pump increases the amount of labour needed to weed because more land is irrigated and more water is applied. Operating the pump has proved to be hard work for women who sometimes hire young boys to do the work. The increase in the amount of vegetables grown also increases the need for better marketing strategies for women.[18] There have been success stories with the use of treadle pumps, but there is a need to address the different challenges faced by women and men in order to make such technology more accessible to women.

Access to and control over wetland resources

Large areas of wetlands, marsh, fern, peat or water, natural or human made are found in the Zambezi basin. Women and men have defined activities in relation to wetland environments. Despite an acknowledgment that women and men use wetlands differently, existing programmes do not take gender into consideration in defining conservation and utilisation of wetlands.

Women harvest renewable resources such as wild fruits and firewood for cooking, grass for thatching, reeds and grasses to make baskets, bowls and other crafts thereby playing an important role in the tourist industry in the basin. Despite this, much of the work on wetland conservation and use has not considered gender issues and the role of women in wetland conservation.[19]

Men on the other hand, in addition to harvesting renewable resources from wetlands, are also engaged in fishing. Men and boys usually do deep-water fishing whereas women fish in shallow water using traps and baskets. Women are also involved in post harvest activities such as fish processing and marketing. In many rural areas across the region fish smoking is an important income earning activity dominated by women. However, in the process of smoking the fish women are exposed to hazardous fumes, which may lead to respiratory infections and difficulties in breathing.[20]

Whilst there are efforts and initiatives in terms of rationalising the access and control of wetland resources, women do not have the same capacity or ability as men to defend their rights over resources hence there is need to enhance women's access to and control over resources.

Environmental policies and programmes

The general understanding of gender has improved in the region but this has not been adequately reflected in policies that directly and indirectly protect the environment.

In assessing the environment, communities are generally treated as a homogenous whole, not differentiated by gender. This gender blind approach to environmental policies and legislation in southern Africa may result in statements in policies and legislation on gender and environment that are not backed by well-articulated plans for implementation.

The SADC Declaration on Gender and Development recognises the promotion of women's full access to, and control over productive resources such as land, livestock, markets, credit, modern technology, formal employment, and a good quality of life in order to reduce the level of poverty among women.

The Regional Indicative Strategic Development Plan (RISDP) of SADC identifies gender as one of the critical crosscutting issues to achieving poverty reduction, improvement of the standard of living of the majority of citizens of the region, prevention and eradication of HIV and AIDS, and regional integration. One of the major areas addressed in the RISDP is the promotion of women's access to and ownership and control over productive resources in the SADC region. Further, the section on gender equality and development in RISDP identifies women as being amongst the poorest and the most affected by poverty.

In the region, several countries have taken a leaf out of international and regional initiatives and put in place environment polices. Initiatives at the regional level have been influenced by international events such as Agenda 21, a blueprint on environment that emerged out of the Earth Summit in 1992. One of the objectives of Agenda 21 is to "formulate and implement clear governmental policies and national guidelines, strategies and plans for the achievement of equality in all aspects of society, including the promotion of women's nutrition and health, women's participation in decision-making positions and in the management of the environment, particularly as it pertains to their access to resources."[21]

Most countries in the region have gender policies and programmes with aspects of environment identified in these policies. The Malawi National Gender policy of 2000, for example, notes that women are hardest hit by the effects of environmental mismanagement because of the gender roles they play in resource mobilisation. The National Gender Policy therefore aims to mobilise campaigns and involve women, men, girls and boys in the planning, design and management of water facilities among others. In addition the policy will enforce women's rights to land ownership and the management of resources.

Zambia's National Gender Policy identifies the lack of access by women to credit, improved technology, land and extension services as an area of concern and proposes action areas in the Plan of Action in water and sanitation, land, tourism, environment and natural resources, and energy.

In Namibia, the government put in place a Water and Sanitation Policy (1993), which "aims to make water affordable and available to all Namibians and allow local communities to manage their own water resources and to facilitate environmentally sustainable water utilisation. Regarding energy, the Namibian government has a stated objective to provide 20 percent of the rural population with electricity and install 6,823 solar energy systems by 2006."[22]

Zambia put in place a Rural Electrification Fund in 2002, but few rural women who farm on a small scale are likely to benefit. The fund is targeted mainly at boosting industrialisation of the rural areas for large-scale agricultural production. Such programmes that do not take into account the differential work areas in the rural economy of women and men are likely to leave women worse off by overburdening them with more work than before such innovations are introduced.

In Zimbabwe, the Environment Management Act (EMA) facilitates the mainstreaming of environment into policies and programmes but does not explicitly identify the gender issues. The Zimbabwe National Water Authority (ZINWA) Act has outlined progressive steps in how gender should be addressed in

New Water Act Box10.4
**promotes decision
making at lowest levels**

Although the New Water Act promotes decision-making at the lowest level, it should be realised that at this level, women do not have equal access to decision-making processes, and special measures should be taken to ensure equal representation of poor women's needs and priorities. Integrated Water Resources Management recommends that rules and procedures for catchments and sub-catchments authorities should facilitate the participation of both men and women with regards to timing of meetings, frequency of meetings and location of meetings. Serious efforts have to be made to include women, especially in community water committees. Strategies have to be formulated to ensure that as more women take up leadership and management roles, men do not withdraw, leaving domestic water supplies as low status "women's sphere" in development. It should be an area in which both men and women are equally involved, thus placing domestic water supplies in a broader developmental context.

SARDC WIDSAA and ZWRCN *Beyond Inequalities 2005: Women in Zimbabwe*, SARDC/ ZWRCN, Harare, 2005

Integrated Water Resources Management (IWRM). "The Act states that granting of water rights and entitlements must be gender sensitive, so should appointments to ZINWA and Catchment Councils and that all personnel in the water sector should have training on gender issues."[23]

However, many constraints to women's equal access to environmental resources still abound at both regional and national level, thereby the need for more concerted efforts to include gender in environmental policy making.

Recommendations

Based on the above situational analysis there is need:

- for collection of disaggregated data on women's and men's resource use, knowledge of, access to and control over resources;
- for gender focal points working in environment management to acquire capacities to formulate and implement policies in line with various international and national protocols relevant to the gender dimension of environmental management;
- to establish, build consensus and raise awareness on procedures for incorporating a gender perspective in planning, monitoring, and evaluating environmental projects;
- to lobby governments for specific targets and timeframes for women to participate in decision-making in environmental policies and programmes at all levels, including roles as designers, planners, implementers, and evaluators;
- to lobby governments for research programmes to study options for renewable energy sources, their access and affordability to women in their respective locations, as well as documentation and replication of best practices;

- for dissemination of information to women so as to strengthen their access and control over natural resources;
- for governments to facilitate women's ownership of resources such as land, water, energy and technology;
- to lobby governments to put in place environmental policies that take into account gender concerns; and
- for governments to create a policy environment conducive for achieving women's rights in environmental concerns by reviewing, harmonising, coordinating environmental-related statutes and policies at regional and country levels and ensure that gender issues are taken on board.

Conclusion

The research undertaken in writing this chapter revealed that there is a paucity of information on the subject of environment as it relates to women. There is little analysis of gender in environmental concerns in the region, thus women's role, participation and benefit in environmental issues remains invisible.

Further, women's effectiveness in managing resources is affected by practices and laws that perpetuate gender discrimination such as tenure systems and inheritance laws, natural resource depletion and land degradation.

In relation to the environment, "women" are classified as one uniform category, namely married women, and this assumes that all (married) women receive sufficient land through their husbands. Intervention on the environment does not take into account the fact that women go through various life cycles, some in which women's access to natural resources are challenged. Rights linked to women's marital status are not sustainable as women often lose these rights through divorce or widowhood.

The resultant effect is that women, the poor and other marginalised groups are less likely to invest time and resources or adopt environmentally sustainable farming practices on land they do not control.

Women's livelihoods are dependent on the exploitation of natural resources such as fuel wood and timber for energy, grass and poles for shelter, and wildlife flora and fauna for food and crafts but these livelihood strategies continue to be threatened by environmental degradation. Measures need to be effected to empower women to acquire ownership and management over natural resources in their own right so as to improve environmental sustainability.

While several polices that directly or indirectly protect the environment exist, very few of such policies incorporate gender, resulting in situations where women's knowledge about use and management of the natural resources is often ignored in planning.

Endnotes

1   Chenje, M. (Ed), *State of the Environment Zambezi Basin 2000*, DC/IUCN/ZRA/SARDC, Maseru/Lusaka/Harare, 2000, p xxi
2   SARDC WIDSAA, *Beyond Inequalities: Women in Southern Africa*, SARDC, Harare, 2000, p 117
3   UNEP, *Mainstreaming Gender in Environmental and Early Warning Systems*, UNEP, Nairobi, 2005, p 14
4   SARDC WIDSAA and UNAM, *Beyond Inequalities 2005: Women in Namibia*, SARDC, Windhoek and Harare, 2005, p52
5   Chenje, M.(Ed), Harare, 2000
6   SARDC and UNAM, p51
9   SARDC andWLSA Malawi , p32
10 SARDC WIDSAA and ZARD , Harare, p40
11 SARDC and UNAM , 2005, p52
12 SARDC IMERCSA, *Communicating the Environment Project (CEP) Fact Sheet No 12*, SARDC, Harare, 1997
13 DFID, Directorate General for
Development European Commission, UNDP and the World Bank Group, 2002, p12
14 SARDC WIDSAA, p 121
15 SARDC WIDSAA and UWC, *Beyond Inequalities 2005: Women in South Africa*, 2005
16 SARDC WIDSAA and ZWRCN, *Beyond Inequalities 2005: Women in Zimbabwe*, ZWRCN/SARDC, Harare, 2005, p7
17 SARDC WIDSAA, *Beyond Inequalities: Women in Southern Africa*, SARDC, Op Cit, p 123
18 Chancellor F, *Sustainable Development and the Gender Question in Southern*, DFID, 2004
19 SARDC IMERCSA, Harare, 1999
20 SARDC WIDSAA, *Beyond Inequalities: Women in Southern Africa*, SARDC, 2000, p 124
21 SARDC WIDSAA, *Beyond Inequalities: Women in Southern Africa*, SARDC, 2000, p 125
22 SARDC and UNAM , 2005, p62
23 SARDC WIDSAA and ZWRCN, *Beyond Inequalities 2005: Women in Zimbabwe*, 2005, p43

References

Chenje, M. and Johnson, P. (Eds.), *Water in Southern Africa*, SADC/IUCN/SARDC, Maseru/Harare, 1996.

Chenje, M. (Ed), *State of the Environment Report: Zambezi Basin 2000*, SADC/ZRA/SARDC, Maseru/Lusaka/Harare, 2000

SARDC IMERCSA, *Communicating the Environment Project (CEP) Fact Sheet No 12*, SARDC, Harare, 1997

Chancellor, F. Sustainable Development and the Gender Question in Southern, DFID, 2004. www.sahims.net/doculibrary/2004/01

Government of Zambia,Gender in Development Division Office of the President, *Republic of Zambia: National Gender Policy*, Lusaka, 2000

Lambrou, Y. and Laub, R. "Gender Perspectives on the Conventions on Biodiversity, Climate Change and Desertification", Gender and Development Service, FAO Gender and Population Division, October, 2004

Meer S. (Ed), *Women, Land and Authority: Perspectives from South Africa National Land Committee and Oxfam*, Oxfam, South Africa and United Kingdom, 1997

SADC, *Regional Indicative Strategic Development Plan*, SADC, Gaborone, 2004

SARDC WIDSAA, *Beyond Inequalities: Women in Southern Africa*, SARDC, Harare, 2000

SARDC WIDSAA and UNAM, *Beyond Inequalities 2005: Women in Namibia*, SARDC, Windhoek and Harare, 2005

SARDC WIDSAA and WLSA Malawi, *Beyond Inequalities 2005: Women in Malawi*, SARDC, Limbe and Harare, 2005

SARDC WIDSAA and ZWRCN, *Beyond Inequalities 2005: Women in Zimbabwe*, SARDC Harare, 2005

UNDP, *Human Development Report 2005: International Cooperation at a Crossroads- Aid, trade and security in an unequal world*, UNDP, New York, 2005

UNEP, *Mainstreaming Gender in Environmental Assessment and Early Warning Systems*, UNEP, Nairobi, 2005

WAY FORWARD AND
STRATEGIES FOR THE FUTURE

11

The southern African region has made progress towards achieving gender equality. However, many challenges remain. Moving from an era of making commitments and promises to an era of implementation and delivery on gender equality, justice and women's empowerment is among the key challenges. The information and strategies for the future that are presented in this book are meant to facilitate the shift from promises to delivery.

The strategies for the future are derived from the information in the chapters as well as from the SADC Gender-Based Regional Integration Plan: Strategic Implementation Framework (SIF) 2006 - 2010, a document developed at a stakeholder's consultative conference on the SADC Gender and Development programme held in December 2005 in Gaborone, Botswana. The conference was aimed at reflecting and re-strategising for gender-based regional integration.

The draft SADC Protocol on Gender and Development will strengthen some of these targets if adopted by the 2008 Summit of Heads of State and Government, following extensive national consultations.

The SIF has clearly defined action areas, targets, specific activities to be undertaken at the regional and national levels with allocated responsibility and a timeframe. The framework, which aligned with the SADC Declaration on Gender and Development and the SADC Regional Indicative Strategic Development Plan (RISDP), will guide stakeholders operating in SADC member states as they plan gender programmes and activities up to 2010. The framework is the region's pro-posed strategy for the way forward to mainstream gender in southern Africa. It is, however, a broad framework that enables stakeholders to develop their own specific actions in line with their areas of competency and their mandates.

Adoption of the draft SADC Protocol on Gender and Development will boost progress towards achieving gender equality in the region, and should advance the achievement of some of the SIF targets. A Protocol is the most binding of SADC legal instruments and is expected to accelerate the implementation of gender commitments.

The idea to follow-up the SADC Declaration on Gender and Development (1997) and the Addendum on the Prevention and Eradication of Violence against Women and Children (1998) with a Gender Protocol was discussed as far back as 2001 and it opens up possibilities of rationalising and enhancing all existing commitments to gender equality as well as providing accountability and monitoring mechanisms.

The draft Protocol has specific time-bound goals and targets to be undertaken between 2010 and 2020. These are meant to ensure accountability in addressing inequalities in constitutional and legal rights; governance; education and training; productive resources and employment; gender-based violence; health; HIV and AIDS; peace building and conflict resolution; and in media, information and communication.

Also in place is a regional gender policy for SADC (2007) that seeks to reinforce and standardise interventions towards achieving gender equality and equity in the region. The purpose of the policy is to provide guidelines to institutionalise and operationalise gender mainstreaming, women's empowerment components and capacity building as key development strategies for gender equality and equity within SADC.

The strategies for the future have been grouped under the following thematic areas:

Strengthening institutional mechanisms

The SIF outlines the following activities and targets:

* all member states to have National Gender Policies and SADC to have a Regional Gender Policy by 2007;
* national gender machineries to be adequately resourced by 2009;
* SADC Gender Unit to be strengthened with capacity to fulfil its mandate by 2009;
* advisory body to be established that will aid in monitoring of gender activities such as a regional Women's Rights Commission by 2009;
* ten percent of each line ministry budget allocated to gender specific activities between 2006-2008;
* regional and national macro-economic and sectoral polices to be engendered (to include planning and budgeting guidelines) from 2006-2007; and
* sensitisation and capacity building for SADC structures and institutions on gender mainstreaming from 2006-2007.

Gender mainstreaming

Specific actions and targets outlined in the SIF are to:

* have a comprehensive audit of non-political decision-making structures across the region by 2006;
* achieve 50 percent in all decision-making positions by 2015 or earlier;
* achieve 50/50 gender balance in the management of the SADC secretariat by 2010;
* ensure affirmative action in all constitutions by 2010;

* establish Gender Parliamentary Forums at national level by 2010;
* undertake a gender audit of parliaments by 2010;
* lobby all political parties to have at least 50 percent representation in all party structures by 2015; and
* develop a tool at regional level for monitoring women's participation in decision-making in the region.

Women's human rights including constitutional and legal reform

The SIF proposes:

* constitutional provisions for gender equality, including the right to dignity, right to life, integrity and security of person;
* the domestication of regional and international instruments and policies;
* gender equality to be enshrined in all constitutions and provisions for gender equality to take precedence over customary law by 2010;
* the removal of all discriminatory legislation by 2010;
* all member states to domesticate CEDAW by 2007; and
* ratification and domestication of the African Protocol on Women's Rights as well as the anticipated SADC Gender Protocol by 2007.

Education, including ending violence in educational institutions

The concerns highlighted on education are around equality of access to education for boys and girls, eradication of illiteracy and the elimination of stereotypes in education curricula. The SADC GU has been tasked to assist in developing action plans and disseminating information on best practices and developing tools for reviewing educational materials from a gender perspective. Activities and targets outlined in the SIF are to:

* introduce state supported early child development in all countries by 2010;

- have all universities and institutions of higher learning offering gender studies programmes by 2010;
- mount zero tolerance campaigns to end gender violence in schools by 2009;
- ensure compulsory primary and secondary education for all children by 2010;
- develop and implement an action plan to eradicate illiteracy by 2006; and
- review all education materials from a gender perspective by 2008 and introduce gender sensitive materials by 2010.

Violence against women and children

Violence against women and children is one of the major concerns in southern Africa. Actions in the SIF to curb this scourge include, halting of trafficking of women and children, strengthening criminal and justice systems as well as fragile social, economic and political environment in parts of the region. Actions and targets outlined in the SIF towards arresting incidences of violence against women and children are to:

- hold a regional consultative workshop on trafficking of women and children in 2006;
- have a dissemination model of legislation on best practices on gender violence;
- have all member states enact laws against gender violence, domestic violence and sexual offences by 2008;
- hold sensitisation of all functionaries in the criminal system and mainstreaming of gender in all their future training programmes by 2008;
- facilitate meaningful and effective involvement of women in peace-building processes and post conflict situations by 2006.

Sexual, reproductive health and rights

The concerns in reproductive and sexual rights are identified as a lack of quality sexual and reproductive health services, resource limitations, poor infrastructure, equipment, facilities and inadequate human resources. The SADC GU is tasked with the responsibility of working with the Social Human Development and Special Programmes Unit of SADC to develop guidelines on sexual and reproductive health. Actions and targets outlined under this concern are:

- provision of free health care for poor and vulnerable sections of society;
- provision of education on emergency contraception including dissemination of information in local languages to communities by 2008;
- development of guidelines for a minimum package for sexual and reproductive health in the region by 2007; and
- reduction of the maternal mortality rate by three quarters between 2006 and 2015.

Gender, HIV and AIDS

Issues of concern around HIV and AIDS include high HIV and AIDS prevalence rates among women and girls, cultural practices that perpetuate HIV and AIDS transmission, and gaps in collaborative efforts between biomedical and traditional medicine in combating HIV and AIDS.

At regional level there is a call for the SADC HIV and AIDS Unit to lead an initiative of adopting a Regional Volunteers' Charter as outlined in the UN Secretary Generals' Taskforce on Women, Girls and HIV and AIDS in southern Africa.

At national level, member states are urged to ensure that HIV and AIDS policies are in place to strengthen programmes and accelerate male involvement in HIV and AIDS initiatives.

Member states are also encouraged to facilitate national discussions on traditional practices that fuel the HIV and AIDS pandemic and ensure wide and free distribution of female and male condoms. There is need to strengthen and increase voluntary counselling and testing (VCT) in rural and urban areas. The targets and actions set out to curb HIV and AIDS in the SIF are:

* halt the spread of HIV and AIDS, as per MDGs six and seven, by 2015;
* reduce incidences of widow inheritance and genital mutilation. Adopt a zero tolerance on minors getting married and reduce by 50 percent the impact of the burden of care on women and the girl child by 2007; and
* create forums to foster negotiations for collaborative partnerships between modern and traditional medicine by 2007.

Economic empowerment
Issues of concern regarding women's economic empowerment contained in the SIF are:

* the need for women to be equally represented in economic policy formulation and women's lack of rights to own property and to inheritance;
* lack of access to credit, capital and land, especially in rural areas;
* the lack of support to women entrepreneurs.

Actions around these concerns are on:

* engendering the SADC Trade Protocol;
* lobbying and negotiating for gender quotas in all trade missions;
* building capacity for financial schemes and markets;
* customs modalities for women cross border traders;
* gender awareness training for customs officials;

Targets outlined in the plan include to:

* have gender balance in all economic policy decision-making structures by 2015;
* establish strategies and action plans for gender mainstreaming in economic policy by 2008;

* end all discrimination against women with regard to property and inheritance by 2010;
* double current levels of women accessing credit by 2010;
* increase equal access to trade opportunities for women by 2015;
* end occupational segregation and all forms of employment discrimination by 2010.

Media and information
The concerns in the region on the media are focused on representation and portrayal of women in editorial content. The plan calls for:

* regional and national campaigns to ensure that gender issues are covered like any other news in the media;
* a gender audit of existing legislation;
* the establishment of code of ethics and media watch bodies.

Actions and targets outlined in the plan are to:

* ensure 30 percent women news sources by 2010 and gender balance in news sources by 2015;
* ensure 50 percent women representation in all areas of media decision-making positions by 2015;
* ensure equal access by women to all dimensions of information technology by 2010;
* integrate gender into all media and ICT polices by 2015;
* develop a Media Action Plan on HIV and AIDS and Gender at regional level by 2006;
* ensure that 80 percent of all media houses have gender and HIV and AIDS polices by 2008.

Women in politics and decision-making
Issues of concern regarding women and politics highlighted in the SIF are representation, participation and policy. The SADC GU was called upon to coordinate an audit of decision-making positions that have not previously been

140

focused on such as the private sector and assist member states to draw up national plans of action to cover all areas of decision-making, emphasising benchmarking and monitoring. Member states are called upon to make provision for affirmative action clauses in national constitutions. Specific actions and targets outlined in the SIF are to:

- have a comprehensive audit of non-political decision-making structures across the region by 2006;
- achieve 50 percent in all decision-making positions by 2015 or earlier;
- achieve 50/50 gender balance in the management of the SADC secretariat by 2010;
- ensure affirmative action in all constitutions by 2010;
- establish Gender Parliamentary Forums at national level by 2010;
- undertake a gender audit of parliaments by 2010;
- lobby all political parties to have at least 50 percent representation in all party structures by 2015; and
- develop a tool at regional level for monitoring women's participation in decision-making in the region.

Communication and information sharing

Due to costs of collecting data, there is a scarcity of data in the region, especially data that is disaggregated by sex, which is vital to monitoring and evaluating gender developments. The framework highlights the need to use research and documentation as a base to strengthen communication and information sharing and monitoring gender developments in the region. In this regard, the following actions and targets have been set:

- SADC GU and its partners to spearhead the publication of an annual SADC Gender Monitor;
- SADC GU in consultation with its partners to set up a gender

and development page on the Internet to facilitate sharing activity reports and updates on national and regional gender activities;
- SADC GU and its partners to embark on annual information gathering processes on gender disaggregated data on SADC directorate areas of focus, on beneficiaries, target groups and line ministries at member state, regional and national levels;
- enhance the capacity of the SADC GU to use monitoring and evaluation tools as of 2006;
- SADC GU to popularise the use of the African Gender and Development Index (AGDI) and the Violence Against Women Index as of 2006; and
- initiate discussion on developing one reporting format to various gender mechanisms as of 2006.

Conclusion

SADC leaders made commitments in various declarations which showed a clear and shared vision and laid the foundation for gender related issues born out of the 1995 Beijing Declaration and Platform for Action (BDPFA). The activities and targets outlined in the SIF and in this book are meant to accelerate gender equality in the region. The realisation and fulfilment of promises on gender equality, justice and women's empowerment in the SADC region will require concerted efforts by all stakeholders, that is, governments, NGOs, civil society groups and the donor community. Strong alliances between governments and its partners need to be forged as a way of coordinating activities. The institutional mechanisms at regional and national level are crucial in overseeing implementation of the SIF thus particular attention needs to be paid to adequate financial resourcing of all gender machineries, staffing, and training staff in gender analysis and mainstreaming.

Table 11.1

Strategy to facilitate implementation of commitments towards gender equality, justice and women's empowerment in the SADC region.

Strengthening Institutional Mechanisms

ACTION AREA	PROPOSED TARGETS	ACTION AT REGIONAL AND NATIONAL LEVEL	WHO IS RESPONSIBLE	TIME FRAME
Strengthen the national and regional gender structures	-Effective National Gender Machinery (NGM) in place by 2010 with adequate resources and budget. -Effective SADC Gender Unit with adequate capacity to fulfil its mandate.	-Implement recommendations of the Capacity Needs Assessment Studies on the NGM that was undertaken in 2003. -Strengthen the capacity of the SADC Gender Unit. -Strengthen the capacity and gender skills of NGMs. -Training of gender focal points in sectoral ministries. -Ensuring that each national gender structure has focused/targeted or specific mandates.	Justice Ministry, SADC Gender Unit, national gender machineries and Gender or Women's Affairs Departments.	2009
Develop and/or strengthen gender policies	-All member states to have National Gender Policies. -SADC Region to have a Regional Gender Policy by 2007.	-Finalise Regional Gender Policy development and facilitate stakeholder consultations. -Coordinate review and development of National Gender Policies. -Facilitate national consultations on Regional Gender Policy draft. -Develop and/or strengthen National Gender Policies	SADC Gender Unit, SADC national committees, national gender machineries and civil society organisations.	2007
Gender mainstreaming Gender budgeting	-Have 10 percent of each line ministry's budget allocated to gender- specific activities.	-Undertake situational analysis and responses capacities in gender budgeting. -Lobbying national governments to allocate 10 percent of each ministry's budget to gender specific activities. -Capacity building for all stakeholders (budget developers in line ministries and ministries of finance and gender) in gender budgeting.	SADC Gender Unit, UNIFEM, UNDP, national gender machineries, civil society organisations and NGOs.	2006-2008
Engendering regional and national macro-economic and sectoral policies to include planning and budgeting guidelines	-Have gender-responsive policies at national macro and sectoral levels, including guidelines by 2015.	-Develop gender checklist for guiding planners for efficient implementation of gender mainstreaming. -Capacity building for gender budgeting, sharing experiences and lessons on best practices in gender budgeting. -Engage partners in gender budgeting initiatives.	SADC Gender Unit, UNIFEM, UNECA, UNDP, national gender machineries, civil society, Ministries of Finance and economic planners.	2007-2015
Sensitisation and capacity strengthening for SADC structures and institutions on gender mainstreaming	-Have gender sensitive SADC secretariat, national machineries and other stakeholders.	-Training of SADC Secretariat staff in gender mainstreaming. -Gender experts working with each Directorate to review and mainstream gender-responsive policies and actions per programme and activity. -Staff at national machinery, stakeholders within the sectors, and SADC national committees trained in gender and gender mainstreaming.	SADC Gender Unit, national gender machineries, civil society and NGOs.	2010

ACTION AREA	PROPOSED TARGETS	ACTION AT REGIONAL AND NATIONAL LEVEL	WHO IS RESPONSIBLE	TIME FRAME
Capacity building for gender mainstreaming	-Strengthened gender mainstreaming skills across relevant and critical stakeholders.	Coordinate, facilitate, support and monitor national capacity building initiatives for gender mainstreaming. -Develop a SADC Gender Mainstreaming Tool Kit. -Translation of declaration, addendum, conventions and other documents into local and user friendly language.	SADC Gender Unit and Corporate Communications Unit, Ministries of Gender, national gender machineries and NGOs.	2006-2007
Harmonisation of gender equality and equity with the socio-cultural and religious environment	-Contribute to the removal of gender gaps in SADC societies.	-Support and monitor national initiatives and progress. -Awareness and capacity building on gender and the socio-cultural and religious environments.	National gender machineries, religious and traditional institutions, civil society and the media.	2006 and ongoing

Women's Human Rights

Constitution and legislation

ACTION AREA	PROPOSED TARGETS	ACTION AT REGIONAL AND NATIONAL LEVEL	WHO IS RESPONSIBLE	TIME FRAME
Constitutional provisions for gender equality including the right to dignity; right to life; integrity and security of person.	-Gender equality enshrined in Constitutions of SADC member states by 2010.	-Coordination and facilitation of gender research and reporting progress made. -Constitutional reviews.	SADC PF, parliament, Ministries of Justice, Gender/Women's Affairs, Information, the Judiciary, and civil society.	2010
Eliminate conflict between customary, religious and codified laws	-Constitutions in SADC member states to state that provisions for gender equality take precedence over customary law by 2010.	-Dissemination and sharing of model legislation and best practices. -Constitutional reviews -Harmonisation of culture and religion on women's human and legal rights issues	SADC PF, Women's Caucuses, parliaments, national gender machineries and the Ministry of Justice.	2010
Review and repeal all discriminatory laws including women's minority status	Have all discriminatory legislation in SADC member states expunged by 2010.	-Facilitate and coordinate national audits and synchronise national findings into a regional report for lobbying and advocacy. -Constitutional reviews of bill of rights and amendment of laws	SADC PF, Women's Parliamentary Caucuses, Parliaments, NGMs, regional and national NGOs.	2007-2010
Domestication of regional and international gender instruments and policies	-Gender and development instruments and policies such as CEDAW domesticated by all member states. -Ratification and domestication of African Protocol on Women's Rights and the anticipated SADC Gender Protocol.	-Coordination, facilitation and monitoring progress. -Develop and implement plan for domestication. -Audits of the extent of domestication of international instruments and policies.	Parliaments, SADC PF, NGMs, Ministries of Gender, NGMs, Ministries of Justice, civil society and regional and national NGOs.	2007

ACTION AREA	PROPOSED TARGETS	ACTION AT REGIONAL AND NATIONAL LEVEL	WHO IS RESPONSIBLE	TIME FRAME
Promotion of and access to legal assistance and legal literacy programmes	-Increased legal awareness and access to legal assistance.	-Translation and simplification of all instruments including local laws into local languages. -Access to legal aid for citizens who are underprivileged to be provided by the state and civil society. -Formulation of legal literacy programmes to educate the critical mass on issues embodied in the protocol and other international legal instruments. -Media to communicate information on women's human and legal rights issues and laws in the language best understood by the majority of the population.	SADC GU, NGMs, national and regional NGOs, civil society organisations working on human rights issues.	2006-2010
Enforcement and Implementation of Laws and other instruments	-Gender budgeting to ensure allocation of resources to enable implementation -Provision of adequate financial and human resources, -Develop targeted programmes and projects.	-Set up a Regional Women's Rights Commission to monitor both implementation and resources allocated for implementation. -Monitoring mechanisms to be developed and used. -Establish or strengthen national law reform commission with adequate representation from the NGMs and women's NGOs in order for gender issues to be taken on board.	SADC Gender Unit, national gender machineries, legislators, and civil society.	2010

Education

ACTION AREA	PROPOSED TARGETS	ACTION AT REGIONAL AND NATIONAL LEVEL	WHO IS RESPONSIBLE	TIME FRAME
Equal access to education	-Introduce state-supported early child development in all countries by 2010. -Eliminate gender disparity in primary and secondary education by 2007.	-Sharing best practices. -Advocate for minimal fees and reduced cost of books and uniforms. -Develop community support systems for families to enable girls to continue with education and not be forced to play reproductive gender roles.	SADC GU, NGMs, Ministries of Education, Social welfare, civil society organisations, UNICEF, UNAIDS and SADC SHDSP.	Plans in place by 2007; target achieved by 2010
Eradicate illiteracy	-Eradicate illiteracy by 2020.	Support national initiatives. -Monitor progress -Develop and implement action plans.	SADC GU, SHDSP, national machineries and Ministries of education.	Plans in place by 2006
Eliminate and challenge stereotypes in education	-All educational materials reviewed from a gender perspective by 2008. -Gender sensitive materials introduced by 2010.	-Develop tools for reviewing educational materials from a gender perspective; sharing best practices. -Review of educational materials from a gender perspective. -Introduce positive material on women that is gender sensitive. -Change mindsets and traditional expectations that limit girls. -Establish scholarships for disadvantaged girls to enable them to remain in school and further their training/education.	SADC GU, national machineries, Ministries of Education, Social welfare, civil society organisations, UNICEF, UNAIDS and SADC SHDSP.	Review by 2008; materials introduced by 2010

ACTION AREA	PROPOSED TARGETS	ACTION AT REGIONAL AND NATIONAL LEVEL	WHO IS RESPONSIBLE	TIME FRAME
Develop quality educational infrastructure and facilities	-Improved access to quality educational infrastructure and facilities.	-Lobby and advocate for increased investment in educational infrastructure and facilities.	Ministries of Education, Finance, national gender machineries, civil society and SADC SHDSP.	2010
Gender studies	-All universities and institutions of higher learning to offer gender studies programmes by 2010.	-Monitoring progress and disseminating information. -Ensure gender studies programmes are in place. -Training of lecturers to enhance academic, vocational and gender equality and equity.	SADC GU, SHDSP, Ministries of Education and institutions of higher learning.	2010

Violence in educational institutions

ACTION AREA	PROPOSED TARGETS	ACTION AT REGIONAL AND NATIONAL LEVEL	WHO IS RESPONSIBLE	TIME FRAME
Eradicate all forms of gender violence in educational institutions.	-Start zero tolerance campaigns on gender violence, which results in no gender violence in schools by 2009.	-Monitoring progress and disseminating information. -Establish policies/ programmes for ending gender violence in schools. -Formulate, strengthen and enforce legislation to deal with teachers who sexually/physically abuse students. -Enlist men's networks.	SADC GU, gender machineries and Ministries of Education.	2009

Violence Against Women and Children

Legal rights

ACTION AREA	PROPOSED TARGETS	ACTION AT REGIONAL AND NATIONAL LEVEL	WHO IS RESPONSIBLE	TIME FRAME
Legislation	-All member states to have laws against gender violence domestic violence and provision, and sexual offences acts by 2008.	-Enact, ratify, domesticate, review and implement specific legislation to end gender violence. -Campaigns against gender violence.	SADC GU, SADC PF, women's caucuses, parliaments, national gender machineries, Ministries of Justice, civil society and the media.	2008
Gender-based Violence (GBV) and HIV and AIDS	-Ensure provisions for survivors of sexual assault to access PEP by 2007.	-Disseminate best practices. -All health centres to have facilities for PEP for survivors.	SADC GU; SADC PF; women's caucuses; parliaments; national gender machineries, civil society.	2007
Trafficking	-Specific legislation or reference to trafficking in specific legislation by 2010.	-Regional consultative workshop on trafficking to be held in 2006. -Enact, ratify, domesticate, review and implement specific legislation to end gender violence.	SADC GU, SADC PF, IOM, UNIFEM, women's caucuses; parliaments, national gender machineries and civil society.	2007
Criminal justice system	-Gender sensitisation of all functionaries in the criminal justice system and mainstreaming of gender in all future training programmes by 2008.	-Dissemination of training materials and best practices. -Plan and actions to ensure that all functionaries in the criminal justice system receive gender sensitivity training.	Ministries of Justice, police services, judicial services, women's caucus and the SADC PF.	2008

145

ACTION AREA	PROPOSED TARGETS	ACTION AT REGIONAL AND NATIONAL LEVEL	WHO IS RESPONSIBLE	TIME FRAME
Women in conflict and post conflict situations	-Meaningful and effective involvement of women in peace building processes and post-conflict situations.	-SADC Gender Unit to work with the SADC Organ on Politics, Defence and Security to facilitate mainstreaming of gender in pre, during and post-conflict situations. -SADC Gender Unit to link with UNIFEM, UNDP, Centre for conflict resolution and the IOM in developing a programme for Angola and DRC. -SADC Gender Unit to take stock and draw lessons from post-conflict situations in the region. -Facilitate the implementation of UN Resolution 1325. -Develop and Implement rehabilitation programmes for women in conflict and post conflict situations.	UNHCR, UNIFEM, SADC Organ, SADC GU, IOM, CCR, UNDP, Ministries of Justice, police services, army, gender machineries, civil society and political parties.	2007
Social, economic, cultural and political environment	-Challenge and eradicate traditional norms and religious beliefs and practices that perpetuate violence against women and children.	-Development of strategic partnerships between civil society, national machineries and the SADC Gender Unit. -Strengthen coordination mechanisms and dialogue where there is convergence to enable effective implementation. -Facilitate capacity building for journalists for greater gender sensitivity, monitoring and reporting. -Adopt zero tolerance policies on gender violence. -Develop information and peer campaigns targeting men. -Enlist men's networks and organisations to lead violence against women campaigns.	SADC Gender Unit, national gender machineries, cultural and religious organisations, media institutions, civil society organisations and the private sector.	2007-2008
Improved quality services for victims, survivors and rehabilitation of perpetrators	-Policy and Practical provision in place. -Resources made available for GBV needs.	-Facilitation, coordination, monitoring documentation of best practices and dissemination of lessons learnt. -Awareness building, advocacy and lobbying to include the development and implementation of campaign strategies. -Establish special units for GBV at police posts. -Establish places of safety for survivors and victims. -Rehabilitation of survivors and perpetrators. -Setting up national funds for women and child survivors.	SADC Gender Unit, national machineries, police and security forces, rehabilitation services, civil society, private sector, and the Ministry of Home Affairs.	2006/07
Sexual, Reproductive Health and Rights and HIV and AIDS				
Improve access to quality reproductive and sexual health services	-Development of guidelines for minimum package for SRH in the region by 2007.	-Gender Unit in collaboration with SHDSP to develop guidelines and disseminate. -Provide free health care for poor and vulnerable sections of society. -Health workers to conduct regular mobile clinics in rural and remote areas.	Ministries of Health, development partners, NGOs, UNFPA, UNAIDS, UNIFEM, and national machineries.	2007

ACTION AREA	PROPOSED TARGETS	ACTION AT REGIONAL AND NATIONAL LEVEL	WHO IS RESPONSIBLE	TIME FRAME
Improve maternal health	-Reduce the maternal mortality ratio by three quarters between 1990 and 2015. -Achieve MDG Goal 5, target 6. -Ensure access to, and use of contraceptives in all rural and urban areas.	-Coordinating and monitoring. -Emergency contraception available at low or no cost in all health centres by 2008. -Education on emergency contraception including dissemination of information in local languages to communities.	Ministries of Health, development partners, NGOs, UNFPA, UNAIDS, UNIFEM, national gender machineries, private sector, ILO and SADC SHDSP.	2008-2015
Development and provision of infrastructure, equipment, facilities and human resources in the health sectors	-Improve and increase access to infrastructure, equipment, facilities and human resources in the health sectors.	-Monitoring progress. -Mobilisation of resources to improve health service delivery.	Ministries of Health, development partners, NGOs, UNFPA, UNAIDS, UNIFEM, national machineries, and SADC SHDSP.	2010
Protecting women and girls with respect to reproductive and sexual health.	-Ensure that female condoms are easily accessible and cost effective	-Wide and free distribution of female condoms at low cost and easily accessible at all retail outlets currently selling male condoms. -Initiate dialogue on legalising abortion at national levels.	SADC HIV and AIDS UNIT, Ministries of Health, private sector and civil society, UNAIDS and UNFPA.	2008-2010
HIV and AIDS				
Reduce HIV and AIDS among women and girls	-Halt the spread of HIV and AIDS and reverse the spread of the virus by 2015.	-Monitor member states to ensure HIV and AIDS policies are in place. -Start a SADC Anti Retroviral Therapy Fund to enable wide access. -SADC HIV and AIDS Unit to coordinate the development of a campaign beyond the current ABCs of AIDS. -Member states to ensure HIV and AIDS policies are in place. -Strengthen HIV and AIDS programmes and accelerate male involvement in such programmes. -Strengthen and Increase VCT centres in rural and urban areas.	SADC HIV and AIDS Unit, Ministries of Health, gender machineries, private sector and civil society organisations, UNAIDS and UNFPA.	2007
Reduce cultural practices, traditions and customs that perpetuate HIV and AIDS	-Reduce incidences of widow inheriting and genital mutilation. -Zero tolerance on minors getting married. -Reduce by 50 percent the impact of burden of care on women and girls.	-Monitoring progress and information dissemination. -SADC HIV and AIDS Unit to lead initiative of adopting a Regional Volunteers Charter (see UN SG Taskforce 2003 UNAIDS). -Awareness raising and sensitisation programmes on the impact of cultural practices on HIV and AIDS. -National discussions on targeted traditional practices. -Communities to expand responsibility of caring for patients to men.	Ministries of Health, private sector, civil society, religious and traditional institutions, UNAIDS, SADC HIV and AIDS Unit.	2007

ACTION AREA	PROPOSED TARGETS	ACTION AT REGIONAL AND NATIONAL LEVEL	WHO IS RESPONSIBLE	TIME FRAME
Strengthen biomedical and traditional medicine partnerships	-Wide provision of health related traditional and bio-medical services.	-Create forums to foster negotiations for collaborative partnerships between modern and traditional medicine.	Ministries of Health, civil society, SADC Gender Unit and traditional doctors' associations.	Initiate by 2007
Women's Economic Empowerment				
Economic policies and decision-making				
Equal participation in policy formulation	-Ensure gender balance in all economic policy decision-making structures by 2015.	-Ensuring gender balance in economic policy structures in line with decision-making targets.	Ministries of Finance, Economic and Development Planning; central banks, UNECA, NGMs and civil society organisations.	2015
Mainstreaming gender in economic policy formulation	-Strategies and action plans for mainstreaming gender in economic policy by 2008.	-Formulate tools and Training of Trainers (TOT) for mainstreaming gender in economic policy formulation. -Formulate processes for mainstreaming gender in economic policy.	Ministries of Finance, Economic and Development Planning; central banks, UNECA, NGM and civil society organisations.	2008
Access to property and resources				
Right to own property and inheritance	-End all discrimination against women with regard to property and inheritance by 2010.	-Establish measures to remove all forms of discrimination with regard to women's access to property and inheritance. -Review land tenure systems by member states by 2008 to enable women to access, control and own land.	Ministries of Finance, Economic and Development Planning; central banks, UNECA, NGM, civil society organisations, Community leadership, SADC national contact points and committees.	2010
Access to credit and capita	-Double current levels of women accessing credit by 2010.	-Removal of all forms of discrimination with regard to women's access to property - credit and capital requirements. -States and international donors to fund women specific initiatives in the agricultural sector.	Ministries of Finance, Economic and Development Planning; central banks, NGM, civil society organisations, SADC Gender Unit and TIFI Directorate.	2010
Support to women entrepreneursl	-Comprehensive plans in all countries to support women entrepreneurs by 2010.	-Develop checklists and guidelines on supporting women entrepreneurs. -Enhancement of Women's Business Associations at national and regional level. -Train women in business. -Set up and/or strengthen national Women in Business Associations.	SADC Gender Unit, NGMs, Ministries of Trade, and TIFI Directorate.	2007-2010

148

ACTION AREA	PROPOSED TARGETS	ACTION AT REGIONAL AND NATIONAL LEVEL	WHO IS RESPONSIBLE	TIME FRAME
Trade and globalisation				
Trade	Women's equal access to trade opportunities by 2015.	-Engendering the trade protocol. -Lobby and negotiate for gender quotas in all trade missions. -Undertake gender audits of existing policies and practices.	SADC trade structures, TIFI Directorate, UNECA, Ministries of Trade and business associations.	Quantified progress by 2010
Globalisation	-Women's equal participation in trade- related negotiations and opportunities created by 2015.	-Initiatives for capacity enhancement, financial schemes, markets, customs modalities for women cross border traders. -Inclusion of gender awareness in customs officials' training. -Initiatives for capacity enhancement, financial schemes, markets, customs modalities for women cross border traders. -Gender awareness included in customs officials' training.	SADC trade structures, UNECA, Ministries of Trade; business associations and TIFI Directorate.	2010
Employment				
Equal access to employment	-Equal share by women in wage employment in the non-agriculture sector. -Achieve MDG Goal 3, target 4, Indicator 11 by 2015.	-Monitoring and information dissemination. -Gender audits of existing policies and practices.	Ministries of Labour, national gender machineries, NGOs, TIFI Directorate and ILO.	2006-2015
Affirmative action and employment equity legislation	-Constitutions to make provision for affirmative action and employment equity legislation including family-friendly practices.	-Monitoring and information dissemination. -Processes to ensure constitutional amendments and relevant legislation. -Monitoring to ensure implementation.	SADC PF, parliamentarians, national gender machineries, civil society organisations , Ministry of Justice and ILO.	2006-2010
Occupational segregation and all forms of employment discrimination	-End occupational segregation and all forms of employment discrimination by 2015.	-Monitoring and information dissemination. -Ensure that laws are enacted and policies to end occupational and employment discrimination are developed.	Ministries of Labour, ILO Parliaments, civil society organisations and trade unions.	2005-2010
Non-remunerated work	-All member States to conduct time-use studies by 2010; formulate policies for reducing the burden of the dual role played by women.	-Coordinate and facilitate study together with TIFI, SHDSP and Statistics Unit. -Formulation of policies around care work at the national level. -Central statistics Offices advocacy initiatives.	Ministries of Labour, parliaments, ILO, UNIFEM and UNECA.	2010

149

ACTION AREA	PROPOSED TARGETS	ACTION AT REGIONAL AND NATIONAL LEVEL	WHO IS RESPONSIBLE	TIME FRAME
Sexual harassment	-Legislation and codes of conduct for ending sexual harassment by 2008.	-Dissemination of model laws and policies. -Processes to ensure the adoption of laws and policies. -Harsh Penalties for offenders.	Ministries of Labour; NGMs, parliaments, civil society, and the private sector.	2008
Social security and benefits	-Ensure the removal of all discrimination in social benefits by 2010.	-Dissemination of model laws and policies. -Processes to ensure the removal of all discrimination in social security/ benefits.	Ministries of Labour, ILO, UNECA, parliaments and civil society.	2010
Representation in unions	-Equal representation of women in union decision-making structures by 2015.	-Collation of data as part of the annual reporting process. -Strategies to ensure gender balance as part of the decision-making plan.	Trade Unions, civil society and ILO.	2015
Informal sector				
Access and support	-Plans, structures and processes in each country for elevating women in the informal sector to more meaningful economic involvement by 2015.	-Civil society organisations advocacy initiatives. -Dissemination of model policies and best practices. -Member States to set in place a ministry or department dealing with the informal sector. -Processes to ensure women's empowerment in small and medium enterprise.	Ministries of Trade and Industries, banks, professional associations, NGOs and TIFI Directorate.	2015
Marginalised groups				
Child labour, migrant women, elderly women, women with disabilities	-Policies and laws to ensure empowerment of marginalised groups. -Policies to ensure	-Model legislation; best practices. -Policies and laws to ensure empowerment of marginalised groups.	Ministries of Economic and Social Development, ILO and UNDP.	2010
Environment				
Environment and sustainable development.	women's equal participation in and benefit from water and sanitation projects.	-Policies to ensure women's equal participation in and benefit from environment/sustainable development projects.	Ministries of Environment and Sustainable Development and SADC FANR.	
Housing	-To achieve a significant improvement in the lives of at least 100 million slum dwellers by 2020	Tools for gathering gender disaggregated data on the achievement of this goal. -Policies, monitoring and evaluation to ensure target achieved for women and men.	-Ministries of Economic and Social Development, gender machinery and SADC SHDSP.	2010

ACTION AREA	PROPOSED TARGETS	ACTION AT REGIONAL AND NATIONAL LEVEL	WHO IS RESPONSIBLE	TIME FRAME
Water and sanitation	-Policies to ensure women's equal participation in and benefit from water and sanitation projects by 2010.	-Gender mainstreaming in SADC sectors responsible for this; tool kits. -Policies to ensure women's equal participation in and benefit from water and sanitation projects.	SADC Gender Unit, FANR, NGMs, Ministries of Water and Sanitation and SADC SHDSP.	2010

Media and Information

Representation and portrayal of women in editorial content of the media

ACTION AREA	PROPOSED TARGETS	ACTION AT REGIONAL AND NATIONAL LEVEL	WHO IS RESPONSIBLE	TIME FRAME
Ensuring that women have equal voice in the media	-Have 30 percent women news sources by 2010. -Gender balance in news sources by 2015.	Monitoring; lobbying and advocacy. -Campaigns at both national and regional levels should be launched to ensure that gender issues are covered like any other news in the media. Gender policies at macro-level and in newsrooms.	SADC information division, NGOs, Editor's Forums, and media regulatory authorities, SARDCWIDSAA.	30 percent by 2010 50 percent by 2015
Challenging gender stereotypes in the media	-Remove all gender stereotypes from the media by 2020.	Monitoring, lobbying and advocacy. -Penalising use of sexist adverts.	Media regulatory authorities and NGOs.	2020
Creating and disseminating gender aware content	-Ensure gender is mainstreamed in all media coverage.	-Monitoring, Lobbying and Advocacy. -Developing and disseminating gender aware content.	Gender structures, gender and media networks, Gender Links, and SARDC WIDSAA	Ongoing
Legislation to enhance a culture and respect for gender equality	-Integrating gender into all media and ICT policies by 2015.	-Gender audit of all existing legislation. -Establishment of code of ethics and media watches. -Lobby and advocate for gender sensitisation by women's caucus, NGMs and CBOs.	SADC PF, women's caucus, SADC GU, Ministries of Communication and Information and relevant structures.	2008-2010
Policy	-Ensure that 80 percent of all media houses have gender and HIV and AIDS policies by 2008.	-Media Action Plan on HIV and AIDS and Gender. -Adoption and implementation of policies.	Southern African Editors Forum, NGO partners, SADC information division, SADC HIV and AIDS Unit, SADC Gender Unit, and Ministries of Information.	2006-2010
Training / Media Literacy	-Ensure that gender is mainstreamed in all media training institutions by 2010.	-Audits and monitoring. -Adoption &implementation of policies (User friendly) -Training of media personnel	Ministries of Information, and media training institutions.	2010

ACTION AREA	PROPOSED TARGETS	ACTION AT REGIONAL AND NATIONAL LEVEL	WHO IS RESPONSIBLE	TIME FRAME
Practical tools	-Develop gender sensitisation handbooks of women experts and sources.	-Disseminate best practices. -Consolidate and disseminate. -Develop handbooks. -Ensure coordinated dissemination and translation into local languages.	Media industry and NGOs.	Ongoing
Research and monitoring	-Repeat the GMBS in 2008 and every five years.	-Coordinating and conducting research. -Disseminate in a user-friendly format / language.	NGOs working with gender machinery and mainstream media, Gender Links, SADC PF and Regional Women's Parliamentary Caucus.	2008 and every two years.
Women within media institutions				
Representation	-Have 50 percent women in all areas and at all levels by 2015.	-Monitoring and information dissemination. -Plans and actions to ensure targets met.	Media houses, Southern African Editors Forum, SARDC WIDSAA, SADC PF and Regional Women Parliamentary Caucus.	2010
Participation	-Have 50 percent women at all levels of decision-making in the media by 2015.	-Monitoring and information dissemination. -Plans and actions to ensure targets are met.	Media houses, SARDC WIDSAA, SADC PF and Regional Women Parliamentary Caucus.	2010
Capacity building	-Policies and resources to develop women leadership in the media.	-Monitoring and information dissemination, monitoring and reporting. -Plans and actions to ensure targets met. -Capacity building of media and other relevant stakeholders and media watches.	Media houses, Southern African Editors Forum, SARDC, WIDSAA, SADC PF and Regional Women Parliamentary Caucus.	2010
Information Technology				
Access, education and training	-Ensuring equal access by women to all dimensions of information technology by 2010.	-Model policies and legislation. -Gender aware policies and legislation. -Review of constitutions and external legislation to include access to information. -Lobby states to refrain from monopolising the public media to ensure that public interests are served.	Ministries of Information and Communication, gender machinery and NGOs.	2010
Women in Politics and Decision-Making				
Representation				
Conduct an audit of areas of decision-making that have previously not been focused on, e.g. private sector	-Comprehensive audit by 2006.	-Coordinate the audit. -Provide information at national level annually.	SADC GU, national machineries, professional associations, NGOs, CBOs, and other stakeholders.	2006

ACTION AREA	PROPOSED TARGETS	ACTION AT REGIONAL AND NATIONAL LEVEL	WHO IS RESPONSIBLE	TIME FRAME
Setting targets for achieving gender balance	-To achieve 50 percent in all areas by 2015 or earlier. -To achieve 50 percent gender balance in the management of the SADC Secretariat by 2010.	-Assist countries in drawing up National Action Plans that cover all areas of decision-making; benchmarking and monitoring these. -Lobby for 50/50 SADC Secretariat management. -Draw up national action plans covering in all areas of decision-making for achieving the target.	SADC GU, SADC PF, gender machinery, women's caucuses, parliaments and civil society.	Action plans in place by the end of 2006-2010.
Affirmative action	-Ensure that all constitutions make provision for affirmative action by 2010.	-Sharing model amendments and best practices from the region. -Constitutional amendments to make provision for affirmative action.	SADC GU, SADC PF, gender machinery, women's caucuses, parliaments and civil society.	2006-2010
Participation				
Leadership positions in structures of governance and decision-making	-Achieve 50/50 balance in leadership positions within decision-making structures by 2030.	-Assist countries in drawing up National Action Plans; benchmarking and monitoring. Draw up national action plans covering- all areas of decision-making for achieving the target.	SADC GU, SADC PF, gender machinery, women's caucuses, parliaments and civil society.	Not later than 2030
Effective inputs into policy development and implementation	-A tool for measuring effective participation by women in decision-making to be in place by 2008.	-Develop a tool that can be used across the region. -Use the tool for monitoring and corrective action.	SADC GU, SADC PF, gender machinery and civil society.	2008-2010
Impact on policy				
Establish or strengthen national gender parliamentary forum to advance gender legislation	-Advanced gender sensitive legislation.	-Sharing best practices. -Develop watchdog mechanism at regional level. -Formation of Gender PF at all national levels. -Audit of gender advancement by all parliaments. -Monitor gender responsiveness of MPs, civil society organisations to monitor parliament debates.	SADC PF, SADC Gender Unit and civil society organisations, Regional Women's Parliamentary Caucus	2010
Legislate the automatic domestication of international instruments on gender and development.	-Legislate or amend legislation and/or the constitution by 2010.	-Share expertise and support best practices regionally and globally. -Lobbying and advocacy by relevant NGOs, civil society, gender and women's parliamentary caucuses.	Judiciary, SADC Gender Unit, parliament, office of the Prime Ministers, Ministry of Communications and Information, Ministry of Foreign Affairs, Ministry of Gender, UN agencies and NGMs, Regional Women's PArliamentary Caucus.	2010

153

ACTION AREA	PROPOSED TARGETS	ACTION AT REGIONAL AND NATIONAL LEVEL	WHO IS RESPONSIBLE	TIME FRAME
Review the electoral system with the view of increasing participation of women at all levels	-Legislate to facilitate gender equality by 2015.	-Assist countries in drawing up legislation and sharing best practices. -Ensure transparency of SADC external and national electoral observers. -Lobbying and advocacy by SADC Gender Unit, national gender machineries, NGOs, and other stakeholders.	Judiciary, NGOs, UN Agencies, NGMs, Home Affairs and relevant departments, SADC Organ on Politics, Defence and Security, SADC PF, SADC Gender Unit, and EISA.	2006-2015
Lobby political parties to have at least 50 percent female representation in all party structures.	-Have gender-sensitive political party manifestos, mechanisms and policies put in place to fast track gender equality by 2015.	-Develop a tool for monitoring progress in the region. -Women politicians, gender caucus, NGOs, CBOs, and relevant stakeholders.	SADC Gender Unit, women gender party structures, NGOs and relevant stakeholders.	2015
Leadership training	-Access to leadership training for women in decision-making.	-Plan leadership training at regional and national level.	SADC GU, SADC PF, gender machinery and civil society.	2006 and ongoing
Gender sensitivity training	-All MPs and key government functionaries to undergo gender sensitivity training.	-Disseminate SADC training kit; train trainers. -Plan and roll out of training at national level. -Monitoring quality of parliamentary debates.	ADC GU, SADC PF, national gender machineries and civil society.	2006 for disseminating kits and TOT; ongoing at national level
Citizen participation				
Public education and awareness on gender and governance	-Voter education on the importance of gender parity for good governance before all elections in the region.	-Work with electoral commissions in developing training packages. -Action plans for conducting voter education.	SADC PF, independent electoral commissions, gender machinery, civil society, and women's gender forum of political parties.	Plan in place by 2006; gender aware voter education before each election in the region by 2010
Constituency consultative processes	-Systematised consultative processes and platforms between MPs and constituencies.	-Develop a model for systematic consultative processes. -Consultations on the model. -National strategy development. -Implementation of the model.	SADC Gender Unit, NGMs, SADC PF, national parliament and civil society organisations.	2008-2010

Communication and information sharing

ACTION AREA	PROPOSED TARGETS	ACTION AT REGIONAL AND NATIONAL LEVEL	WHO IS RESPONSIBLE	TIME FRAME
Strengthen communication and information sharing	-Research and Documentation	-Publish SADC Gender Monitor annually. -Publicise Regional Implementation Framework 2006-2010. -Develop a gender and development page on the internet to share activity reports and updates. -Gender Unit together with Statistics Unit to embark on an information gathering process on gender disaggregated data on directorate's areas of focus of beneficiaries, actors and target groups at national and regional levels. -Develop periodic reports on outputs, outcomes, lessons learnt from implementing the regional gender agenda. -National level researches on thematic areas.	SADC Gender Unit, Statistic Unit, Corporate Communications, SARDC-WIDSAA, national machineries and civil society organisations.	Annually

Drawn from the SADC Gender-based Regional Integration Plan: Strategic Implementation Framework (SIF) 2004-2010 . Note that some of the dates have changed considering the drafting of the Protocol on Gender and Development that set new targets for gender equality goals.

www.ingramcontent.com/pod-product-compliance
Lightning Source LLC
Chambersburg PA
CBHW080250030426
42334CB00023BA/2762